Theatre History Studies

2011 VOLUME 31

Edited by

RHONA JUSTICE-MALLOY

PUBLISHED BY THE MID-AMERICA THEATRE CONFERENCE
AND THE UNIVERSITY OF ALABAMA PRESS

Designed by Todd Lape / Lape Designs
Typeface: Minion
Articles appearing in this journal are abstracted and indexed in *Historical Abstracts* and
America: History and Life.

∞

The paper on which this book is printed meets the minimum requirements
of American National Standard for Information Sciences-Permanence of
Paper for Printed Library Materials, ANSI Z39.48-1984.

Theater History Studies is an official journal of the Mid-America Theatre Conference, Inc. (MATC). The conference encompasses the states of Illinois, Indiana, Iowa, Kansas, Michigan, Minnesota, Missouri, Nebraska, North Dakota, South Dakota, and Wisconsin. Its purposes are to unite people and organizations within this region and elsewhere who have an interest in theatre and to promote the growth and development of all forms of theatre.

Theatre History Studies is devoted to research in all areas of theatre history. Manuscripts should be prepared in conformity with the guidelines established in the *Chicago Manual of Style*, and emailed to rjmalloy@olemiss.edu, or submitted in duplicate, and sent to Rhona Justice-Malloy, Editor, Dept. of Theatre Arts, 110 Isom Hall, University of Mississippi, Box 1848, University, MS 38677-1848. Consulting editors review the manuscripts, a process that takes approximately four months. The journal does not normally accept studies of dramatic literature unless there is a focus on actual production and performance. Authors whose manuscripts are accepted must provide the editor with an electronic file, using Microsoft Word. Illustrations (preferably high-quality originals or black-and-white glossies) are welcomed. Manuscripts will be returned only if accompanied by a stamped, self-addressed envelope bearing sufficient postage.

This publication is issued annually by the Mid-America Theatre Conference and The University of Alabama Press.

Subscription rates for 2011 are $15 for individuals, $30 for institutions, and an additional $8 for foreign delivery. Back issues are $29.95 each. Subscription orders and changes of address should be directed to Allie Harper, The University of Alabama Press, Box 870380, Tuscaloosa, AL 35487 (205-348-1564 phone, 205-348-9201 fax).

Theatre History Studies is indexed in *Humanities Index, Humanities Abstracts, Book Review Index, MLA International Bibliography, International Bibliography of Theatre, Arts & Humanities Citation Index, IBZ International Bibliography of Periodical Literature,* and *IBR International Bibliography of Book Reviews,* the database of *International Index to the Performing Arts.* Full texts of essays appear in the databases of both *Humanities Abstracts Full Text* and *SIRS.* The journal has published its own index, *The Twenty Year Index, 1981–2000.* It is available for $10 for individuals and $15 for libraries from Rhona Justice-Malloy, Editor, Dept. of Theatre Arts, Isom Hall 110, University of Mississippi, Box 1848, University, MS 38677–1848.

CONTENTS

CONTENTS

BOOK REVIEWS

CONTENTS

CONTENTS

ILLUSTRATIONS

In Memoriam

Vera Mowry Roberts (1913–2010)

—MILLY S. BARRANGER

The diminutive woman in the hat, known to all as Vera, was a giant in educational theatre for over fifty years. She came into our lives as a teacher, stage director, theatre historian, editor, academic administrator, church elder, mentor, and friend. Her confident voice, guiding and encouraging, echoes in remembrance.

Her accomplishments were legion. A native of Pittsburgh, she served her country as an officer in the United States Naval Reserves during World War II, received a doctorate from the University of Pittsburgh, and began a teaching career in the late forties in Washington, D.C. In 1950 she was one of the founders of Arena Stage, which augured the rise of professional regional theatres in America. While at Arena, she married actor Pernell E. Roberts (they divorced in 1960) and their son J. Christopher was born. Relocating to New York City, Dr. Roberts joined the speech and theatre faculty at Hunter College of the City University of New York (CUNY) in 1955; she served as chair of the new Department of Theatre and Film for ten years (1970 80). During her tenure at Hunter she wrote two textbooks *(On Stage: A History of the Theatre* and *The Nature of Theatre),* coedited a biographical dictionary *(Notable Women in the American Theatre),* and launched another phase of her career in support of professional organizations.

As president of the American Theatre Association, Vera became widely known among her peers for her work to establish standards for degree programs in theatre and to initiate programs in support of senior citizens and women in theatre. In recognition of her work, she garnered a number of honors and awards, including induction into the College of Fellows of the American Theatre, the

American College Theatre Festival's Gold and Silver Medallions, a Career Achievement Award from the Association for Theatre in Higher Education, and President's Medals for Excellence from Hunter College and the CUNY Graduate School. Toward the end of her life, she established a professorship and a scholarship fund in the CUNY Graduate School, where she had been executive officer of doctoral programs in theatre and held graduate seminars until her retirement.

Despite the many demands of her profession, she never neglected her spiritual life, which sustained her at the death of her beloved son. Long active in the Presbyterian Church, she became the first woman elected to Moderator of the New York City Presbytery in its two hundredth year. In 1998 she documented the history of her spiritual home, Rutgers Church on West Seventy-third Street, in *The Story of Rutgers Church.*

In a lifetime of meritorious efforts on behalf of colleagues and students, she fervently believed that the separation of professional and educational theatre was a false dichotomy. From the cofounding of Arena Stage to her leadership of the Theatre and Film Department at Hunter, she persisted in her conviction that professional artists and educators *merge* their passions and talents in the nurture and practice of theatre as an enduring form of art. Vera Mowry Roberts leaves the pursuit of this common goal as her legacy to future generations.

Class Act(resses)

How Depression-Era Stage Actresses Utilized Conflicting
Gender Ideals to Benefit Their Community

—KELLY CAROLYN GORDON

During the mid-eighteenth century, when professional theatre companies first began to appear in the United States, dominant culture held that women must devote their time and energy strictly to the private sphere: home, church, and charity. Historians refer to this era as having an ideology of "ideal" or "true" womanhood. Historian Barbara J. Harris defines "true womanhood" as "a compound of four ideas: a sharp dichotomy between the home and economic world outside that paralleled a sharp contrast between female and male natures, the designation of the home as the female's only proper sphere, the moral superiority of women, and the idealization of her role as a mother."[1] Ultimately, this collection of ideas held that women were the natural, moral guardians of their husbands and children.

However, implicit in the true woman ideal was the notion that a woman's moral superiority was fragile and easily destroyed. Exposure to the corruption of the public world of business, government, education, and entertainment might very well transform true women into depraved and wanton hussies, destroying not only their moral nature but also that of their husbands and children and, by extension, society as a whole. The ideology of true womanhood was a dominant belief upon which Western society depended.

Toward the end of the 1800s, this concept of true womanhood was severely challenged by the suffrage and abolitionist movements and the changing realities of women's lives. Gradually, myriad opportunities emerged for women in the public sphere, a domain that had previously been closed to most women. Women began to carve out a stronger place for themselves outside the home, joining the workforce, the political realm, and institutions of higher education. Historian Deborah S. Kolb points out that "the abolitionist cause trained women orators and writers and demonstrated the power which organized women might yield. Within twenty years, from 1865 to 1885, America saw the opening of Vassar (1865), Smith (1875), Wellesley (1875), and Radcliffe (1882), and women were also accepted into more than fourteen state universities. The dearth of men due to the Civil War and to westward migration, in conjunction with the opening of industry and higher education to women, instilled a new feeling of self-reliance and independence in women."[2] The ideal of the "new woman" provided U.S. culture with a new "sense of the female self; independent, athletic, sexual and modern."[3] The new woman was "unafraid to challenge male decisions and male dominance. While she might retain the status of wife and mother, [she] frequently demanded new respect and responsibility as career woman."[4] The period of the new woman culminated in the passing of the Nineteenth Amendment in 1920, which gave women the right to vote. After the amendment was passed, feminist Carrie Chapman Catt aptly stated, "We are no longer petitioners, we are not wards of the nation, but free and equal citizens."[5]

With the 1929 collapse of the New York Stock Exchange came a backward step in the progress that women had been making during the 1920s. Having won their fight to vote, attended college, and joined the workforce in increasing numbers, women were now told, "Don't take a job from a man." One example of this pervasive attitude was the firing of married female teachers and government employees, who were given the rationale that each family really needed only one breadwinner and that the breadwinner should be a man. The main question on the minds of many suffragettes was posed by Genevieve Parkhurst in the title of her article published by *Harper's Magazine* in 1935: "Is Feminism Dead?"[6] Clearly, the Depression era marked a return to the true woman ideal; the era of new women had been short-lived.

Throughout the decade of the Great Depression, as American culture returned to the ideal of true womanhood, a number of ingenious projects were implemented to help unemployed theatre workers. For the most part, these charities were created and run by women. Playwright Rachel Crothers created the Stage Relief Fund, which raised money for theatre professionals in need. Much has been written about Hallie Flanagan's leadership of the Federal Theatre Project, a branch of President Roosevelt's Works Progress Administration specifically designed to put theatre professionals back to work. Lasting from 1935 to 1939, the work of the Federal Theatre Project not only provided jobs for countless theatre employees but also brought high-quality theatre to the American public at little or no cost.

Historically, less attention has been paid to actress-driven charities designed to help the theatre community in New York during the 1930s; in particular, little has been noted about Selena Royle's creation and leadership of the Actors Dinner Club, which was closing just as the Federal Theatre Project was beginning. As women workers during the Depression era, actresses were in a unique position. They received pay and worked hours equal to their male counterparts, an ideal of new womanhood. However, onstage, in the media, and often in their private lives, actresses appeared to uphold the values of the true woman ideal, prioritizing domesticity and morality. Actresses who created and ran charitable organizations like the Actors Dinner Club made the best of this dichotomy. On the one hand, charity is a central value of the true woman ideal. Conversely, these women used their professional know-how and connections to gain valuable leadership experience, blazing a trail for future generations of women. Actresses who started charities for the theatrical profession during the 1930s benefited from both the true woman and new woman ideals; as a result, they made invaluable contributions to their field.

The Actors Dinner Club was one of the most collaborative and imaginative endeavors created to assist out-of-work theatre professionals during the Depression era. Located in New York City, this dinner club was established in 1931 by actress Selena Royle, who conceived of the idea while performing in John Galsworthy's *The Roof* with Actors Dinner Club cofounders Bessie Beatty and William Sauter. Royle envisioned a place where unemployed and employed actors alike could enjoy meals seven nights a week, from 5 to 8 P.M., while being entertained.

Furthermore, Royle thoughtfully set up a system that would prevent anyone from knowing who had paid for their dinner and who had not, a system that the *New York Times* described as "a triumph of generous tact."[7] Tickets to the dinner club were available not only at the door but also at the offices of such organizations as the Actors' Equity Association and the Actors Fund of America. Those who could not afford to buy a ticket could discreetly ask for one at the Actors' Equity office, for example. When the ticket was presented at the dinner club, no one knew whether the ticket-holder had paid for it or not.

In the beginning stages of the project, not even Royle's father, a well-known playwright, believed in the Actors Dinner Club. In an October 9, 1932, *New York Times* article, Edwin Melton Royle wrote, "Frankly, I was one of those who did not believe in it, and I advised my daughter to abandon the project."[8] Apparently, however, Selena Royle had ample gifts of persuasion, earning the commitment of aid from several theatre organizations and actresses such as Helen Hayes, Katherine Cornell, and Ethel Barrymore. Barrymore served on the dinner club's board of directors. Several other famous actresses, including Mary Pickford and Mae West, contributed by giving free performances.

The dinner club was staffed primarily by volunteer Actors' Equity Association members, led by Royle, and underwritten by the Actors Fund of America.[9] Other organizations that contributed time and money included the Catholic Theatre Guild, the Episcopal Actors' Guild, the Jewish Theatrical Guild, Chorus Equity, the Lambs Club, the Friars Club, the Players Club, and the National Vaudeville Artists. Various restaurants and hotels donated food and supplies.

For the opening season, Rev. C. Everett Wagner of the Union Methodist Episcopal Church, a church that had a long history of supporting the theatre, donated the use of his church's hall, which had a capacity of seventy-four. The dinner club was so successful that it needed to move to larger quarters, eventually relocating five times and ending up at the Hotel Woodstock.

According to the *Billboard,* "during the first week, following its opening December 7, [1931,] The Actors Dinner Club served more than 1,400 persons."[10] On opening night, many patrons waited for up to forty-five minutes. The large number who attended and their willingness to wait in line demonstrated the great need for such aid. Tickets could be purchased at the door for fifty cents (one dollar for the general public) or were available for free at the various theatrical guilds, Actors' Equity, or the Actors Fund offices.[11] About half of every dollar made went toward free meals. The average dinner included soup or fruit cocktail, an entrée (chosen from two meats and one fish), three vegetables, dessert, and tea, milk, or coffee. Although most of the meals served were free, there were also many working actors who attended and made generous donations.[12]

A May 1934 article in *Stage Magazine* described the exciting environment of the Actors Dinner Club: "The waiters are actors and actresses out of work, who are glad to carry trays for seven dinners a week and no tips. You are as likely as not to have Mary Pickford or Irene Franklin, or Mae West, Frances Alga, Ruth St. Denis, Cornelia Otis Skinner, or almost anybody else doing their stuff while you dine. . . . It is as about as gracious a way of giving and taking charity as has ever been devised."[13] The dinner club was not just a venue to receive much-needed charity and to enjoy dinner and a show. Casting announcements were read, agents came looking for new talent, and tourists came to star-watch. According to Edwin Melton Royle, in one case a theatre manager spotted a man peeling potatoes in the kitchen and cast him in a new show. Overall, Royle pointed out, "First, last, and always it is a place to eat, but it is more than that. It is a place of contacts and human relationships. Men cannot live by bread alone.

To men or women who are out of a job, who need shelter or clothes or food, who have exhausted their own resources and those of their friends, the place is a godsend."[14] The club also provided some jobs for those who needed them. A destitute actor could "get a basement room, rent free, by doing janitor service. He [could] pick up a little money here and there shoveling snow."[15] These services were available to actresses as well as actors; however, unemployed actresses were more likely to be found working in the kitchen than shoveling snow.

The Actors Dinner Club provided free meals for countless theatre professionals for three and a half years. Ultimately, the club fell victim to the economic crisis. Due to rising food costs and consistently serving more free dinners than paid for, the club was forced to close its doors in 1935. During its brief existence the club had struggled financially, despite many benefits thrown on its behalf by stars such as Fanny Brice, Bob Hope, Jack Benny, and the Marx brothers. The dinner club, indeed, had much support from the theatrical profession, but the need of free meals for theatre employees was too great a problem to be solved by such a small organization. One *New York Times* reporter responded to the closing of the dinner club, saying: "Unsuccessful, to be sure, is a harsh word, for no organization which has steadfastly functioned through three years of national misery and fulfilled its mission in that time can be said to have missed success, no matter what its final fate may be. . . . [T]he popularity of the Dinner Club . . . is attested by the figures on the ledger. Since that opening night so long ago it had served in the neighborhood of 332,000 meals, more than two thirds of which were free."[16] The club was unique in many ways, not the least of which was that it was run and supported primarily by actresses, many of whom went on to continue charitable work in their field. In the 1940s, Selena Royle organized the Stagedoor Canteen, which provided free meals and entertainment for servicemen during World War II.

Since heightened morality and compassion were part and parcel of the true woman ideal, this ideal served Selena Royle and others like her very well. While compassion is not exclusive to women, perhaps being incubated in the values of the private sphere is part of what has given them a special role in the theatre. Combining the leadership training and skills of the new woman with values of the true woman enabled women in theatre to blaze trails not only for other women in the field but for men as well. These women who rose to leadership in charitable theatre organizations during the Depression also helped to remove the vestiges of the association of actresses with prostitutes and the general notion of theatre as a morally suspect place.

Throughout history, following in the footsteps of female leaders of charitable organizations like Selena Royle, actors and actresses have traditionally given performances to benefit those in need, whether to help survivors of Hurricane Katrina in 2005 or to fight inhumane conditions in Darfur. Considering that theatre is a difficult profession even in the best of times, the charitable spirit of theatre workers is quite remarkable. It is important to note that, rather than depending solely upon aid from others, members of the theatrical profession have used their imagination and skills to support their own community as well. The Actors Dinner Club lasted a short time, but the spirit that created it lives on today. Projects like Broadway Cares/Equity Fights AIDS, the healthcare support provided by Fractured Atlas, and the Actors Fund of America retirement homes uphold the legacy of the charities created by actresses during the Great Depression. Today, as the United States once again faces a time of economic crisis, theatre workers will do well to follow the example of pioneers like Selena Royle.

Notes

1. Barbara J. Harris, *Beyond Her Sphere; Women and the Professions in American History* (Westport, Conn.: Greenwood Publishing Group, 1968), 32.
2. Deborah S. Kolb, "The Rise and Fall of the New Woman in American Drama," *Educational Theatre Journal* 27 (May 1975): 150.
3. Ibid., 157.
4. Ibid., 149.
5. Chapman Catt quoted in S. J. Kleinberg, *Women in the United States 1830–1945* (New Brunswick, N.J.: Rutgers University Press, 1999), 282.
6. Genevieve Parkhurst, "Is Feminism Dead?" *Harper's Magazine*, May 1935, 735.
7. "Actors Must Eat, Too: At the Dinner Club in Forty-eighth Street the Profession Takes Care of Its Own," *New York Times*, December 9, 1931.
8. Edwin Melton Royle, "Actors Must Eat: Mr. Royle Writes of the Dinner Club, the Theatre's Own Restaurant," *New York Times*, October 9, 1932.
9. "Actors Dinner Club Will Have Many Players as Guests for Meals," *Variety*, December 1, 1931, 37.
10. "Splendid Work of Actors Club," *Billboard*, December 26, 1931, 25.
11. "Actors' Free Dinner Club Cheerful Locale for Laughs and Stories," *Variety*, December 15, 1931, 35.
12. Ibid.
13. "The Actors Dinner Club," *Stage Magazine*, May 1934, 37.
14. Edwin Melton Royle, *New York Times*, October 9, 1932.
15. *Variety*, December 1, 1931, 37.
16. Bosley Crowther, "The Actors Dinner Club Bows Out," *New York Times*, March 17, 1935.

Storytelling, Chiggers, and the Bible Belt

The Georgia Experiment as the Public Face
of the Federal Theatre Project

—ELIZABETH OSBORNE

Their feet are still in the mud. They live in indescribable want, want of food,
want of houses, want of any kind of life.... Their one entertainment is an
occasional revival meeting, so when I get excited, tear around and gesticulate,
they think it's the Holy Ghost descending upon me. It isn't. It's a combination of rage that such conditions should exist in our country, and chiggers,
which I share with my audience.
HERBERT STRATTON PRICE, director of the Georgia Experiment

One of the most frequently repeated stories of the Federal Theatre Project's
rural activities centers on a community puppet theatre in Georgia. Hallie Flanagan writes in *Arena: The Story of the Federal Theatre:*

In many places in Georgia the children were taught to make puppet theatres and
puppets, and one day Herbert Price made a discovery. A little girl tried to smuggle the
puppet she had been making home under her ragged dress, and when it was discovered
she refused to give it up.

"Hit's mine. Hit's the onliest thing I ever had what was mine." The theatre changed
its activity temporarily, and for the first time every child in the vicinity had a doll—a
corncob doll dressed in gay clothes made of old sugar sacking dyed with the berries of
the region.[1]

That Federal Theatre Project (FTP) personnel were able to integrate themselves into this rural southern community to such a degree is testament both to the power of theatre as a universal device and to the agency of the communities that embraced the project. This simple example shows the needs of a single child altering—if only temporarily—the activities of the local FTP; she stole a doll, refused to give it back, explained her reasoning, and soon all the local children had their own dolls courtesy of the FTP. The veracity of this story notwithstanding, it is a charming tale of the FTP's effect on the small communities in Georgia and of the mythology that surrounded the project's efforts.

The story of this young puppet thief appears repeatedly in the FTP literature and epitomizes the goals of the project on national, regional, and local scales. This essay examines the so-called Georgia Experiment in terms of its goals and achievements, and then contextualizes it within the mythology of the FTP as a whole. In the Georgia Experiment, three distinct threads become tangled, resulting in an example of slippage between stated goals, reality, and the public face of the FTP. Why was this story so vital to the public face of the FTP? Moreover, what does it mean that no archival evidence for this particular event appears to exist? To examine these questions, it is first necessary to discuss the overriding intentions of National Director Hallie Flanagan with respect to the FTP as a national entity and then to look more closely at FTP activities in Georgia. I then juxtapose the reality of the Georgia Experiment with the public mythology of the project in the aforementioned anecdote.

The FTP was the most massive, semi-cohesive national theatre ever seen in the United States. Under Flanagan's leadership, it employed more than thirteen thousand theatre professionals throughout the country, brought theatre to an audience of more than thirty million, and fought to provide locally relevant theatre to a predominantly working-class audience. Flanagan's task—to create a theatre that was "worthy of its audience" in quality and devoted to their lives and "immediate problems"—demanded a decentralized program that would capitalize on local talents and themes.

Although controversial productions such as *The Cradle Will Rock, The Swing Mikado,* and the "Voodoo" *Macbeth* garnered more press, I argue that these productions operated not in the mainstream but on the fringes of the FTP—the exceptions rather than the rule. Indeed, I suggest that the heart of the FTP—the plays and projects that had the potential to be both national and local in scope—beat in the wilderness of the theatre world. Tent theatres, traveling troupes, and the many small companies that performed in the more rural sections of the country brought theatre to the people who were unlikely to attend Broadway-style performances in the city. A study of the FTP's goals in creating locally relevant theatre is incomplete without discussion of its rural efforts. After all, one of Flanagan's expressed intentions was to create a theatre that was national in scope but regional and local in emphasis; for Flanagan, this meant that the FTP had to go beyond the nation's urban centers. Thus, these comparatively rural, decentralized FTP units would provide fertile ground for a grassroots, community-based theatre. Ironically, since these performances are often the most difficult to research, they are the least likely to appear in scholarly analysis.[2]

In the summer of 1936, an Englishman by the name of Herbert Stratton Price appeared in Flanagan's Washington, D.C., office and asked for "something hard to do." Ideally suited for an adventure in community drama development, Price had experience in acting, directing, and stage management as well as knowledge of sociology and interest in rural community drama.[3] He had been working as a liaison between the FTP and the Recreation and Resettlement Project; in this capacity, he traveled throughout the twelve southern states attending conferences, demonstrating techniques, initiating and developing an extensive network of contacts throughout the Works Progress Administration (WPA), and building up local and regional interest in recreational and community drama. Flanagan challenged Price to detail a viable proposal for an experimental recreational drama program. Price's plan would extend beyond the urban centers and into the vast countryside, focusing primarily on smaller cities and towns in the Deep South. "The ideal achievement is for the plays produced by the Community Drama Groups to draw color and background from the life, desires, and ambitions of the community itself," he wrote. "The ultimate aim is not chiefly the production of plays, but the encouragement of the people in the free exercise of their imagination."[4]

Price emphasized the same traits that Flanagan herself highlighted in her national plans for the FTP. The Georgia Experiment would draw from local issues and concerns in a way that invited community members to shape their own theatre, thus providing agency to a group of individuals who had received little opportunity to shape their own public personas since the Depression began. In this way, community drama would provide a form of recreation and develop skills, work, and talents, as well as offer much-needed moral support to a struggling nation while using only a few key individuals to lead the organization in the South. While the Georgia Experiment itself relied on the strength of the foundation that Eugene Bergmann (in his role as a community drama consultant to the state) and Price developed in their travels, the experiment could serve as a model for expansion to other communities in Georgia, the South, and the country.

Once Price convinced the national administration that the project would satisfy a local need, employ theatre artists, and help to stabilize the FTP's apparently perpetually unpredictable position in Georgia and the South, he received approval for a ninety-day experimental collaboration with the Division of Recreation Projects and Women's and Professional Projects. These drama consultants would remain on their current FTP project payrolls at their current salary but would work locally in specific Georgia towns and cities for the duration of the Georgia Experiment; if successful in instigating the development of a community drama program, each consultant would have the option to remain in Georgia to continue their work after the ninety days.[5] Price chose five individuals from the New York Community Drama Program[6] with the assistance of the program supervisor, Madalyn O'Shea. The FTP sent these five drama consultants—Mary Dirnberger (Savannah), Charles Carey (Columbus), Joseph Fetsch (Augusta), Howard Gantier (Albany), and Edward J. Hayes (Rome)—into Georgia communities as drama consultants. Eugene Bergmann, an industrious Georgian who began his career with the FTP via a letter-writing campaign as an advocate for theatre in his state, had initially been assigned to develop community drama for the state of Georgia; he was reassigned to Atlanta when the other five drama consultants arrived, bringing the total number of recreational theatre projects to six. The project mission was "to organize and develop Community Drama Groups."[7] More specifically, these six people had three months to travel into the small cities and communities of Georgia, incite or capitalize on local interest in theatre, and create drama that the people of the community would support financially once the three-month experiment ended. As Price explained, "the ultimate aim was to have the various communities support their own Drama activities without Federal aid."[8]

Many interested parties followed the Georgia Experiment. In addition to Flanagan and the national FTP administration, Frances Nimmo Green (director of the Southern Play Bureau), Gay Shepperson (administrator in the Division of Recreation Projects), D. G. Nichols (district director of Savannah's Women's and Professional Projects), and numerous WPA officials requested repeated updates on the project.[9] In a letter to Price, Shepperson wrote: "Thank you very much for keeping me informed and abreast of events. I want to make a special trip to see the effects of this work personally, which I plan to do before long. On my recent trip North I stopped in the Washington office and found the entire office intensely interested in this Georgia experiment and . . . very anxious to get first hand information of the progress of the experiment. From the evidence of publicity in your letters there seems to be no question about its ultimate success."[10] Certainly, the Georgia Experiment was buoyed by the optimism of the FTP, the Division of Recreation, and the WPA.

Although the Georgia Experiment varied somewhat based on location, the basic outline of the project's goals and methods remained consistent. For the purposes of this essay I will focus on one of the five experiment centers: Rome. Neither the most successful nor the least successful, the Rome project appears to have been average in community response, challenges, and relative successes. Located in northwest Georgia, just a few miles from the Alabama border, Rome was the leading industrial city of northwest Georgia and boasted a population of approximately twenty-two thousand.[11] FTP community drama director Edward Hayes arrived on February 22, 1937. Like most of the other drama consultants, he was sent from New York and arrived in Rome with little more than a suitcase and the name of the local recreation supervisor. His belongings were in storage, he had no lodgings, and travel and expenses came out of his own sparsely populated pocket, as his travel reimbursement and paycheck were to arrive at a later date.[12] Hayes and his family stayed with the local recreation supervisor for a week, seeking affordable accommodations and attempting to establish a rapport with the locals.

Certainly, Hayes encountered numerous challenges during his ninety days in Rome; yet he experienced a number of successes as well, as evidenced by his reports to Price and local newspaper records. Hayes's early reports to Price list many problems. Upon arrival he found that the Community Drama Committee of Rome was poorly organized and had little overall interest in the project. As he described it, his invitations in the decidedly anti-administration newspapers went unanswered, so he was forced to "go out into the highways and byways to secure members and arouse some enthusiasm."[13] Compounding Hayes's challenges as an outsider in a moderately sized southern town was the conspicuous absence of the project's front man and supervisor, the personable and experienced Herbert Stratton Price, who was off in the Mississippi Valley spearheading a campaign to bring theatre to the thousands of flood refugees following the Great Flood of 1937—one of the most disastrous floods in U.S. history.[14] Price engineered the Georgia Experiment in a series of staggered beginnings in January and February 1937, which allowed him to make initial introductions for each drama consultant locally and help to smooth the consultants' entrance into the community. Since Price conceived of the program and laid the foundation for its success with his numerous trips and vast network of local contacts, both at the community level and within the administration of the state WPA offices, his absence left a gap for those drama consultants who arrived in late January and throughout February.

It is interesting to note the contrast between Hayes's perceptions and those of the "poorly organized" Community Drama Committee and other citizens of

Rome. In a letter to Price, Assistant Recreation Supervisor R. H. Elliott reported that the "first week's work by Mr. Hayes in Rome has produced much interest and much organization progress." According to Elliott, the committee built up Hayes's arrival in the newspapers, arranged for office and auditorium space, and secured initial funding for the program. Elliott personally introduced Hayes to members of the drama committee, radio stations, and newspapers and arranged for Hayes to stay in his home until Hayes could arrange suitable accommodations at the local hotel.[15]

Elliott's perception of the local interest in the program is validated by the accounts printed in the *Rome News-Tribune,* the anti-Roosevelt daily that was the town's only newspaper in the 1930s. The *News-Tribune* printed a surprisingly large number of articles related to the FTP's experiment in Rome and serves as one of the few remaining chronicles of those activities outside of the National Archives and the Library of Congress. Although none of these articles were attributed to a specific writer, as was the case with nearly all of the paper's articles, the writer did not seem particularly anti-FTP, anti–Georgia Experiment, or anti-Hayes (although the paper habitually decried Roosevelt's New Deal, the WPA, Social Security, the U.S. Supreme Court, and many of the more liberal political policies). The first article, printed a week before Hayes arrived, referred to the recent visit of the Atlanta Theatre Guild, which incited local interest in the theatre and looked forward to Hayes's arrival. The advisory committee, which had formed months earlier to engage Price, the FTP, and the WPA in discussions about a community theatre in Rome, featured a number of prominent Romans who would eventually play major roles in the FTP production of *The Fool* and in the numerous radio plays and religious dramas.[16] Repeatedly, the newspaper articles noted the excitement of the community, the exotic nature of the New Yorker sent to their town by the FTP, and the fact that Rome was one of only five points in the state to receive this "recognition and opportunity." As Hayes and the drama committee announced decisions regarding the choice of Channing Pollock's *The Fool* and the other opportunities the recreational program would offer Romans, the articles betray a distinct pride; *The Fool* "made theatrical history," and the fact that their recreational drama program planned to take on "one of the most difficult of productions" placed Rome on a cultural footing parallel to Atlanta and Savannah. In fact, the paper optimistically predicted "one of the finest amateur performances in the history of Rome when the curtain rises on the first act of 'The Fool.'"[17]

By mid-March, the recreational drama unit in Rome had its own name— the Community Drama Players of Rome—and continued to appear regularly in the newspaper with tidbits about radio dramas, religious programming, and rehearsal updates. Articles pointed to the town's positive attitude toward the players, the high quality of the stage sets (created by Romans for their production of *The Fool*), the talent of their community drama director (Hayes), and the skills of the Romans involved in the production. In fact, by the time the ninety-day Georgia Experiment concluded in Rome it seems that Hayes had successfully won over the "anti-administration newspaper" he referred to in his initial report to Price.

This disparity between the different perspectives is striking; Hayes insisted that the community's apathy jeopardized the project, while the local perception via Elliott and the *News-Tribune* reported that the project was proceeding well. About a month after his arrival, Hayes reevaluated his difficulties: "The principal obstacle or difficulty to the Drama movement in Rome, as I see it . . . is not the lack of interest, but the CLASS barrier, there is a very distinct social strata in this town and it's going to be a hard job to hurdle it, I consider this the real problem, but I really believe that I [am] making some headway . . . and altho the results are not what I should like them to be, I think that I will eventually succeed in leveling the barrier to some extent."[18] This statement points to several issues of interest. First, note that local apathy was no longer an issue. Instead, Hayes highlighted the issue of class—leaving out all mention of race, which was also a highly charged issue in Rome. Perhaps most intriguing is the implicit assumption that the project was already enjoying success with one class and that Hayes wanted to expand his program across class barriers to include a larger portion of the community. Considering the obstacles Hayes faced upon his arrival in Rome, this speaks to an extraordinary level of success in a single month of work.

Notwithstanding these widely varying initial impressions, it is clear that Hayes's success swelled as the experiment continued. In three short months he put together a production of Channing Pollock's *The Fool*, spoke at a number of local schools and churches, and created a broadcast that went out over the local radio station every Sunday. In addition, as the *News-Tribune* explains, Hayes spearheaded a free seven-week series of "religious dramatic presentations" held Sunday afternoons in a local community auditorium. "All plays," asserted the newspaper, were "endorsed by local ministers" and "carry vivid Biblical messages."[19] A special Mother's Day production included exclusive seating and complimentary transportation for any mothers who wished to attend the performance of *A Mother's Memories*, based on Luke 1:40–48.[20] Other works included *He Is Risen* (a radio drama designed to "show how the disciples groped their way out of perplexity and sorrow into belief and understanding and to give us listeners a deeper appreciation of the Risen Christ"),[21] *The Prodigal Son, The Liv-*

ing Christ, The Widow's Mite, and *The Stranger at the Gate.* Each of these plays was based on enacting and illuminating specific Bible verses. These religious plays were so popular with audiences that they carried on for several weeks after Hayes returned to New York City at the end of May. Hayes worked with a group of about sixty-five people during the first month. He cast thirty-seven Romans in *The Fool,* used more to build the production, and set up classes for those interested in playwriting, design, and other theatrical activities. Like the other recreational drama leaders, Hayes worked with children and saw interest spike in subsequent months.

One additional activity lends credence to Hayes's ability to build a recreational community drama in Rome: a sister town's request that Hayes create a similar program for its own community. A group of women from Marietta, about fifty miles southeast of Rome, visited Hayes and asked that he organize and lead a community drama program in their town. Approval for their request arrived through official FTP channels, and Hayes described Marietta's enthusiasm for the program as dwarfing what he found in Rome. He chose another Channing Pollock play, *The Enemy,* cast it, and began the rehearsal process in mid-March 1937.[22] In fact, Hayes's efforts to build a program in Marietta were important enough to appear in the *Rome News-Tribune,* which noted that rehearsals were being held at the Episcopal church and that "leading citizens of Marietta [were] identified with the movement there."[23] The situation in Marietta proved difficult for Hayes, though, as was shown in one of the few letters to Price from the latter period of Hayes's work in Rome. Hayes found it "absolutely impossible to serve the Marietta District under the present arrangement . . . I can not see how I can give them any more time in Marietta as they are requesting without neglecting the Rome program." Hayes cited two specific difficulties: the two-dollar fare to Marietta (and the lack of timely reimbursement of these funds) and the time required to run two individual programs in two different cities.[24] His involvement with the community drama program in Marietta appears to have ended around this time, as subsequent FTP correspondence demonstrated an unwillingness to fund his travel expenses, and Hayes was unable to pay the fare.[25]

Hayes's experience in Marietta raises two specific questions. First, why did the community members from Marietta travel to Rome to invite Hayes to spearhead their community drama movement, when Atlanta was a mere twenty miles away and possessed both superior resources and a recreational drama consultant in a position parallel to that which Hayes held in Rome? Eugene Bergmann, the Atlanta drama consultant, had traveled throughout the state in his capacity as a statewide drama consultant, so it is probable that he was familiar with the

Marietta community. Since the request received approval at both the state and regional administrative levels within the FTP, the choice of Hayes over Bergmann was likely a conscious one that was at least tacitly reinforced by the approval of the FTP. In what way(s), then, was Hayes a more appealing candidate than Bergmann? Second, local newspapers show no record of performances of Pollock's *The Enemy* in Marietta; there is, however, record of a community theatre group, led by Bergmann, rehearsing and performing August L. Stern's *The Hired Husband* in late May.[26] Just as the *Rome News-Tribune* predicted *The Fool*'s success, so did the *Marietta Journal* anticipate *The Hired Husband* to be "one of the best ever produced in Marietta"; the cast celebrated opening night with a spaghetti dinner.[27]

While archival records and other primary sources fail to address these questions, I suggest that Hayes and Bergmann offered distinct programming choices to their respective communities, and that Hayes was more appealing to the community of Marietta—until Hayes found himself unable to continue due to financial hardship. Bergmann's choice, *The Hired Husband,* was a light, Broadway-style comedy. His own work throughout the state was expansive, ranging from storytelling and holiday pageants to the staging of three original programs in Waycross's Slash Pine Festival; D. G. Nichols, district director of Savannah's Women's, Service, and Professional Projects, touted Bergmann's role in the festival, writing, "I think he did more for us in putting over the value of the recreation program to a large group of representative people from all over the state than anything we have done so far."[28] This was certainly a notable accomplishment, and one that led ultimately to the conceptualization and realization of the Georgia Experiment. However, Bergmann's productions tended toward lighter fare—comedies, marionettes, and children's theatre being the most common.

In contrast, the program Hayes offered in Rome consisted almost exclusively of drama with a clear and respectful focus on religion, much of which (according to newspaper accounts) was actually approved by the ministers of the local churches; in fact, two of the five core members of Rome's Community Drama Committee—Rev. John H. Wood and Rev. H. F. Joynet—were local pastors. Moreover, what I have been able to glean of Hayes's personal background suggests that he would be uniquely suited to the creation of a community drama program with strong religious overtones. Hayes directed the Broadway Temple Players in New York City in a production of the one-act drama *The Widow's Mite* at the Broadway Tabernacle Methodist Episcopal Church in 1934, prior to his induction into the FTP's Community Drama Program in 1936.[29] It seems that Hayes grew up in a theologically minded family. His brother, Rev. Thomas J. Hayes, was a professor of philosophy at St. Anselm's College, and his sister, Anna M. Hayes, became the reverend mother of the Western Province of the Order of the Little Sisters of the Poor, a Roman Catholic religious order for women.[30] Hayes's direction of the Broadway Temple Players demonstrated a link (whether or not his own religious proclivities tended in this direction) to the Methodist Episcopal Church. His ability to integrate religion and theatre likely served Hayes well in his capacity as drama consultant in Rome. During the 1930s at least 16 percent of Floyd County residents over the age of fourteen were members of the various branches of the Methodist Episcopal Church. Another 25 percent were members of branches of the Baptist Church, all of which were categorized as evangelical Protestant religions. According to the 1930 U.S. Census, Rome made up just under half of the Floyd County population. The statistics for Marietta (Cobb County) paralleled those of Rome in this area.[31] Certainly, religion could not be ignored as an identifying characteristic in these communities; Hayes's ability to unite religion and community drama deferentially was likely one of the keys to his success in Rome, as well as one of the factors that drew the women of Marietta to him rather than to the light comedies of Bergmann.

In many ways, Hayes's experiences in Rome were representative of the Georgia Experiment as a whole. Most of the drama consultants met initial resistance of varying degrees, depending on their familiarity with the issues of their communities and the groundwork laid by Bergmann and Price. Although Price knew it could pose a problem, he was forced to send New York directors and organizers to lead four of the five rural projects, as he could not find any Georgians who were qualified as both relief workers and community theatre directors and willing to lead the projects in these small towns.[32] As Price would argue in his assessment of the program, "it is obviously difficult, if not impossible, to competently judge any experiment or project without personal knowledge of community problems, attitudes, and resources."[33] This lack of firsthand knowledge of the region, compounded by Price's absence because of the ill-timed flooding of the Mississippi and Ohio Rivers, stymied several of the projects during the crucial formative weeks. Moreover, Price noted that several of the projects took place in communities that already had some basic interest in theatre (and in some cases, infrastructures in place for the production of community theatre), while others did not. In Savannah, Columbus, Atlanta, and Rome, drama consultants built on the interest or organizations already in place; this was one of the keys to success in such an intense, brief experiment in recreational theatre.[34] Since the experiment lasted for only three months, the drama consultants could not develop leisurely relationships with members of the community in addition to building a recreational drama program. Price highlighted the need to train local personnel and emphasized the importance of flexibility in theatre recreation projects: "One thing which this experiment has revealed is the desirability of using more than one method of approach and more than one method of organization. There should be freedom to adopt that method of approach and organization which would appear to be the most effective in a community in light of local conditions."[35]

Price's argument—that each project director should be empowered to adopt the most effective method of approach for his or her local community—recalled Flanagan's ideas regarding the need for a decentralized, locally relevant focus to the FTP as a whole. For both Price and Flanagan, these practices required personnel in each location to learn about their communities in visceral, individualized ways so that they could tailor recreational drama programs to the community's needs. This knowledge was particularly crucial in the South, which operated more than any other region with the "flying squadron method."[36] Developed due to the limited resources in the South, this method focused the disbursement of personnel through the region as needed but suffered the unfortunate side effect of distancing these traveling artists and administrators from the communities in which they produced FTP work.

Price's ideas were so successful, and coincided so well with Flanagan's goals for the FTP as a whole, that they excited interested in Pennsylvania, West Virginia, and North Carolina. WPA administrators from these states watched the progress of the Georgia Experiment with interest and approached Price regarding the possibility of a recreational program in their states. With the approval of the national administration, Price began preliminary work in North Carolina and West Virginia. Applying the principles learned in the Georgia Experiment, he sought professional FTP personnel native to each state to spearhead the movement.[37] In May 1938 Price wrote of his success building a parallel program in North Carolina. It was only when repeated threats to his job coincided with the prohibitive cutbacks in the summer of 1937 that these projects stalled.

The previous sections discussed the Georgia Experiment's goals, execution, and achievements through a case study of Edward J. Hayes's activities in Rome; but what of the mythology that has grown up around the program? In a 1938 letter to Flanagan, Price described the success of his recent trip to North Carolina and broached a dilemma: the International Grenfell Association had offered Price a position in community organization in northern Newfoundland. Yet his reluctance to leave the FTP shone through: "As you well know I have pioneered in the field that now appears to be on the brink of real development. I should, of course, like to remain with you if you feel there is a spot for me in this new and broader program."[38] Two months later, Price did not hesitate to chastise Flanagan for her assessment of the Georgia Experiment: "If we had followed through on our original plan in community drama in other sections of the country—servicing key communities outside of the larger cities—these centers would today be our outposts in the field and our touring companies would have representatives strategically placed." A handwritten note in the margin, presumably by Flanagan, stated only, "True."[39]

And so, the Georgia Experiment was reduced from the proverbial apple of the FTP's eye—a golden opportunity for meaningful collaborations between the FTP and sister WPA agencies, as well as a chance to realize Flanagan's goals for a relevant, community-based national theatre—to a few apocryphal stories. But what of the mythology that has grown up around the Georgia Experiment? Recall the story of the young girl who stole her corncob puppet doll and changed the activities of the entire community drama group. This story became representative of the Georgia Experiment and, with it, FTP activities outside of the large urban centers; yet there is no archival evidence of this specific event, and it is unlikely that the FTP supplied funds for a mass-puppet-making endeavor. This story is in Flanagan's personal history of the FTP, *Arena*, *Federal Theatre Magazine*, *Federal One*, and in countless other locations (although its source is never cited).[40] In fact, the story is so frequently repeated that another FTP worker named Herbert Price saw it in print and felt it necessary to write to Lorraine Brown and the George Mason University Oral History staff to correct the record; as he explained, he had never traveled to Georgia, let alone "helped little 'hill' people to make good dolls, as a side issue of puppetry, for their first possession of that type."[41] Although research demonstrates that the FTP did, in fact, have two individuals named Herbert Price employed simultaneously, this Price's insistence that he has nothing to do with this story is interesting.

Yet the problem of the anecdote about the poor little girl who allegedly changed the face of the Georgia FTP remains. What can the scholar make of this (very likely false) story serving as the public face of the FTP's rural exploits? It is easy to see why this story is repeated; it demonstrates the versatility and power of the FTP. If true, it suggests that the FTP was in the process of integrating itself into the community in a physical and ideological way. The corncob dolls, distributed to every child in the area, would serve as tactile reminders of the FTP's presence and interest in the local population. More than that, these dolls were actually created by the children and became their sole possessions. Here was a kindred spirit—a struggling, plucky, federal organization that cared enough to identify what the children needed and then find a way to give it to them in spite of the obstacles. The appeal cannot be ignored.

In a 2003 essay, Thomas Postlewait debates the place of anecdotes in theatre history: "Even the most diligent scholars have recognized that the distinction between facts and anecdotes (or records and legends) is impossible to maintain consistently in any examination of historical documents; many records are not factual; many anecdotes not only contain a kernel of factuality but also express representative truths."[42] While I cannot designate the story of the young puppet thief as fact, I also cannot dismiss it as fiction. It is certainly possible that the story contains a "kernel of factuality," and quite likely that it evokes a "representative truth." If this story is a "representative truth," what does Flanagan's inclusion of it in *Arena* say about the role she wanted the FTP to play in rural and national theatre?

I suggest that the story of the FTP adapting to the needs of a poor, young girl was chosen to show a specific relationship between the FTP and its audience. The child was poor, clearly a member of the impoverished "people" who made up much of the FTP's audience. In this story, the FTP not only listened to her needs but adapted its own function to serve those needs. The FTP prioritized serving the community on its own terms; no mention is made of the extensive bureaucratic process required to change activities, the loss in potential box-office revenue, or the additional expenditure involved in making dolls that would then be given to the community (as opposed to being maintained in the service of the government). The mythological FTP, free from the constraints the real FTP was forced to operate under throughout its existence, was able to become the people's theatre without concern for the consequences. This image of a true people's theatre, coveted by Flanagan during her time as national director of the FTP, emerges superbly from this story. Hence, if this story is fabricated, it is easy to see why this slippage between the actual and the mythological FTP was so appealing.

Vital to the study of the Federal Theatre Project as both national theatre and as a reflection of the constantly evolving relationship between the FTP and its surrounding communities, the Georgia Experiment provides a case study for examining both the "real" and the mythological public faces of the FTP. While the reality of the Georgia Experiment laid a successful foundation for further community drama activities, both in Georgia and as a model for parallel structures in other states, the program did not survive cuts to funding and manpower. According to Price, the energy of the Georgia Experiment fizzled when the drama consultants departed for New York and FTP support evaporated.

However, if this anecdote is resituated as part of the mythological public face of the FTP, the program takes on a different cast. In this light, the Georgia

Experiment becomes an ideal example of the decentralization and local relevance that Flanagan prioritized. It employed relief workers, cost the government very little, raised public morale, helped develop FTP audiences, and played to public sympathies. The story of the child puppet-thief is an icon of Depression-era America; an innocent and youthful American, put down by economic strife and struggling to maintain her individuality and imagination, stands up for her rights and single-handedly makes her corner of the world a better place. This represents the best the FTP would have to offer—locally relevant and desperately needed activities for American communities. And so, while the Georgia Experiment itself sputtered into obscurity, the mythology provided evidence of the virility of the Federal Theatre Project. Thus, as the public face of the Federal Theatre Project, the Georgia Experiment endures.

Notes

Epigraphs: Price quoted in Hallie Flanagan, *Arena: The Story of the Federal Theatre* (New York: Duell, Sloan, and Pearce, 1940), 91–92; Josef Lentz, interview by John O'Connor, April 7, 1977, New Orleans, p. 21, WPA Oral Histories Collection, Special Collections and Archives, George Mason University Libraries.

1. Flanagan, *Arena*, 92.
2. The only study of the Georgia Experiment that I have located to date is in John Russell Poole, "The Federal Theatre Project in Georgia and Alabama: An Historical Analysis of Government Theatre in the Deep South" (Ph.D. diss., University of Georgia, Athens, 1995).
3. Flanagan, *Arena*, 91.
4. Herbert S. Price, "Federal Theatre Community Drama Program in Georgia," "Price File—Rome," Box 523, Entry 952, Correspondence of Herbert S. Price—Coordinator for Community Drama, Record Group 69, National Archives and Records Administration [hereafter NARA].
5. Four of the five drama consultants were a part of the Community Drama training program in New York City at the time of their assignment, earning $95.44 monthly. Mary Dirnberger, the representative assigned to Savannah, was working in North Carolina at the time of this assignment and continued on that salary at $125 monthly while working in Georgia. Herbert Price to Ellen S. Woodward, undated memorandum, "Price File—Community Drama, General," Box 523, Entry 952, Correspondence of Herbert S. Price—Coordinator for Community Drama, Record Group 69, NARA.
6. The New York Community Drama Program was linked to a training program for community theatre directors and run by Madalyn O'Shea out of the New York City offices and New York's Provincetown Playhouse. The program was so popular, and their theater so overcrowded, that O'Shea finally resorted to banning visitors from the space entirely.
7. Herbert S. Price, "Federal Theatre Community Drama Program in Georgia (Rome to be

included)," "Herbert S. Price, Correspondence," Box 523, Entry 952, Correspondence of Herbert S. Price—Coordinator for Community Drama, New York City, Record Group 69, NARA.

8. Price to Dorothy Braley, undated memo, "Community Drama—Herbert Price," Box 5, Entry 839, General Correspondence of the National Office, 1935–1939, Record Group 69, NARA.

9. Early in the process, Shepperson expressed interest in a loose partnership between the FTP and the Division of Recreation Projects. She and Price communicated about this for some time, both before and during the Georgia Experiment.

10. Shepperson to Price, January 26, 1937, "Price File—Community Drama, General," Box 523, Entry 952, Correspondence of Herbert S. Price—Coordinator for Community Drama, Record Group 69, NARA.

11. *Georgia: A Guide to Its Towns and Countryside,* Compiled and Written by Workers of the Writers' Program of the Work Progress Administration in the State of Georgia, American Guide Series (Athens: University of Georgia Press, 1940), 443.

12. According to a December 1, 1936, memo, each of the five drama consultants was to be preapproved for travel expenses and a per diem of three dollars for the first twenty-one days in the field. However, subsequent communications between the drama consultants and various FTP administrators document that this process—if it indeed did come to pass—was not a smooth one, and that the drama consultants were forced to place their belongings in storage, live in cheap hotels or with new acquaintances, and fund their work-related travels for the majority of their time in Georgia. Herbert Price to Madalyn O'Shea, December 1, 1936, "Price File—Community Drama, General," Box 523, Entry 952, Correspondence of Herbert S. Price—Coordinator for Community Drama, Record Group 69, NARA.

13. Hayes to Charlotte Holt, Received March 23, 1937, "Price File—Rome, Georgia," Box 523, Entry 952, Correspondence of Herbert S. Price—Coordinator for Community Drama, Record Group 69, NARA.

14. Just as the Georgia Experiment began, a massive flood struck a number of states along the Mississippi River. Price proposed a plan for a flood tour, and the FTP appointed him the leader of a company that traveled throughout the flood zone, offering entertainment. The company performed in three states and before more than twelve thousand refugees in less than a month. For a more detailed study of the flood tour and of Herbert Stratton Price, see my article "A Nation in Need: Revelations and Disaster Relief in the Federal Theatre Project," *Journal of American Drama and Theatre* 20, no. 2 (2008): 49–64.

15. Elliott to Price, March 1, 1937, "Price File—Rome, GA," Box 523, Correspondence of Herbert S. Price—Coordinator for Community Drama, Record Group 69, NARA.

16. "Federal Theatre Director Arrives Here February 22," *Rome News-Tribune,* February 14, 1937, 12.

17. "Details of Federal Theatre to Be Given," *Rome-News Tribune,* February 17, 1937, 2; "Federal Theatre Director Comes to Begin Duties," *Rome News-Tribune,* February 24, 1937, 2; "Federal Theatre Begins In Rome with 'The Fool,'" *Rome News-Tribune,* February 26, 1937, 10; "Cast Announced for 'The Fool,' Federal Drama," *Rome News-Tribune,* March 21, 1937, 11.

18. Hayes to Charlotte Holt, received March 23, 1937, "Price File—Columbus, GA," Box 523, Correspondence of Herbert S. Price—Coordinator for Community Drama, Record Group 69, NARA.

19. "Religious Plays to Be Presented by Drama Players," *Rome News-Tribune*, April 20, 1937, 2.

20. These verses focus on the meeting of Mary, future mother of Jesus Christ, and Elisabeth, future mother of John the Baptist, during Elisabeth's pregnancy.

21. "Rome Drama Unit to Present Play Sunday Afternoon," *Rome News-Tribune*, March 26, 1937, 2.

22. Hayes to Charlotte Holt, received March 23, 1937, "Price File—Rome, GA," Box 523, Correspondence of Herbert S. Price—Coordinator for Community Drama, Record Group 69, NARA.

23. "Cast Announced for 'The Fool,' Federal Drama," *Rome News-Tribune*, March 21, 1937, 11.

24. Hayes to Price, April 6, 1937, "Price File—Rome, GA," Box 523, Correspondence of Herbert S. Price—Coordinator for Community Drama, Record Group 69, NARA.

25. Traveling the one-hundred-mile roundtrip to Marietta for rehearsals of a production, even two to three times per week, would have required approximately 15 to 20 percent of Hayes's pretax monthly salary of $95.44.

26. Unfortunately, the records of the *Marietta Journal* are incomplete, particularly for January, February, and March 1937, and, as such, fail to chronicle the search for a community drama consultant or Hayes's efforts to work within the Marietta community; however, the records for April and May are nearly complete. "Theatre Group to Present Play May 21–22," *Marietta Journal*, May 7, 1937, 3.

27. Bergmann and his wife attended the spaghetti dinner to celebrate the opening of *The Hired Husband*. "Theatre Group to Present Play May 21–22," *Marietta Journal*, May 7, 1937, 3; "Theatre Guild Gives Spaghetti Supper for Cast," *Marietta Journal*, May 24, 1937, 3.

28. Nichols to Gay Shepperson, November 17, 1936, "Price File—Community Drama, General," Box 523, Entry 952, Correspondence of Herbert S. Price—Coordinator for Community Drama, Record Group 69, NARA.

29. Note that Hayes chose to produce *The Widow's Mite* again in Rome on May 30, 1937, although this was after he had returned to New York City. "Church Programs in the City Today," *New York Times*, July 1, 1934, N6.

30. Obituary, *New York Times*, September 4, 1935, 19; "Rev. Mother Blandine," *New York Times*, May 20, 1937, 21.

31. These data are, according to the cautionary note on the census, "seriously incomplete"; hampered by lack of funds and cooperation from churches, the survey resulted in "significant undercounts for many denominations throughout the South," noting particularly the strangely low numbers of the Southern Baptist Convention and the Methodist Episcopal Church, South. Thus these percentages are likely lower than an accurate count would have been. In calculating these percentages, I excluded all individuals under age fourteen because the numbers provided by the Census of Religious Bodies considered only those individuals who were of age and official members of the church. The 1930 U.S. Census calculated the total population of Floyd County at 48,667 and the population of individuals age fourteen or over at 33,146. I have also combined the many different branches of the Baptist and Methodist Churches into a single percentage for the sake of clarity. For the complete, detailed results of this survey see Department of

Commerce and Labor, Bureau of the Census, *United States Census of Religious Bodies, County File, 1936*, Association of Religion Data Archives, http://www.thearda.com/Archive/Files/Downloads/1936CENSCT_DL.asp; U.S. Census Bureau, *Census of Population and Housing*, Population—Georgia, Table 13, Composition of the Population, By County, 1930, http://www.census.gov/prod/www/abs/decennial/1930.html.

32. The most notable exception to this was Mary Dirnberger, consultant to the successful Savannah unit, who was on loan from North Carolina's FTP. Her background likely enhanced her ability to connect with the Savannah community. The project in Savannah appeared to be the most successful of the five initial forays into the smaller cities and towns of Georgia. Eugene Bergmann, based in Atlanta, continued his work there even after the Georgia experiment ended.

33. Price immigrated to the United States at age eighteen in 1920 and passed through Ellis Island on his way to Philadelphia. Within a few years he returned to New York and became a broker. At the onset of the Depression he shifted his focus to community entertainments and recreation, serving as the entertainment coordinator for the local Civilian Conservation Corps before joining the FTP in 1935. Like John Houseman (an immigrant from Romania), Price experienced a series of firings and hirings by the FTP in 1937 because he was not a full citizen of the United States; Flanagan and numerous others repeatedly requested special consideration for him because of his expertise in the area of community drama. Herbert Stratton Price, "Personal History Statement," November 20, 1935, "Price, Herbert Stratton—Personnel," Box 39, Entry 840, Correspondence of the National Office with FTP Personnel and Individuals Concerned with the FTP Programs, Record Group 69, NARA; Herbert Price to Hallie Flanagan, "The Georgia Experiment in Community Drama," April 5, 1937, "Community Drama—Herbert Price," Box 5, Entry 839, General Correspondence of the National Office, 1935–1939, Record Group 69, NARA; "Herbert Stratton Price," July 17, 1920, Statue of Liberty-Ellis Island Foundation, Inc., Original Ship Manifest, The Celtic, 1093–4, online at http://www.ellisisland.org (accessed February 10, 2007).

34. Herbert Price to Hallie Flanagan, "The Georgia Experiment in Community Drama," April 5, 1937, "Community Drama—Herbert Price," Box 5, Entry 839, General Correspondence of the National Office, 1935–1939, Record Group 69, NARA.

35. Price to Dorothy Braley, undated memo, "Community Drama—Herbert Price," Box 5, Entry 839, General Correspondence of the National Office, 1935–1939, Record Group 69, NARA.

36. Flanagan, *Arena*, 82.

37. Charlotte Holt to Mary McFarland, April 29, 1937, "Community Drama—Herbert Price," Box 5, Entry 839, General Correspondence of the National Office, 1935–1939, Record Group 69, NARA.

38. Price to Flanagan, May 4, 1938, "Community Drama—Herbert Price," Box 5, Entry 839, General Correspondence of the National Office, 1935–1939, Record Group 69, NARA.

39. Price to Flanagan, July 15, 1938, "Community Drama—Herbert Price," 4, Box 5, Entry 839, General Correspondence of the National Office, 1935–1939, Record Group 69, NARA.

40. *Federal One* is the periodical produced by the Institute for the Federal Theatre Project at George Mason University (GMU). Initiated with the arrival of the lost Library of Congress Federal Theatre Project collection, *Federal One* featured articles about the progress

of GMU's oral history collection as well as current studies on the FTP. The article Price responded to was a brief excerpt of the story told by Flanagan in *Arena* and was printed following the "Curator's Column" in *Federal One*, October 1976, 16.

41. Herbert Price to Lorraine Brown and Laraine Carroll, July 31, 1980, "Price, Herbert," WPA Oral Histories Collection, Special Collections and Archives, George Mason University Libraries.

42. Thomas Postlewait, "The Criteria for Evidence: Anecdotes in Shakespearean Biography, 1709–2000," in *Theorizing Practice, Redefining Theatre History,* ed. W. B. Worthen and Peter Holland (New York: Palgrave Macmillan, 2003), 65.

Shakespearean Celebrity in America

The Strange Performative Afterlife
of George Frederick Cooke

—RICK BOWERS

In November 1810, New York theatre fans could hardly believe that George Frederick Cooke, the star of Covent Garden, was booked to appear as Richard III on the Park Theatre stage. For two seasons in the United States, until his sudden death in New York in September 1812, Cooke triumphed in Shakespearean roles. Having crossed the Atlantic, stormed the stages of Boston, New York, Baltimore, and Philadelphia—creating deep public animosity but also eliciting fervent admiration wherever he went—and married for the third (or perhaps fifth) time, this virtuoso Shakespearean expired with all the conflicted public mourning usually accorded to deceased royalty. Years later, it was rumored that Yorick's skull on the Park Theatre stage was in fact Cooke's skull. And it *was*—on at least one occasion.[1] More recently, in November 1980, Cooke's skull appeared in a Mercer Community College production of *Hamlet* in West Windsor, New Jersey. Moreover, as Cooke biographer Don B. Wilmeth reports, the owner of Cooke's skull in 2010, Jefferson University Medical School in Philadelphia, not only displays the relic proudly in its library, but will also "make the skull available on loan to responsible institutions, with a bond required of $25,000 for its safe return."[2]

This macabre twist on Cooke's career might not seem so strange in the light of his outrageous celebrity in relation to theatre and audiences. Indeed, his unprecedented assertions of self willed celebrity—onstage, offstage, and within his own self-mythologizing imagination—pitched themselves beyond the parameters of theatrical, social, even natural, life. Embodying conflict and contradiction within his art, Cooke lived and died in terms of radically contested histrionic self-performances—performances that, I argue, contributed to, even as they mirrored, post-Revolutionary American culture on the virtues, necessities, and dangers of asserted extremes. In this regard, I will adduce previously unconsidered biographical evidence from contemporary American periodicals and elsewhere that vividly attests to paradoxes of performance regarding the personal, national, and theatrical identity of this great actor. As the first publicly available virtuoso celebrity, Cooke could *never* leave the stage. A variety of media constantly reinforced his immortal significance as Shakespearean star, and his skull—on the Park Theatre stage or at Jefferson University—continues as after-image of his eternal and controversial "performance."

When Cooke arrived in America he was already England's foremost Shakespearean actor in the tradition of Garrick, Macklin, and Kemble. But he exceeded those great actors through an energetic, emotionally committed style as well as a special reputation for menacing villainy onstage and drunken recklessness offstage. Born of obscure origins in Dublin or London, Cooke was raised by relatives in the northern town of Berwick-upon-Tweed. Throughout the 1780s and 1790s he developed as a professional actor on provincial stages before, in 1800, hitting the London stage at Covent Garden, where he would play Richard III, Shylock, Iago, and Macbeth. His reputation included triumph and disappointment, both as a result of his alcoholism and mercurial personality and because of his risky, often aggravating, but also original performance style. His career had declined by 1810, but his reputation for good and bad both preceded and pursued him upon arrival in America, where Cooke's new brand of celebrity would encourage both good and bad in that paradoxical quality of abnormally interesting people, lately theorized by performance critic Joseph Roach as "It."[3]

Theatre historian William Dunlap, who acted as Cooke's personal handler, may have lacked the semiotic vocabulary, but he certainly understood that, in terms of revenue-generating star power, Cooke had "It." Dunlap puts it succinctly in *A History of the American Theatre from Its Origins to 1832:* "The theatre was in a decline; when lo! George Frederick Cooke arrived, and all was well again," unconsciously inflecting his praise with terms that would have much greater purchase within later celebrity culture. "It must be remembered that the *stars* took care to share the profit with the managers, except the greatest of all stars, George Frederick Cooke, and the profits of his performances were secured by those to whom he had bound himself."[4] In fact, according to Wilmeth, the total receipts for Cooke's appearances in America totaled approximately $250,000—an enormous sum at that time.[5] Cooke's arrival definitely initiated the star system in American professional theatre, and Dunlap, as theatre manager, sometime playwright, and judgmental friend of Cooke, was intimately involved. He even penned a popular two-volume biography of Cooke first published within a year of the great actor's death.[6] Cooke's overwhelming celebrity suggested a *public* intimacy, created by his image as an elite performer, that remains unavailable to most people. Dunlap's romantic overstatement and personal morality would collide in a new celebrity culture that was broadcast through Cooke's powerful performance characterizations. Everyone knew there was something radically new and exhilarating about Cooke's performances, their creation of public interest, and their complex relation to American publicity.

As the first international, transatlantic artist, often misunderstood but constantly exploring performance, Cooke energized the American theatre and made it something new. In *Shakespeare on the American Stage,* performance historian Charles H. Shattuck calls Cooke's original influence "a welcome antidote to the classical dignity of the Kemble school or to the idealizing and sentimentalizing tendencies of the day."[7] Moreover, the American theatre public seemed to intuit that, with Cooke, something different and difficult to digest was happening on their stages. Dunlap describes an intense histrionic atmosphere shared by performer and audience from the moment of Cooke's first appearance onstage in New York as Richard III: "He returned the salutes of the audience, not as a player to the public on whom he depended, but as a victorious prince, acknowledging the acclamations of the populace on his return from a successful campaign" (*Life,* 2:180). A year and a half later in Boston, the *Polyanthos* newspaper was still at a loss for criticism in describing his effect, as in the following account of Cooke's performance in *The Merchant of Venice,* January 20, 1812:

Mr. Cooke, after the recess of a week, owing to a severe indisposition, appeared in Shylock, and was welcomed with rapturous applause. Our present limits will not permit us, nor will it perhaps be thought "germain [*sic*] to the purpose," to say much of a performance, which all who have seen, have declared to exceed anticipation. Memory cannot retain the impression of all its beauties; nor, if retained, can they be suitably described.

> To those who saw them not, no words can paint,
> And those who saw them, know all words are faint.[8]

The reviewer's trim couplet effectively concedes that the only suitable description of Cooke in performance necessarily involves Cooke's own words and actions in performance. As well, the reviewer admits to learning something new in Cooke's complicated interpretation of Macbeth:

> Mr. Cooke's Macbeth is a very unequal performance, often rising above, and as often falling below expectation. The best of his acting is unquestionably in the banquet scene, the whole of which he plays in an undertone. Instead of driving off the ghost with rant and bravado, he addresses it,
>
> > Hence, horrible shadow!
> > Unreal—mockery, hence;
>
> In a tone scarcely audible, which is undoubtedly more proper for a man conscious of guilt.[9]

Herein, heroic bravado yields to deeper introspection regarding guilt as a worm of regret that gnaws internally and grows to revulsion only after many tormented revisitings. Radically subjective in performance, Cooke imposed himself on his material to elicit equally subjective but compelling responses in his audiences. He connected emotionally and somewhat uncomfortably with audiences. Through bold emphases in diction, unusual tonal shifts, and swift transitions of meaning, Cooke purposely broke the rhythmic declamatory style then prevalent on the professional stage to combine with audiences in a new brand of celebrity—onstage and offstage—that embraced paradoxes of mass reportage and mass consciousness, a consciousness that both craved and reviled his constantly available celebrity image.

Recent theoretical work links celebrity image-making to production, consumption, and media representation of value through the concepts of "ascribed," "achieved," and "attributed" celebrity.[10] In 1810, Cooke embodied all three concepts. As an English star performer—especially in kingly and heroic roles—Cooke's reputation preceded him in celebrity that was ascribed as firmly as if he were royalty. He had It. He may not have been born great, but he had certainly achieved greatness and continued to have it thrust upon him with unconscionable ease. Like English royalty, Cooke combined charisma with stigmata in American public consciousness, especially as enacted within elite Shakespearean roles. As the predominant Shakespearean actor in 1810 America, Cooke literalized even as he constantly performed the role of Shakespearean role-icon. For 1810 America, Cooke performed the role-icon of "tragedy king." He was first to do so there, and his "auratic presence" literally enriched stage managers and newspapers even as it culturally enriched theatregoers within wider complications of public consciousness. That his most notable and oft-reported role was

as the attractively malicious king Richard III suggests the unstable and paradoxical nature of his firmly achieved celebrity in America.

At that time, according to American cultural historian Lawrence Levine,
Shakespearean entertainment suffused public consciousness in complex and intensely popular ways.[11] Ripe for parody but also revered as the ultimate in literary expression and cultural value, Shakespeare signaled a heritage of English
cultural power newly reproduced within the public consciousness of nineteenth-
century America. Cooke's celebrity as the foremost Shakespearean actor—in England or the United States—clarified and reinforced this burgeoning American
sense of itself as audience in relation to culture and to performance, especially
within a shared language and a shared, as well as deeply contested and triumphant, revolutionary history. The greatest actor was in the "house" of America,
and as the greatest, he could "do it all." He could perform great triumph, tragedy,
value, and significance, but also great distress, unpredictability, ridiculousness,
and outrage. As role-icon of elite Shakespearean performance, his versatility
transcended the usual lines of business to thrive on the paradoxes of celebrity. And although he burned out at fifty-seven years old, he succeeded in ignit-
ing a new and complicated public consciousness through his performances of
"Shakespeare" in America. This new public consciousness thrived likewise on
Cooke's live performances as well as on his images as reported after his death. In
this regard, Cooke's cultural reputation was as immortal as the parts he played.
He could never "die," and American periodicals reveled in reporting both the
good and the bad of his unprecedented celebrity.

Don B. Wilmeth concludes his 1980 biography of Cooke by quoting the following "unofficial" epitaph:

> Pause, thoughtful stranger! pass not heedless by,
> Where Cooke awaits the tribute of a sigh.
> Here sunk in death those powers [of] the world admir'd,
> By nature given, not by art acquir'd.
> In various *parts*, his matchless talents shone;
> The one he fail'd in was, alas! his *own*.
>
> M. F.[12]

Noted merely as an "unidentified clipping" in the Harvard Theatre Collection,
the poem first appeared in London as "EPITAPH *On the late Mr. Cooke*" in the
Gentleman's Magazine over the initials M. F., "*Finsbury-Square, Dec. 25, 1812*."[13]
Reprinted in *Analectic Magazine*, Philadelphia, and in the *Olio*, a New York

weekly, before the end of 1813, this vaguely satirical epitaph conveyed the reckless power of Cooke's performances both on and off the stage.[14] Through its anonymity and reprinting, however, it also reinforced Cooke's celebrity status within culture even as it circulated judgment regarding his moral character. This new democratic power of print, as argued by Michael Warner in *Letters of the Republic,* suggested a new public consciousness shaped by an idealized anonymous voice of shared information. Hereby print discourse enables a people to imagine itself publicly in distinction from the state.[15] In the case of Cooke, democratic print creates a public consciousness about an actor in distinction from the stage. Ironically, the voice of democratic print creates a personality that dominates public consciousness through paradoxical celebrity performance. As will be seen, Cooke's "various *parts*" created his public image, but that image was also widely circulated, reported, reinforced, and constantly reproduced through popular print. And while the epitaph quoted above credits Cooke as the sum of his performance "*parts*" at the same time as it pities and praises him as a failed coherent personality, it misses its own point that such notoriety asserts celebrity in surprisingly nuanced and tortuous ways.

For Cooke, it had always been thus. His reputation in England, developed over thirty years on professional stages, was one of great dramatic intensity coupled with self-destructive urges manifested in chronic alcohol abuse and deeply vindictive behavior. Everything about him was extreme: his rude loquaciousness, his sociable gentility, his explosive rages, and his overwhelming talent. During Cooke's final season in London, the *Satirist* registered its perplexity about him as follows: "Were we to judge by the fondness of the public, this man would appear to be the best actor we have. . . . And yet no man has treated his audience with such insolence and contempt as this very person. His frequent inebriety, his impertinent speeches, his non-acknowledgement of applause, his unpopular cast of characters, and his extreme want of the *suaviter in modo*—all these circumstances would naturally lead one to suppose, that Cooke must be much disliked."[16] But Cooke clearly thrived on this art of transgression, which he imported to America and performed as a powerfully suggestive, paradoxically romantic motif that he manifested onstage in his most celebrated roles as Richard III, Iago, and Shylock and manifested offstage in reports of his shameful attention-getting behavior. Besides, for every critical note objecting to Cooke's behavior an equally laudatory one survives, as in the following epitaph from the *New York Weekly Museum* for Saturday, December 5, 1812:

EPITAPH ON G. F. COOKE, ESQ.
Stop! reader, stop! and give one farewell look,

Where lies the body of *George Frederick Cooke;*
A celebrated tragic player of his age,
As trod the boards of any stage.
Oh! drop one tear upon his grave, now dead,
Who living caused so many to be shed.[17]

The great romantic actor deserves at least a single tear in recompense for stimulating waves of ennobling grief in the theatre. And yet, offstage, reveling in the self-elevating pleasure of displeasing others at will, Cooke asserted his art with little regard for consequences. Love him or hate him (and he seems to have stimulated both emotions with ease) this controversial figure was not soon forgotten or easily explained. His indiscretions as well as his performances were constantly reported and infinitely reproduced through print. They were also significantly mourned at his death by an American public consciousness receptive to such emotional extremes, especially as played out in public with a firm sense of Shakespearean cultural entitlement.

In his biography, Dunlap attempted simply to reconcile Cooke's contradictory behavior by defining him as an alcoholic. Meeting personally with Cooke in Philadelphia in 1811, Dunlap allowed his subject to peruse the following unflattering personal summary, about which the actor was reportedly "mortified":

No two men, however different they may be, can be more at variance than George Cooke sober and George Cooke in a state of ebriety. At these times his interesting suavity of manners changes to brutal invective; the feelings of his nearest and dearest friends are sacrificed; his best benefactor wounded, either in his own person or that of his tenderest connections, and the ears of delicacy assaulted by abuse of the grossest nature. Such are the unfortunate propensities of this singular man;—unfortunate, I say because he seems incapable of avoiding them, although they have a tendency to ruin his health, injure his property, and destroy his social connections. (*Life,* 1:50–51)[18]

No wonder Cooke was mortified. But beyond simple vanity, Cooke's mortified response also registered protest against external personal description in favor of his own cultivated public image—an elite image circulating widely in the absence of his own person. Yet Dunlap merely, if somewhat clumsily, presented the actor with two basic sides of his complex personality. Hereby, Cooke's grandiose self-perception seems always to have blinded him to the moment, as in his condemnation of President Madison's attendance at a performance in Baltimore. Dunlap reports that Cooke referred to Madison as "the contemptible King of the Yankee Doodles" before exploding, "I'll be damned if I play before him. What I? I?—George Frederick Cooke! who have acted before the Majesty of Britain, play before your Yankee President!" (*Life,* 2:348–49). Monumentally selfish, Cooke hereby identifies and extravagantly performs himself with all the eternal nature of royalty as opposed to the more humble and momentary purview of a presidency. And yet such contradictory personal performance relates both to romantic freedom within acting style and to American audacity within performance culture.

Like a pre-photographic tabloid celebrity, Cooke and his misbehavior were constantly reported in what Dunlap refers to as "the English fugitive publications" (*Life*, 2:176) as well as in the newspapers of America. The *Port Folio*, a Philadelphia monthly, was especially informative in its retailing of anecdotes on the nature of Cooke's many contradictions. Reporting his "Bacchanalian insanity" in a variety of modes, the paper mentions Cooke's many public arguments, social blunders, disregard of cash, and recklessly quotable wit; but it also dwells on Cooke's complex performance of self: "The severity of his language was sometime almost without a parallel. On some controversy with a gentleman, which ended in a personal combat in which Mr. Cooke was foiled, he craved a suspension of hostilities. Taking his own portrait from his bosom, he presented it to his antagonist with these words: Do me the favour, sir, to wear this; and whenever you look upon it, remember that *the original called you a scoundrel*."[19] A better description of self-dramatized romantic excess could hardly be imagined. Remarkably (and apocryphally), Cooke carries his own image on his person—doubtless a portrait miniature—which he foists upon his antagonist as both gift and insult. He *lives* the role of a villain-hero.

Cooke was clearly and enigmatically inseparable from his roles. Consider his first obituary, published a week after his death in the *New York Weekly Museum*:

"OTHELLO'S OCCUPATION'S GONE."

On Saturday morning the 26th ult. COOKE took leave of this worldly stage. George Frederick Cooke, in the fifty-seventh year of his age—The celebrity of this universally excellent player has received the approbation of all ranks and countries in so public and extensive a manner, as to bid defiance to eulogium. We need only remark, that "The Man of the World" has quitted it forever—Sir John now feigns not the sleep of death, and there may he in quiet lay till the last act when "Richard will be himself again."[20]

Unnoted by Cooke's previous biographers, this remarkable notice enters into "role play" with Cooke in multiple characters. His reality, even his mortality, is accessible only through his starring roles in the theatre: Sir Pertinax MacSycophant in Macklin's *The Man of the World,* and the Shakespearean roles of Sir John Falstaff, Richard III, and Othello. Yet Cooke, having crossed the Atlantic to appear in America, really *is* a man of the world, and this obituary notice purposely blurs his roles into each other to the point of otherworldy performance. Factual reportage yields to the gushing tones of a stage-struck fan, referring to Cooke strictly in terms of histrionic fame. Moreover, Cooke's remarkable talent forces this new criticism through the extremity of his performance style. In the celebrity-generating terms of popular print, Cooke's roles precede his reality to the extent that the above-quoted notice reads more like another publicity review than an obituary. Instead of final reporting of a life lived, the obituary reproduces Cooke's multifaceted and reproducible celebrity performance image.

Intensity, disbelief, and defiance constantly circulated around Cooke's public image in America from his very first appearance in New York on November 21, 1810, wherein many theatregoers thought the advertisement of Cooke appearing in person at the Park Theatre to be a hoax. As contemporary reporter William Dunlap observed, "It appeared as impossible to many, that the great London actor should be removed to America, as that St. Paul's Cathedral should be transported across the Atlantic" (*Life,* 2:175). The crush at the doors of the Park Theatre that opening night was dangerous, involving too many people, too few seats, and more than one fistfight before Cooke himself appeared at center stage as Richard III. Dunlap, who accompanied Cooke to the theatre that night having already witnessed him in private at his drunkenly dissipated worst, describes the impression Cooke created: "His appearance was picturesque and proudly noble: his head elevated, his step firm, his eye beaming fire. I saw no vestige of the venerable grey-haired old gentleman I had been introduced to at the coffee house; and the utmost effort of the imagination could not have reconciled the figure I now saw, with that of imbecility and intemperance" (*Life,* 2:180). And yet this figure of complete control could barely get out of the dressing room that night. As Dunlap reports, "Previous to his going on, Mr. Cooke's agitation was extreme. He trembled like an untried candidate who had never faced an audience" (*Life,* 2:181). These barely reconcilable extremes of behavior, emotionality, and reputation come to characterize Cooke most fully in America, even as Dunlap quietly and shrewdly observes of his subject, "He was conscious that but a small portion of George Frederick Cooke as a private man was true" (*Life,* 1:51); however, the *truth* as circulated by his public image and enacted within his roles involved Cooke as role-icon, as virtuoso romantic Shakespearean actor. Despite Dunlap's observation, Cooke was never "a private man" in America. Instead, he harnessed fears and nervous energy to refract his art in explosive colorations of emotion on the stage. His actions, so natural in mimetic character, constantly elicited interest even as they generated celebrity publicity—publicity not subject to personal control.

It comes as little surprise, then, that this public and "picturesque" performance artist was also the subject of a rare full-length portrait by the American master painter Thomas Sully. Painted in the spring of 1811 in Philadelphia, this celebrated portrait of Cooke in the role of Richard III still hangs in the Pennsylvania Academy of Fine Arts. Cooke had to be preserved whole. A 1983 retrospective of Sully's art refers to the painting as "a true masterpiece of the artist's early years," adding, "its celebrity was augmented by the death of Cooke in New York in September 1812."[21] But the celebrity portrait was "celebrated" prior to Cooke's death as well. In July 1812 the *Port Folio* art reviewer complained about the impossibility of capturing Cooke's features on canvas:

[A] *whole length portrait of the celebrated Mr. Cooke, in the character of Richard III. By T. Sully.* This picture deserves much praise, as far as relates to the composition and general arrangement. . . . [B]ut the artist has not been so fortunate in preserving the likeness; indeed it is hardly fair to expect a correct likeness of any celebrated actor in character, because the best performers possess so much command of features as to appear altogether different persons in different characters. There is something peculiarly striking in the figure of Cooke; in this I think the artist defective; but I believe that he deviated from nature with a view to improve his picture, a circumstance that has rather operated against him, as far as it regards a faithful resemblance of this admirable and well known actor.[22]

According to the reviewer, Sully's masterful portrait, "exquisitely fine" in overall effect, captures everything *but* Cooke. The actor's complex, chameleon exterior negates any attempt to capture inner truth with anything resembling a credible finality. He contains powerful "differences" within himself that are not subject to visual display.

And yet at Cooke's death the painting itself was pressed into icon-like service for a memorial performance to celebrate the passing of the great actor. On October 1, 1812, actors at the Chestnut Street Theatre in Philadelphia advertised a performance to be presented the following Friday night, a "respectful remembrance of their deceased favorite" involving a tableau that included the Richard III portrait, a statue of Shakespeare, busts of Macklin and Ben Jonson, two actors in grief portraying Comedy and Tragedy, as well as "persons properly habited, bearing Mourning Banners of Mr. Cooke's principal plays."[23] Cooke gains apotheosis as performance art. The portrait itself represents the centerpiece of performance and gets further mention as being on display daily at the Pennsylvania Academy. If Cooke's mortal remains lay in New York, his artis-

Figure 1. Portrait of George Frederick Cooke as Richard III by Thomas Sully, 1811–12. Courtesy of the Pennsylvania Academy of the Fine Arts, Philadelphia. Gift of friends and admirers of the artist.

tic remains were everywhere alive in a new spirit of professional theatre in the United States.

Poetic effusions followed without restraint. "The Seat of the Muses" column of the *New York Weekly Museum* gave vent to rhapsodic mourning of "The Celebrated Tragedian" in terms of romantic sentiment, of deep and ancient Celtic melancholy—a grief surpassed only by direct recourse to the tragic muse Melpomene as well as to Shakespeare himself through King Lear. The final two verses are representative:

> Alas! old Lear, the gods again hath shut thee up in gloom;
> And all thy wrongs with Cooke, lie buried in the tomb,
> No more thy phrenzy will awake the bosom's throb,

But thou shalt live, oh! Cooke, while memory holds her seat,
Or for departed genius, the heart with life can beat,
And Shakespeare and Cooke, shall posterity repeat,
And still the sigh, awake the heart-felt sob.

O soft shall midnight dews weep o'er thy lowly grave,
And soft shall sweet nature, her lov'd son's bosom lave,
Oft shall thy couch, oh! Cooke be wet with tears,
Soft shall Cynthia's beam play on thy shrouded breast,
Soft shall the Shamrock wave its green glowing crest,
And soft shall be thy pillow, in eternal rest
While friendship its monumental tribute rears.   C.[24]

Poetically clumsy but deeply felt, "C.'s" memorial passion above attempts to convey elegiac perceptions about life, and death, and theatrical art—and about Cooke's "role" in essential terms of character performance. Lear dies with Cooke but lives forever paired with Shakespeare in romantic mourning that expresses itself in tears of dew upon the grave. As well, the shamrock of evergreen friendship figures Irish affiliation within Cooke's own blurry biographical, ethnic, and national experience. Herein, old English and new American nationalism combine and assert themselves with all the cultural power and significance of undying Shakespearean tragedy.

More playfully, and perhaps more tellingly, the Boston paper *Polyanthos* was punningly irreverent and worth quoting in full:

Epitaph on the late George Frederick Cooke.

The devil sends us *Cooks,* they say;
Mere *Cooks* to roast, perhaps he may,
To boil or fricassee;
Such common *kitchen stuff* may swarm,
But when will *fire* as fervid warm
Another *Cooke* like thee!

Was there no *sage in herbs* to save—
No *balm* to snatch thee from the grave—
The *cooks of cooks* restore?
None. The rich *feasts* that Shakespeare's pen,
That Macklin gave the sons of men,
Shall be *recook'd* no more.

Rum fellow! may some jug, we pray,
Full shortly animate thy *clay*—
Still may it bumpers share;
Oh! may thy jovial *spirit* glide

Securely o'er some nectar's tide,
And help to *toast* the fair.[25]

With Cooke's death, the metaphorical recipe for virtuoso acting has been lost. Hot, spicy, and entertaining, but not to every taste, he contained within his art the multifarious feasts of dramatic action. Like that "rum fellow" Falstaff whom he often played onstage, Cooke could be the cause of wit in other men. The comic detail, rhythm, and tone of the above-quoted poem suggest Cooke's gift for comedy as well as his versatile impact as a tragedian. Not only preeminent, his performances can never be duplicated, never "*recook'd.*" Moreover, the demon that drove him—whether alcoholic, artistic, or totemic—still represents dangerous possibilities within the romantic imagination.

Earlier in Cooke's American sojourn, published verse had been lively, descriptive, and suggestive of his complicated art, as in the following excerpt from "*Tributary verses to Mr. Cooke*" published anonymously in the *Philadelphia Repertory*"

No "strutting player," do we behold in you,
'Tis Richard's self, when Richard you appear;
In Pertinax, "a true born Scot," we view;
And in the injured King, not Cooke, but Lear.

Skill'd in the softer keys that touch the soul,
In virtue's cause your words can steal the sigh,
Or make, when vice demands it, sternly roll
The fiery ball of indignation's eye.[26]

Heroism, comedy, pathos—as always, Cooke's "life" resides in his feelingly artful performance of character. He conveys a natural and lifelike sense of stage action hitherto unknown on the American or English stage. In fact, Cooke's virtuoso performances represent the histrionic *reality* of key characters on the contemporary stage. Where others are merely actors, Cooke, as living virtuoso, is the *real* thing. He embodies and conveys powerful variety and suggestive paradox within his performances.

Unconsidered in previous biographical work, the above-quoted poetic elegies intensify Cooke's charismatic reputation from beyond the grave. While living, Cooke projected a more complicated celebrity wherein his behavior was as radical, unpredictable, and laden with stigmata as his art. His fellow performers often felt his terrible intensity, especially the justly celebrated Thomas Abthorpe Cooper. In both London and America, Cooke triumphed as Richard

III and Lear with audience favorite Cooper as Buckingham and Kent. Audiences thrilled to their performances together in a variety of roles. Moreover, as co-manager of the Park Theatre, Cooper, along with New York impresario Stephen Price, had been instrumental in signing Cooke up for his lucrative two-season tour of America. And yet, having received an anonymous letter extolling Cooper's power and virtue, Cooke reportedly exploded in a drunken rant against Cooper and the American theatre in general. Dunlap quotes him verbatim: "I will never play in New-York again! They have got their Cooper there to play for them! . . . Blast them!—No! I'll never play for them again! He says that Cooper tells the people of New-York that I am engaged to him for three years. Am I?—I'll show him! I'll write such a pamphlet on my return to England— I'll not forget the American theatres and their managers! I, play with Cooper!" (*Life*, 2:315–16).

Such outrage goes beyond mere competitiveness. The blustering intensity of these lines is almost palpable. Cooke's triumphant persona onstage, seemingly so natural, reverts offstage to overwhelming petulance and sense of injured merit. He fantasizes grandly about composing a written counterattack from across the seas in England. Alcohol and imagined self-assertion hereby combine to medicate Cooke's resentment and inadequacy as an interactive personality in petty real time without a script and without applause. He lashes out with Lear-like rage.

And yet, Cooke's reported selflessness could be just as uncomfortably intense. A mere six months after his death, the *Port Folio* reminisced about a strange episode of tenderness on the part of Cooke, about how he once burst into tears at the mere thought that his fellow actor (unnamed, but probably Cooper) was playing to an empty house: "This ludicrous association may thus be accounted for. Mr. C. had laid it down as a fundamental point that he was unquestionably the better actor of the two. Suddenly recollecting that his rival was then treading the boards, and as he was himself absent, he predicted, as a matter of course, a thin house. Knowing what a crowded audience his presence had always collected, he was prompted by the impulse of his insane humanity to propose to give his attendance *and fill the house.*"[27]

One can only imagine the stir occasioned by Cooke's arrival. Again, he grandiosely asserts himself as proof against his own internal lack of consequence offstage. Acknowledging the dangers of actorly success, modern performance theorist Bruce Wilshire vividly captures the paradox: "His success as an actor—his being loved as a character—will prevent him from acknowledging that he is afraid to be desired, loved, and judged as an actual individual with a life unrolling indefinitely in time. His success traps him in exhibitionism."[28]

Cooke, trapped within his own star power, could fill any theatre in America just as his presence, drunk or sober, could fill any room regardless of the circumstances. And with Cooke involved, the circumstances could be dramatic indeed. Dunlap reports another stunning instance of Cooke's extraordinary behavior:

About ten o'clock in the morning of the 19th of February, 1811, after one of the most inclement nights of one of the coldest of our winters, when our streets were choked with ice and snow, a little girl came to the manager's office at the theatre with a note scarcely legible, running thus:—

"Dear Dunlap, send me one hundred dollars.

G. F. Cooke." (*Life*, 2:229)

In 1811, one hundred dollars was a lot of cash. Suspicious, even somewhat fearful, but taking the money and the peremptory note in hand, Dunlap followed the child to a dark tenement in Reed Street. There he encountered a group of local people: a couple of sheriff's officers; a sick widow; and a drunken, disheveled, dissolute, and crying George Frederick Cooke. "His skin and eyes were red, his linen dirty, his hair wildly pointing in every direction from his 'distracted globe'" (*Life*, 2:232). In a surge of drunken indignation, Cooke insisted that Dunlap pay off the sheriff's officers to avoid their repossessing the widow's furniture for nonpayment of rent. This, from the world-famous actor who had just performed Richard III the night before. What sort of payoff or bribe was transpiring here? What was Cooke, clearly on an overnight binge, doing in this part of town? Was the "widow" some sort of bootlegger or prostitute? Was the child? Curious onlookers that morning must have read Cooke's performance in a variety of ways. Yet Cooke clearly attempts to elevate himself above the circumstances, to perform grandly and emotionally within a tragic discourse of character that reflects his own role in positive terms. And yet he finds himself deeply, perhaps even criminally, implicated in the gritty reality of new urban America.

But Cooke had always mollified his excessiveness by moving on to another role. Dunlap, in his diary account, purposely avoids mention of Cooke's sexual exploits but refers often and abashedly to Cooke as an "old beau," mentioning incidents of whoring and Cooke's ordering a coach to go to a Boston brothel.[29] Moreover, Dunlap recounts that incident with the widow and child in New York as an example of Cooke's reckless generosity. Cooke's inexplicable behavior that night is reminiscent of his sudden decampment during the 1789 summer season at Newcastle-upon-Tyne where, having gone missing, he was discovered some ten days later in the nearby village of Swalwell in a state of intoxicated delirium. In fact, Cooke seems to repeat these extremes of behavior: theatrical triumph followed by self-destructive public intoxication, followed by massive remorse and expressions of shame. Consequently, his public reads him as both mercurial and wonderful, a natural force within theatre and within culture. Cooke's radical self-performance always signaled extremity, and official pronouncements at his death reveal an equally extreme range of moral tone.

Morality (and mortality) aside, however, Cooke's real "home" was on the stage. If in death he could no longer excite audiences in person, his spirit, as avatar of virtuoso performance, was called on to bless American theatres and help them thrive. Such is the appeal in a public prologue dedicated to the opening of a new theatre in Albany, New York, and published in the January 1813 issue of the *Polyanthos*. As with the elegies at his death previously quoted, this piece insists on Cooke's ever-living quality even as it surveys a history of theatre from early Greece and Rome through Shakespearean times on to early-nineteenth-century America, where the Muse gets personal and exclamatory on the peregrinations of George Frederick Cooke:

> But ere my Muse, great Cooke! her flight has stay'd,
> Shall she not rev'rence thy departed shade!
> Thou Star of Tragic fame! whose rising beam
> Gilded the fluent wave of Liffey's stream,
> Then spread its light to Albion's classic shore,
> That Garrick's shade might wonder and adore!
> Till proud, exulting in the MILLION'S smile,
> It spurn'd the limits of Britannia's isle!
> Wide o'er th' Atlantic pour'd its orient blaze,
> And made Columbia mourn its parting rays![30]

Paradoxically, Cooke's "departed shade" elicits mourning but still lives to establish this "Infant Stage" in Albany with all the appropriate classical blessings. In his 2005 work on early American theatrical prologues, Gary Jay Williams notes the constant motif of the muses moving to America.[31] But with Cooke, the spirit had already arrived and thrived. The Albany dedication centers on the living spirit of Cooke's performances. Moreover, this moment of dedication gets widely reported. In fact, with its first issue the *Olio* actually scooped the *Polyanthos* by reproducing precisely the lines quoted above: "A new Theatre was opened in Albany on Monday evening the 16th inst. when an appropriate address, written by the editor of the 'Albany Register,' was delivered by Mr. Southey, from which the following lines, on the celebrated George F. Cooke, Esq. are extracted."[32] Cooke had already metaphorically "left the building" but his influence on American stages was strong, and newspapers competed to report on his influence even after his death. In America he enacted romantic passion with deeply bardic powers of expression, identity, and performance that reflected itself within a newly ascendant power of self-determination. In this regard, Cooke both informs and creates the conditions for new cultural energy within American theatre.

In fact, reporting just a month before on the current state of the theatre in Philadelphia, an anonymous but well-informed contributor to the *Port Folio* was already nostalgic about Cooke and the post-Cooke state of theatre in Philadelphia: "The company is sufficiently large to fill, with good effect, most of the plays now in vogue, and is certainly selected with a judgment and employed with a discrimination equally creditable to the managers and the actors. There are indeed no Cookes—and I have enthusiasm enough on that subject to believe that there are not many even within the limits of Covent Garden or Drury Lane."[33] Through such intimate reporting, Cooke's image as elite performer remains before the public, circulating within and informing American cultural life in terms of significance and even preeminence. With Cooke, the American professional stage had experienced the best and achieved significant maturity. Americans were clearly aware that one of the world's greatest actors had just passed by in their midst and conferred international, "world class" status upon their venues.

As American cultural tastemaker, Washington Irving knew it all along and had been saying so from the time of Cooke's arrival in America. Having witnessed Cooke's interpretation of Macbeth in Philadelphia in April 1811, Irving felt moved personally and with a sense of fan familiarity to describe the effect in his letter to Henry Brevoort:

I stopped in accidentally at the theatre a few evenings since, when he was playing Macbeth; not expecting to receive any pleasure, for you recollect he performed it very indifferently in New York. I entered just at the time he was meditating the murder, and I remained to the end of the play in a state of admiration and delight. The old boy absolutely out-did himself; his dagger scene, his entrance to Duncan's chamber and his horror after the commission of the deed, completed a dramatic action that I shall never forget as long as I live; it was sublime. I place the performance of that evening among the highest pieces of acting I have ever witnessed.[34]

Irving continues on the nature of Cooke's distinctive acting style, even speculating on his contribution to American dramatic art: "The more I see of Cooke, the more I admire his style of acting; he is very unequal, from his irregular habits and nervous affections; but when he is in proper mood, there is a truth and, of course, a simplicity in his performance that throws all rant, stage-trick, and stage-effect completely in the background. Were he to remain here a sufficient time for the public to perceive and dwell upon his merits, and the true character of his playing, he would produce a new taste in acting."[35]

Truth, simplicity, and direct naturalness—all three qualities on the stage impress Irving both as theatre critic and as contemporary arbiter of taste, and all three relate to a new sense of American romanticism in the theatre. No longer distant and declamatory like the English school of Kemble, Cooke's style interpenetrated American consciousness. Onstage, offstage, and within public print, Cooke created, performed, and served the effects of a new American cultural life massively disseminated through celebrity.

Irving also voiced his positive but complicated sentiments publicly if, as seems likely, he is the author who reviewed Dunlap's biography of Cooke in the *Analectic Magazine* in June 1813. In words very similar to the above phrasings, the bulk of the review—never before reprinted—focuses on Cooke's performance style: "The performances of Cooke have awakened a new taste in acting. . . . [Audiences] beheld a man that neither stamped, nor started, nor slapped his breast, nor threw himself into attitudes; one so devoid of stage mummery, so free from rant, so like the life, in a word, *so good,* that they were utterly at a loss what to think of it."[36] Conscious of a new virtuoso naturalism but also unable critically to pinpoint Cooke's effect, Irving's concluding "it" unconsciously enunciates "It." He broadcasts an aporia of admiration similar to that of the *Polyanthos* reviewer who described Cooke's Shylock and Macbeth. Cooke's overwhelming, somewhat confusing, but remarkably credible cultural virtuosity represents a new paradox of publicly available, publicly intimate performance in America.

As cultural commentator, Irving had just become editor of the *Analectic Magazine* in January 1813 and, as his most recent bibliographer put it, "must have written or had a hand in writing much that cannot now be identified."[37] He doubtless had a hand in crafting the American performance image of George Frederick Cooke. Irving witnessed Cooke onstage both in England and America and even met the actor once or twice in person.[38] Hence perhaps the decidedly personal tone near the end of this review, combining typical Irving-like grace, balance, and goodwill with a searching sensibility:

It was Cooke's great misfortune that his ruling propensity became notorious, and that he had no longer the apprehension of discovery to make him cautious in his excesses;

he, therefore, gradually became familiar with disgrace and regardless of public exposure. The good-humoured indulgence with which he was received by polite audiences, after repeatedly insulting them by drunken desertions from the theatre, or, what is worse, by drunken exhibitions, led him to magnify his own importance in the public eye. He seemed to think that there was a redeeming spirit in his performances that atoned for every fault.... In a word, he appears to have been one of those unlucky beings who are nobody's enemy but their own.[39]

But Cooke's "enemy" status to self represents paradoxical friendship with his various public roles. He lived always for the audience, returning to his audiences an arrogant freedom and energy modeled in the various outrageous roles he played. Irving's personalized sentiments and perceptions above make it unsurprising that he would be first in America to publish the previously quoted "Epitaph on the Late Mr. Cooke" that first appeared in London in the *Gentleman's Magazine* in April 1813.

Irving, however, also touches on a key aspect of Cooke's notoriety that suggests a nuanced relationship to the public, a sense of emotional immediacy that connected to the audience's imagination in a new and visceral way. Cooke asserted a new credibility beyond the polite aristocratic balance of American federalism to suggest a new American permissiveness, individualism, and consciousness of exploration as a good in itself. Herein, in a new urban democracy of energetic action and individual rights the usual rules of engagement no longer applied with the same comfort as they once did. Indeed, for post-Revolutionary America, Cooke *freed* Shakespeare on the democratic stage. As the greatest contemporary Shakespearean performer, Cooke actually performed a powerful democratic function that Leo Braudy encapsulates in *The Frenzy of Renown*: "To be seen was to be free, to be heroic, to be American."[40] While Cooke might not be an American national, he certainly, through the high visibility of performance and celebrity, liberated an old world of stratified, patronizing, polite Shakespeare to assert a new, rudely energetic, and passionately expressive American form. Herein Shakespeare rises above cultural transnationalism in a new sense of romantic performance at once powerful and vulnerable. Arising from a variety of sources both onstage and off, Cooke's celebrity performance suggested itself in a variety of responses—good and bad—that were assembled and modified by a fascinated public. Moreover, Cooke's questionable public image put him in constant democratic dialogue with audiences and critics in which moral frailty and vulnerability are shared even as they are excoriated.

Cooke's death, at the height of his celebrity, seared his image fully within

American public consciousness. Shattuck's estimation is as accurate as it is synoptic: "Cooke's early death saved his reputation in America. His professional irresponsibility, together with his barbarous social behavior—his quarrelsomeness, his contempt for 'Yankee rebels,' his drinking and whoring—could never have been mended and would not have been endured much longer. But in the American memory these faults diminished into astonishing eccentricities, something to gossip about, while his powerful acting became a legend of excellence against which to measure actors of the future."[41]

Literal measurement began immediately. A death mask was cast in plaster and is now in the Harvard Theatre collection.[42] Cooke's skull, as the repository of his remarkable genius, was examined with great care at the autopsy and doubtlessly handled with critical reverence during later phrenological lectures. Beyond such quantitative "science," the skull contained a loosely anthropological sense of *mana* or spiritual power related structurally to the complications of celebrity and popular culture. But Edmund Kean, Cooke's heir as star performer in England and America, required more. Traveling to New York in 1820, Kean saw to it that Cooke's remains were moved from the Strangers' Vault at St. Paul's to the place in the churchyard where they rest to this day under the same impressive monument. For his trouble, Kean returned to England in possession of Cooke's right index finger—"that dictatorial finger," as Dunlap called it—declaring, "I have something that the directors of the British Museum would give ten thousand pounds for; but they sha'n't have it."[43] Any "piece" of Cooke, reported, represented, or physically displayed, still performed as cultural artifact and precious relic containing power. In this regard Kean, as a fan, merely literalizes what Roach argues as a way "to preserve a sense of the relationship with the past by making physical contact with the dead."[44] Kean did so when he absconded with Cooke's actorly pointing finger. Dr. Francis and the Park Theatre did so with Cooke's skull. Then as now, everyone "wants a piece" of the celebrity, and Cooke's skull—still available to view at the Scott Library, Jefferson University—represents both democratic possibility as well as an enduring Shakespearean cultural distinction that America could claim as its own.

At once brilliant and degenerate, loquacious and sullen, controlled and chaotic, even English and American—but also Irish—Cooke inhabited liminal zones of instability and threshold edginess that further enhanced his celebrity. As actor, he embraced the contradictions of celebrity to live as an image beyond the term of his own natural life. Indeed, Cooke seemed impossible to contain, and the epitaph on his ornate monument, still standing in St. Paul's, New York, reinforces both his massive influence but also his temporality:

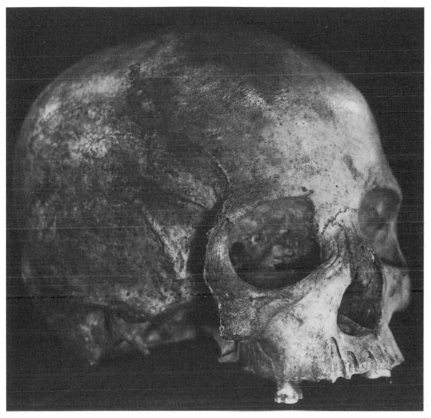

Figure 2. George Frederick Cooke's skull. Photo courtesy of the Archives and Special Collections, Thomas Jefferson University.

> Three Kingdoms claim his birth
> Both Hemispheres pronounce his worth.

Cooke clearly thrived on the instabilities of performance and celebrity. While no record of his actual birth exists, the afterimages of his constant performance suggest that he was "born" upon the stage. He was the first star performer to triumph on both sides of the Atlantic, and he died in America at the height of his renown. Contemporary journalism reinforced his complicated art, sometimes literally as in Sully's portrait, at times farcically in retailed anecdote, often sentimentally in romantic poetic effusion, but always in terms of celebrity publicity. Herein, he was as publicly available offstage as he was onstage. His various, at times misunderstood, identities raged with emotional surprise and credibility, linked to Shakespearean performances as well as to the complexities of personal interaction, popular romance, and star power. As self-conscious cultural celebrity, Cooke was the great progenitor. His decline from popular consciousness only clarifies his unprecedented significance as celebrity, prior to the invention of photography, the arrival of Booth and Barrymore, or even the idea of Hollywood celluloid.

Notes

1. See Don B. Wilmeth, *George Frederick Cooke: Machiavel of the Stage* (Westport, Conn.: Greenwood, 1980), 275–86. Cooke's physician, Dr. John W. Francis (who also performed the autopsy), did lend Cooke's skull to the Park Theatre on one occasion and also used the skull in a lecture on phrenology. See John W. Francis, *Old New York* (1865; reprint, New York: Benjamin Blom, 1971), 292–93.

2. Don B. Wilmeth, "The British Actor Invasion of the Early American Stage," in *Extraordinary Actors: Essays on Popular Performers,* ed. Jane Milling and Martin Banham (Exeter: University of Exeter Press, 2004), 78. It should be noted that Cooke's skull is no longer available for "rent," according to Michael Angelo, University Archivist and Special Collections Librarian at the Scott Memorial Library, Jefferson University. I am very grateful to Michael Angelo for his hospitality and information during my visit in November 2007. For online note and photograph of the skull see, http://jeffline.jefferson.edu/Education/forum/02/12/articles/end.html, which includes a link to Thomas Sully's 1811 portrait of Cooke as Richard III. (accessed August 4, 2008).

3. My debt to Joseph Roach's work *It* (Ann Arbor: University of Michigan Press, 2007) will be apparent throughout. Roach clarifies usage on page 1: "For the sake of clarity, let *it,* as a pronoun aspiring to the condition of a noun, be capitalized hereafter, except where it appears in its ordinary pronominal role."

4. William Dunlap, *A History of the American Theatre from Its Origins to 1832,* ed. Tice L. Miller (Urbana and Chicago: University of Illinois Press, 2005), 362, 354. On early theatre structure and management, and on Cooke's place within it, see *The Cambridge History of American Theatre,* vol. 1, ed. Don B. Wilmeth and Christopher Bigsby (Cambridge: Cambridge University Press, 1998).

5. See Wilmeth, *Cooke,* 256.

6. See William Dunlap, *The Life of George Frederick Cooke,* 2 vols., 2nd ed. (1815; reprint, New York: Benjamin Blom, 1972); cited parenthetically in the text as *Life.*

7. Charles H. Shattuck, *Shakespeare on the American Stage* (Washington, D.C.: Folger Shakespeare Library, 1976), 32.

8. *Polyanthos,* February 1812, 58.

9. Ibid., 62. On Cooke's performance in another key role, see Rick Bowers, "Cooke's *Hamlet* in Performance, 1785," *Dalhousie Review* 82 (2002): 347–63.

10. See Chris Rojek, *Celebrity* (London: Reaktion Books, 2001), 13–14, 17–20.

11. See Lawrence W. Levine, *Highbrow/Lowbrow: The Emergence of Cultural Hierarchy in*

America (Cambridge: Harvard University Press, 1988), esp. chapter 1, "William Shakespeare in America," 13–81.

12. Wilmeth, *Cooke,* 273–74. In line 3, "of" makes the line awkwardly hypermetric and does not appear in any other version.

13. *Gentleman's Magazine,* April 1813, 360.

14. See, specifically, *Analectic Magazine,* October 1813, 349, and *Olio,* November 6, 1813, 328. A few years later the epitaph reappeared in England in a compendium of comic writings compiled pseudonymously by John Bull, Esq., *The Laughing Philosopher* (London: Sherwood, Jones, 1825), 413. My thanks to Dr. Paul S. Smith, who brought this 1825 document to my attention and thereby initiated my research into Cooke's posthumous reputation.

15. In this regard see Michael Warner, *Letters of the Republic: Publication and the Public Sphere in Eighteenth-Century America* (Cambridge: Harvard University Press, 1990).

16. Quoted in Wilmeth, *Cooke,* 254.

17. *New York Weekly Museum,* December 5, 1812, 123.

18. For readability, I have lightly modernized punctuation when quoting from nineteenth-century texts.

19. *Port Folio,* March 1813, 280–81.

20. *New York Weekly Museum,* October 3, 1812, 87.

21. Monroe H. Fabian, *Mr. Sully, Portrait Painter: The Works of Thomas Sully, 1783–1872* (Washington, D.C.: Smithsonian Institution Press, 1983), 14. See also Christopher M. S. Johns, "Theater and Theory: Thomas Sully's George Frederick Cooke as Richard III," *Winterthur Portfolio* 18, no. 1 (1983): 27–38. My thanks to Gale Rawson, Registrar, Pennsylvania Academy of Fine Arts, for her information and hospitality during my visit in November 2007.

22. *Port Folio,* July 1812, 21–22.

23. *United States Gazette,* October 1, 1812, 2.

24. *New York Weekly Museum,* January 23, 1813, 152. Similarly lengthy effusions followed Cooke's death almost immediately, including "Lines on the Death of G. F. Cooke, the Celebrated Actor," *Polyanthos,* December 1812, 158–59. Melancholy, popular, and touchingly identified as written "by a young lady not yet fifteen years of age," the poem reappeared the following year in *Port Folio,* March 1813, 281–82.

25. *Polyanthos,* February 1813, 253–54.

26. *Philadelphia Repertory,* June 15, 1811, 30–31.

27. *Port Folio,* March 1813, 277.

28. Bruce Wilshire, *Role Playing and Identity: The Limits of Theatre as Metaphor* (Bloomington: Indiana University Press, 1982), 272.

29. See *The Diary of William Dunlap,* ed. Dorothy C. Barck (1930; reprint, New York: Benjamin Blom, 1969), 443–44, 449.

30. *Polyanthos,* January 1813, 222–23.

31. See Gary Jay Williams, "Athenian Prologue to an American Theatre," in *Staging Nationalism: Essays on Theatre and National Identity,* ed. Kiki Gounaridou (Jefferson, N.C.: McFarland, 2005), 48–62.

32. *Olio,* January 27, 1813, 5.

33. *Port Folio,* December 1812, 635–36.

34. Pierre M. Irving, *The Life and Letters of Washington Irving* (New York: G. P. Putnam, 1864), 1:278.

35. Ibid.
36. *Analectic Magazine,* June 1813, 517.
37. Edwin T. Bowden, *Washington Irving: Bibliography in The Complete Works of Washington Irving,* ed. Richard Dilworth Rust, vol. 30 (Boston: Twayne, 1989), 679.
38. See *The Diary of William Dunlap,* 437, 439.
39. *Analectic Magazine,* June 1813, 522–23.
40. Leo Braudy, *The Frenzy of Renown: Fame and Its History* (Oxford: Oxford University Press), 453.
41. Shattuck, *Shakespeare on the American Stage,* 35–36.
42. See photograph in Wilmeth, *Cooke,* 276.
43. Ibid., 278. See also Dunlap, *History,* 394.
44. Joseph Roach, "History, Memory, Necrophilia," in *The Ends of Performance,* ed. Peggy Phelan and Jill Lane (New York: New York University Press, 1998), 29.

Burns Mantle and the American Theatregoing Public

—DOROTHY CHANSKY

In 1920, Burns Mantle interviewed Dorothy Dalton, a now-forgotten screen star who was making her Broadway debut in an orientalist stage spectacle called *Aphrodite.* Mantle's piece, published in *Photoplay Magazine,* helped shore up Dalton's theatrical bona fides in what has become a time-honored way, as he asked her about her preferred performing venue. Said Dalton, "If I were forced to make my choice between the screen and the stage, other things being equal, I would unhesitatingly choose the stage." Coaxing her to continue, Mantle writes, drawing us in with his use of the first person, " 'It's the applause?' I ventured."

" 'It's the fascination,' said she, 'and the satisfaction. It is the inspiration the actress in the theater gets from her audience, that the actress before the camera never feels. It is the lights, the stage, the voice, the human contact. It is—' "

Mantle fills in the blank. " 'It is the theater,' I said, and she agreed."[1]

At this point, readers of a scholarly persuasion are quite possibly holding two simultaneous thoughts in their minds. One is that the term "theatre" cries out here for critical, historicized unpacking; the other is probably—whether we like to admit it or not—a sense of recognition and identification. The theatre. Of course.

My project in this short essay is to look at Burns Mantle's understanding of the American theatregoing public, which, for the last thirty-seven years of his life, meant largely the Broadway theatregoing public. As with "theatre," there are often unspoken, present-day assumptions about this particular public that go unremarked under rubrics such as "mainstream" or "commercial." Mantle struggled to understand and define this audience. His efforts are of interest not only because he was in a privileged position to observe this public but also because of the perspective he brought to his task and who he was to become for theatre historians. Both his optic and the particulars of his descriptions may tell us more than we would like to know (or how much we would like to repress) about the public that supports American theatre in its largest, most visible and influential venue.

Burns Mantle is known to any scholar of the twentieth-century American theatre as the founding editor of the *Best Plays* volumes, started in 1920, hailed in 1967 as "the oldest continuous record of theatrical activity on Broadway and environs," and still going strong in 2011.[2] Mantle founded the series at the request of editors from Small, Maynard in Boston, who were looking for an analogue to their existing *Best American Short Stories* yearbook.[3] He retained the editorship for twenty-seven years, overlapping his work as a daily critic for the *New York Daily News* from 1922 until 1943. As yearbook editor, Mantle established the practice not only of selecting and redacting the ten "best" plays of every season but also of providing what Joseph Wood Krutch lauded as a record "astonishing in its completeness" and analogous to those in other specialist fields but previously nonexistent for theatre. Each volume listed, "in the order of their first nights, every New York theatrical production for the year—with its cast, its run, and a brief synopsis of the plot. Moreover, all this [was] indexed and supplemented by various other compendia of information."[4] Lewis Nichols declared Mantle's position in 1946 to be "comparable only to the worthy writers who put out 'Moody's Industrials'";[5] Edward Albee asks rhetorically on the current *Best Plays* website, "Is there a more complete and useful record of each year's American theater life?" He answers, "I doubt it."[6]

Besides the prodigious data Mantle compiled, however, he left a record of his intermittent thoughts about the people who were presumably among his readers, and who, crucially, whether they bought his books or not, were loyal theatregoers. Mantle spent fifty years as a critic of commercial theatre, starting in Denver in 1892, moving to Chicago in 1902, and taking up residence in New York in 1911, where he first wrote for the *New York Evening Mail.* He continued, after his retirement in 1943 until a few months before his death in 1948 at age seventy-four, to attend every Broadway opening. His apprehension of the Broadway public was, like the understanding of "theatre" he elicited from Dorothy Dalton (which he appeared to share), firmly felt yet something for which he offered allusions more than any single definition. His sense of Broadway audiences was something he discussed in shorthand and piecemeal over at least a thirty-year period yet never quite fully explained. Still, the gestalt that emerges in this mosaic is the result of the knowledgeable placing of an experienced finger on the pulse of a specific American cohort to diagnose its predilections and peccadilloes with care and expertise. One might also add, with sympathy, as Mantle was known for being a critic who was as much like an average and gentlemanly person in the audience as he was like his professional playgoing colleagues.

Mantle's thoughts about his fellow audience members are of interest not only because they are there for the taking but also because of Mantle's position and reputation among theatre critics. A 1930 piece profiling in thumbnail sketches the major New York drama critics writing for dailies saw Brooks Atkinson of the *New York Times* as "analytical" and "scholarly," Percy Hammond of the *Herald Tribune* as "smugly content" in demeanor while offering "vitriol" in his reviews, and Mantle as "a mild-mannered gentleman, whose reviews, for the most part, are just as mild-mannered. The homely, unpretentious, pleasant plays appeal to him, apparently, for they usually lure his applause."[7] (Missing from this list, as he did not write for a daily paper, was the hugely influential, often sarcastic, educated, and scornful George Jean Nathan.) An article printed in 1943, not long after Mantle announced his retirement from daily reviewing, described him as the "gentle, professorial Mantle," "pink-faced [and] blue-eyed," wearing "the sort of suit that looks at home on Wall Street" (i.e., "no crazy lapels or tucks"), cultivating a "conscientious aloofness," "avoiding friendships in the theatre," a reformed smoker, and a drinker of orange juice or milk, save "an occasional cocktail, [which] usually waits for the annual Dutch Treat Party."[8]

Professorial he may have looked, with his monogrammed shirts, but Mantle enjoyed neither formal education nor class privilege. His father died when young Mantle, first named LeRoy Willis and born in upstate New York in 1873, was five or six, and his mother moved the family first to Denver, then to a kind of pioneer colony in Mexico, and shortly thereafter—when the colony scheme failed—to California, where she was a music teacher. Mantle, renamed Robert Burns, which had been his father's preference for his son (a grandmother overrode the choice), started delivering newspapers via horse and wagon to earn money to contribute to the household. He became a typesetter when he learned that he could increase his income by 50 percent. Bob, as Mantle was known, moved (back) to Denver at the age of nineteen.[9] The story he told about his start there as a critic was that he helped get the paper out on time when a drama review by the regular critic came in with handwriting so illegible that Mantle, who had seen the play in question himself but was unable to make out the review, rewrote the piece as he was typesetting it. Happily for him, it met with the regular critic's favor. Mantle was, quipped one pundit commenting on the *Best Plays* editor's start as a Linotype operator, "the only dramatic critic who ever wrote his story straight on one of those frightening contraptions that only printers understand."[10] Mantle never gave up his affiliation with the printers' union, and in 1941 he was toastmaster at a dinner given at the Manhattan Center for typesetters who had been union members for fifty or more years.[11] He and his wife, Lydia, whom he wed in 1903 and with whom he lived until his death forty-five years later, resided in Forest Hills, a pretty—one might even say suburban—area of Queens that still takes at least forty minutes to reach by subway from midtown. They adopted a daughter, and in later years Lydia's two sisters lived with them.[12] Mantle never became a Manhattanite. His reputation was that he was likable, considerate, kind in print, and, overall, a safe critic. Indeed, a 1934 profile of Mantle said that Small, Maynard selected him for the *Best Plays* project when he won the most votes from a producer, a press agent, and a playwright who were queried by the publisher's representative. The losers were Alexander Woollcott (model for the hypersophisticated, egomaniacal *Man Who Came to Dinner*) and Heywood Broun, both members of the Algonquin Round Table.[13]

How did the seemingly middlebrow but indisputably knowledgeable Mantle see the public for whom he wrote? A 1914 profile of Mantle in the *New York Dramatic Mirror* allowed him to expound on his ideas about critics and the public. The critic, he opined, was a professional playgoer whose primary task was conveying information for "that percentage of the readers of his paper interested in the theater. He should first of all be a good reporter." He asserted that about 10 percent of a paper's readers made up the public for whom theatre criticism was written, and he saw that group as comprising three "distinct publics. . . . First, the public that isn't present at the performance being reviewed, second, the public that is present, and finally, the professional crowd, inside and out, that is in the theatrical know. Obviously the public to reach is the big aggregation outside that knows nothing of back-stage. They want a clear impression of the play, and an opinion concerning it, nothing more."[14]

At first blush, Mantle, in devising classifications, was doing little more than other critics of his era. Thomas Dickinson, a faculty member at the University of Wisconsin, founder of the Wisconsin Dramatic Society, and a Little Theatre movement activist, similarly staked out a specific segment of the public who attended theatre, but Dickinson criticized and categorized them in terms of a definite value system. "Puritans" influenced the theatre by virtue of being part of a large cohort that basically disapproved even while attending. "Theatregoers" were dismissed for failing to discriminate between vaudeville, movies, and legit. "Connoisseurs"—also known as highbrows—were problematic because they offered more over-refined criticism than they did actual support. Dickinson's target group was "theatre-lovers," because they had "taste" but favored enjoying the theatre over judging it. Dickinson's project was to exhort the aesthetically fit to support the serious and experimental theatre of the day, which he defined as "a place of entertainment for intelligent people."[15]

Mantle, the non-professor, situated himself neither above nor in a separate category from the public. Recall that he defined the newspaper critic as a playgoer—albeit a professional one. "The drama will never be saved by the critics," he wrote. "The ultimate disposition of it rests with the public. . . . The public, however, isn't studious and doesn't want to be instructed. It may be educated, but it doesn't want to be conscious of the proceeding."[16] Like Dickinson, he flattered the playgoing public's intelligence, but unlike Dickinson, he recognized that neither instruction nor effort characterized what the putatively educated (the term is never defined) public wanted out of theatregoing. Whatever it did want, though, Mantle knew he had to contend with it. The interview concludes with his stab at defining the ideal critic: he should be an authority "on literature, dramatic technique and what the public wants."[17] Mantle would comment intermittently over the years in his annual introductory essays in the *Best Plays* volumes on the difficulties of triangulating these areas of expertise. Equilateral though he might have wished his constructions to be, when looking for "the best" he recognized a tendency toward the isosceles and was not always comfortable with the idea of the public's tastes being equal in value to literature and dramatic technique (although he did not always find both these latter in plays he admired).

Virtually from the beginning of his *Best Plays* tenure Mantle referred to the playgoing public as "my collaborator," crediting them with controlling the "disposition" of the commercial theatre but simultaneously noting that this same theatregoing community was not necessarily disposed to good literature.[18] He would wrestle with this in essay after essay. "The intention [of the Best Plays series] frankly has been to compromise between the *popular success,* as representing *the choice of the people who support the theater,* and the success with sufficient claim to *literary distinction of text or theme to justify its publication*" (emphasis added).[19] Two years into the series (1922) he upped the importance of the "educated" but anti-intellectual audience by reminding his readers that his yearbook existed "to serve the playgoing public. . . . [Therefore] it should represent the popular or so-called commercial theater, which is the theater of the people. To do this it should be concerned with the most popular as well as with the 'best' plays judged by the higher literary standards, because it is the popular plays that represent the preferences and tastes of the public which it is our hope to reach. Parenthetically, therefore, the book's title probably should read 'The Best (of the Successful) Plays' . . . [T]here were several plays which had achieved long runs . . . which we did not feel were entitled to inclusion in our list of ten."[20] Among these, for example, was A. A. Milne's *The Truth about Blayds*, which did not make the "ten best" list and was characterized a little sarcastically as "an immediate success with what is known slangily as the *intelligencia*."[21] Lest this sit poorly with anyone who might like to think of him- or herself as a member of the intelligentsia but who missed (or misunderstood) or disliked the Milne play, the next year's volume stroked egos with reference to Karel Capek's *RUR*, saying the play "represents the taste of a theatre-going public that is constantly growing in America, particularly eastern America."[22] Taste—manifested by an affinity for a politically committed, futuristic drama set in a world of science and industry—is now subtly different from mere preference and we can all feel good that it is growing, although readers are quietly reminded that the most progress is being made in the East, so one had best look there to avoid being left out in the cultural cold.

Mantle the middlebrow was not afraid to characterize part of the theatre-going public as "morons" (those who were "confounded" by *Six Characters in Search of an Author*) or to use shorthand (or stereotypes) as a means of letting readers (presumably not among the "morons") feel superior and in the know: "Worried businessmen" like musical reviews; their "sentimental mates flock to the heavier drama."[23] A "typical audience" early in the theatre season is "a third professional, a third resident and a third wide-eyed tourist."[24] (Beware appearing wide-eyed is the presumable message.) He acknowledged "those most consistent of drama supporters, the women playgoers," although if by "drama" he meant "serious drama" this both praises women's intellectualism (despite his preferred adjective above: "sentimental") and marks them as outside the mainstream.[25] He has categories called the "woman's play," something to which "menfolk" needed to be "dragged" (his example here was Zoe Akins's 1935 Pulitzer Prize–winning *The Old Maid*), and the "man's play," something with "limited appeal to women playgoers" (his example was Maxwell Anderson's 1933 inside-the-Beltway satire, *Both Your Houses*).[26] The strict gender division in these presumably entirely legible examples problematizes his notion of a "public," or at least admits that it is a segmentable market.[27] And Mantle would occasionally insist on a bit of intellectual roughage (it's good for you), as when he included Maxwell Anderson's 1936 *High Tor* among the ten best despite its not having done well at the box office, diplomatically saying in this instance he felt "that a considerable number of serious-minded patrons were outvoted and in a way overwhelmed by this season's rush of highly amusing but essentially trivial comedies."[28]

Mantle certainly had a priggish strain, objecting to profanity and acknowledging his "puritan" heritage.[29] But he balanced his stance with support for the good fight of the "protesting realists" who want "a finer freedom of expression than has ever before existed."[30] He was capable of developing with the times, and gently informed readers of what was emergent and what was old-fashioned, as when George S. Kaufman and Edna Ferber's 1932 *Dinner at Eight* embraced newish dramaturgy. A turntable facilitated a changing mise-en-scène to support the play's episodic unfolding and multiple locales, although even with smooth scenic changes Mantle was relieved that the scenery served "to minimize the handicap of a frequently broken interest on the auditor's part." Still, he wrote, determined to keep up with evolution in dramatic structuring, "only those older playgoers, accustomed to the set forms of an earlier drama, were disappointed in the lack of emotional sweep. . . . Playgoers, trained in the ways of the motion picture and the story of frequently broken sequences, admired it greatly."[31]

The playgoing public, then, were men and women with distinct gendered preferences. They comprised morons and an intelligentsia. They were older and nostalgic and they were informed and progressive. They were New Yorkers, suburbanites, members of the theatre industry, filmgoers, and wide-eyed tourists. They also included Jews, characterized as audiences as "numerous and show-minded"—although it would be Mantle's immediate successor, John Chapman, who collaborated on Mantle's final *Best Play* volume, was trained by Mantle, was his assistant for twenty years at the *Daily News,* and succeeded him as daily critic on the paper, who would say this.[32]

Perhaps Mantle's most telling statement about the playgoing public appeared in 1934, when he wrote, "it is emotional satisfaction for which playgoers pay most cheerfully and most consistently in the theatre. . . . The intellectual drama must always be content with small audiences in the people's theatre. . . . The year book of the drama in America, I feel, should be principally concerned with those plays that represent the whole theatre rather than with laboratory experiments of special types in which the larger playgoing public is seldom interested. At the moment it seems to me to be the duty of a year book editor to report trends rather than to attempt to direct them."[33]

Whatever the duties of the yearbook editor, Mantle seemed to understand the playgoing public writ large in a way that still speaks to us in 2011.[34] Moreover, his brief observations suggest a kind of research about audiences that remains minoritarian at best, looking as it does beyond the generic traits of Americans who support the arts. Surveys that seek information about theatregoers' spending habits, income, interest in restaurant dining, magazine subscriptions, and educational levels tell little about the theatregoing public that is not largely equally applicable to the ballet-going public, the symphony-going public, the museum-going public, the jazz-supporting public, or, for that matter, the gourmet-dining public. What is it about *theatre* that creates an imagined community of Broadway supporters at once intelligent and expecting to have its intelligence flattered; at once interested in the new (perhaps in areas of technology or their own professions) but commonly invested in sentimentality when they are in the playhouse?[35]

I am not suggesting that Mantle knew the answer to these questions but refused to go on record. Nor am I suggesting that I am the first to ask them. I am suggesting, however, that as we—and here I include commercial producers, academics, and avant-garde practitioners—continue to worry about future audiences, we might do well to consider the wisdom offered by the past. John Chapman, Mantle's successor, worried in 1951 about how few young people attended the theatre, positing that this was not due to any lack of interest but to the high price of tickets. "The true stage addict," opined Chapman, "should be caught and trained in his formative years, but with ticket prices as high as they are the youngster can't afford to go to a play very often, if ever."[36] Familiar (and comforting) though this idea may be, we ought to be able to see in hindsight a glaring flaw—one that may not have been evident to Chapman at the time but that ought to be quite plain sixty years later. Namely, if the teenagers and twentysomethings of 1951 seemed to a concerned theatre professional to be outnumbered by bluehairs and graybeards, we ought to be able to figure out with relative ease that it is precisely those youth who stepped into their elders' shoes, as the same mantra of woe has continued to be repeated decades later. Might it be that theatregoing in the mid- and late twentieth and early twenty-first centuries is an adult, later in life, acquired taste?

Mantle considered age differentials in theatre audiences once in a *Best Plays* introductory essay. In 1925 he mused about audiences of the future and how they might divide themselves into two camps: supporters of theatre and moviegoers: "In another ten or fifteen years, when you and I are content to stay at home and take our entertainment from the phonofilm, the more forward young folks will be discussing with bated breath and amazing words the latest soul analyses of the theatre."[37] He imagines the young going to exciting theatre and the middle-aged at home with an as-yet-nonexistent product that sounds presciently like television, video, or DVDs. Yet Mantle may not have been wrong with regard to his idea of the "more forward young folks" being precisely those who create and follow "the latest" in the theatre, leaving their elders shaking their heads.[38] Today one need only attend any production coded as alternative, experimental, or otherwise presumably progressive in any American city and compare its audience with any Broadway or most musical comedy audiences to see (or have reconfirmed) that the young far outnumber the middle-aged or older when "forward" is in operation. Chapman's worries a quarter century later notwithstanding, it may be worth considering that one simple reason for theatre audiences' graying is that much theatre fare (or theatre fare designed to turn a profit on Broadway or keep an organization with a large payroll afloat elsewhere) is designed to appeal to a grayhaired demographic. Yet no group is so well (even over-?) represented in non-mainstream theatre as under-thirty-fives. Perhaps the youthful audience about whom administrators and educators fret is alive, well, and simply waiting for representatives of its own cohort to take over and shape a theatre that will speak to them as equals rather than a population in need of instruction.

Why join the theatregoing public? Theatre, and all cultural goods, notes Paul DiMaggio, "are consumed for what they say about their consumers to themselves and to others, as inputs into the production of social relations and identities."[39] We do it because our family and friends and, perhaps most importantly, those to whose status we aspire do or recognize or approve or admire it. Alice Goldfarb Marquis, reporting on a major study, makes the prescient observation in her book *Art Lessons: Learning from the Rise and Fall of Public Arts Funding* that "No matter how many schoolchildren were 'exposed' to the arts, no matter how many low-priced tickets were given away, only those near the upper levels of income and education were drawn to more than an occasional visit. . . . Analysis . . . show[s] a direct correlation between interest in attending theater and a high level of education. . . . [P]articipants did not view a theater visit as an aesthetic or educational event but rather as a social experience."[40] Ronald Berman, chair of the National Endowment for the Humanities during the Nixon years, called art simply "an ennobled form of middle-class entertainment," noting that the idea of creativity described, more than any achievement, "an attitude about the self."[41] DiMaggio parses this notion superbly, historicizing the rise of high art culture in the United States in the latter part of the nineteenth century and its arrival and dissemination in American universities in the 1920s, just in time to butt heads with the arrival of a robust popular culture in the form of (among many other things) radio, jazz, talkies, and an explosion in creative advertising.[42] Choosing theatre shores up (whether this is conscious on the part of the theatregoer or not) a sense of self that other activities do not. And it does so with minimal intellectual difficulty, at least compared to, say, abstract art, twelve-tone music, or opera in foreign languages.

We might be tempted to pooh-pooh such notions—that class and sociality trump all and that an attitude about the self supersedes an investment in aesthetics—but any marketer knows that such dismissal would be disastrous. My question, then, is how a specific understanding of the emotionally satisfying, intellectually flattering but not bracingly difficult, socially embedded experience that is "theatre" culls the imagined community that is Broadway's playgoing public? How can we "know" what Mantle knew? If we do know it, how can we accept rather than criticize it? (And I recognize that many do simply accept it, even if some also scratch and shake their heads over it.) One major difference between Mantle's era and our own is that the golden age of theatre during which he was a critic did not have television as a competitor for audience attention. This golden age, which Ethan Mordden situates between 1919 and 1959, was characterized by glamorous opening nights, sophistication expected in stars and in musical lyrics, numerous New York daily newspapers, and theatre figuring routinely in cultural analysts' lists of what belonged in the thinking person's habitus.[43] Today's Broadway audiences simply have more entertainment options, including, obviously, those for which they need not leave home. They also encounter a product comfortable with consumers in casual wear and arguably shorter attention spans.[44]

It is also worth remembering that Mantle reported on experimental and non-Broadway work, perhaps most notably on productions offered by the Federal Theatre Project in the 1930s. The Broadway of his day included not only what is now simplistically called "mainstream theatre"; it was also the address for experimental European imports and verse dramas, among many, many other things. Was his Broadway "public" more inclusive than ours simply because its constituents had fewer alternatives? Perhaps. But few theatregoers who identify as such today see or enjoy only one kind of play, and most like it that way, even among those who may not stray far from Broadway and the well advertised. Moreover, I can think of no theatregoer who does not also see movies, read books, enjoy some kind of music, watch some kind of television, and usually pay attention to some kind of professional sports. Theatregoers then, as now, had and exercised multiple options.

Mantle's observations and career are a reminder that every theatregoing public is multifaceted. Even the idea of choosing theatre because it is a sanctioned kind of cultural capital within one's social milieu does not obviate an individual occupying several positions within his or her social stratum. The woman who loves a chick flick with girlfriends is not, on account of this activity, incapable of parsing abstract poetry, wallpapering a house on her own, organizing a political campaign, understanding hedge funds, or self-identifying as a basketball junkie. Her tastes in theatre may or may not seem to mesh with any one of these interests. They may mesh with more than one of those interests, leaving her subject simultaneously to the approval and the chiding of a the-atre critic who might decry the likes of *Shrek* and extol the virtues of *Red*, ig-noring the fact that one and the same theatregoer attended both (as, by the way, did the critic, by necessity).

Those bitten by the theatre bug often, like Mantle himself, start buying tickets in their teens and shelve their last program shortly before shuffling off this mortal coil. If they are not eternally young, nor, usually, eternally progres-sive, they suggest in the aggregate a musical metaphor. The playgoing public comprises a melodic and harmonic mix of varying preferences in discourse and style layered over the shared bass line of wanting magic, stimulation, and trans-formation when the lights go down. This symphonic recipe makes the theatre-going public both hard to pin down on any particular show and somehow com-fortingly predictable in the aggregate.

Mantle's Broadway playgoing public—varying IQs, gender differences, anti-intellectualism and all—actually resembles a dream come true for Maurice Browne, founder in 1912 of the Chicago Little Theatre and a key player in the American Little Theatre movement. Browne, an unapologetic aesthete, saw theatre as the "temple of a living art," but his view of its worshippers sounded less spiritual than pragmatic. He wanted "about one per cent of the population going to the theatre about once a month as a matter of course and preferring to enjoy itself while there." This assemblage should comprise average Americans: "men and women, without overmuch money or brains, but with a great deal of that splen-did, pitiful, underrated quality which is common to all—ordinary humanity; your cousins . . . my aunts . . . Mrs. Lake Avenue's cook's young man . . . store-clerks and college professors and club-women and policemen . . . all of whom are compact . . . of the laughter and tears and the divine childish gift of 'let's pretend.' "[45]

Between Browne's era and our own (and including the years of Mantle's entire New York career), theatre as an art gained the traction that would result in a plethora of university and college programs: the regional theatre network that burgeoned in the 1960s and 1970s, the National Endowment for the Arts (started in 1965), the various state arts councils that emerged in the NEA's wake, and what DiMaggio calls a "managerial revolution" in the arts.[46] It is this mana-gerial revolution that may have caused us to stray from assessing audiences as Mantle did. Managerialism, DiMaggio explains, is a kind of carcerism suscep-tible to the logics of privileging access and continuation over artistic vision or excellence; of creating the sort of administrative systems that shore up the im-portance of bureaucracy in the eyes of funders and work to the disadvantage of arts collectives (among others); and the logic of boosterism for the arts in general, again with less interest in individual endeavors than in keeping systems visible and going. These sorts of "collective efforts of arts administrators to enhance their status, authority, and career opportunities" favor audience studies that can be systematized or duplicated and that yield quantifiable data.[47] They also favor programs such as education and outreach, which, as discovered in the study noted by Marquis, may do little or nothing to increase the number of people interested in (among other things) playgoing, but do bring in grants.[48]

A recent *New York Times* article suggests that Broadway producers, despite their present-day concerns for niche marketing and their alliances with nonprofits (the managerials), actually do think in terms that pick up on Mantle's observations about emotional satisfaction being the most prized product for the playgoing public and about that satisfaction emerging from a delicate mixture of visual, aural, bodily, and kinesthetic facets of attending a Broadway show. In choosing a theatre in which to open a show, producers worry about the way individual Broadway houses *feel*, noting that a happy marriage between the mood of the show and the essence of the theatre space has something to do with audiences responding positively. "Few factors can be as consequential to a show's success as a theater's seating capacity," writes Patrick Healy. "Too many seats, for instance, can be a mood killer if some go empty and audience members feel they are at a show no one else wants to see."[49] "Moods" are not culture-free phenomena, of course. But without resorting to a kind of census-like examination of who will be in the audience for a given show, producers nonetheless have not just a demographic but also a gut sense of who makes up their public, fragmented and fickle though it may be. Certainly producers think about the appeal that individual plays will have for particular cohorts (women, men, racial and ethnic groups, morons, intellectuals, out-of-towners) qua cohorts. But they also see these cohorts in their role as Broadway-bound playgoers for whom "the theatre" promises an experience that, at least some nights of the year, tops any other, "other things being equal," as Dorothy Dalton said.

Because he was not directly responsible for selling tickets, booking a theatre, or making ends meet via his own dramatic output, Mantle's perspective on the audience could be one of participant-observer. If his categories do not seem to add up, it may be because, diverse though they are, they share a kind of DNA that allows for tremendous differences within the extended family. If he deplored certain spectator preferences or what he saw as group lapses in reception abilities, he knew that in the aggregate, the audience was his partner and that there would be no dance without them. Perhaps Samson Raphaelson (known now as the author of *The Jazz Singer*) made it into Mantle's *Best Plays of 1934–1935* for his observations about the Broadway theatregoing public in *Accent on Youth,* a valentine to New York and theatre. The comedy ran a respectable although hardly earth-shattering 204 performances, but Mantle called it "the most appealing romance of a season that was weak in this type of play, retelling the love story of sentimental bachelors and romantic middle-aged professors to the great delight of a playgoing public that is itself largely middle-aged and reminiscent."[50] What Raphaelson told that public about itself resembles what Mantle and Dorothy Dalton shared about "theatre" in that its writer knew he would not need to explain it: "You mustn't hate audiences. . . . Hate human beings if you want to, but not audiences. People are drab, they're petty, they spend their days serving each other and loathing each other. But in the evening— . . . after they have dined, when they get into street cars, subways and taxis and come together in the theatre, when the lights go out and the footlights go on— in other words when they become an audience—they cease being human; they become divine."

Would Burns Mantle agree with this assessment of his partner in theatre-going? I only wish I had his direct dial.

Notes

1. Burns Mantle, "The Voice in the Dark," *Photoplay Magazine,* May 1920, 35, 36, 128.
2. Harold L. Cail, "Burns Mantle Would Hardly Know Yearbook He Created," *Portland (Maine) Sunday Telegram,* December 17, 1967, 15D. In ninety years there have been just six editors. Mantle was succeeded by John Chapman, his longtime assistant. The subsequent four included Louis Kronenberger, Henry Hewes, and Otis Guernsey, who edited thirty-six volumes. The sixth, Jeffrey Eric Jenkins, assumed the post in 2001.
3. Small, Maynard sold the project to Dodd, Mead in time for the 1924–25 volume.
4. Joseph Wood Krutch, "Mr. Mantle's Annuals," *New York Times Book Review,* December 24, 1944.
5. Lewis Nichols, "Mr. Mantle's Accolades," *New York Times Book Review,* December 1, 1946.
6. http://www.bestplaysonline.com/bestplayseditor.html. The criteria for "best" and the cities and media on which the volume reports changed over the years, but the yearbook remains influential and its editor casts a wide net.
7. Louis Sobol, "Your Broadway and Mine," Tuesday, December 23, 1930, unidentified clipping, "Critics and Criticism" file, Billy Rose Collection, New York Public Library, Lincoln Center for the Performing Arts.
8. "The Dean of Drama Critics Will Meet No More Deadlines," unidentified clipping, September 11, [no year given but definitely from 1943, as that was the year Mantle retired, which is the impetus for the feature], "Clippings, Burns Mantle" file, New York Public Library, Billy Rose Collection, Lincoln Center for the Performing Arts.
9. John Chapman says Mantle was called Roy, but this is the single reference I found saying so. Still, Chapman clearly knew him well, as the brief article mentioning this makes

clear that Mantle's family knew Chapman from the day the latter was born. "To Clara, with Love, from John," by John Chapman, unidentified clipping in "Clippings, Burns Mantle" file, Billy Rose Collection, New York Public Library, Lincoln Center for the Performing Arts.

10. "The Dean of Drama Critics Will Meet No More Deadlines."

11. "'Big Six' Honors 50-year Veterans," February 3, 1941, unidentified clipping, Billy Rose Collection, New York Public Library, Lincoln Center for the Performing Arts.

12. See "To Clara, with Love, From John."

13. Ben Pinchot, "They Tell Us What We Think: A Series of Portrait Studies by Ben Pinchot: No. 4," *Stage*, May 1934. The manager was Crosby Gaige, the press agent was John Peter Toohey, and the playwright was Earl Derr Biggers. All three are non-names today, although Biggers created the character of Charlie Chan in a series of novels on which the later films are based. Sidnew Skolsky, "Tintypes," *New York Daily News*, September 25, 1931.

14. Arthur Edwin Krows, "Burns Mantle Separates Critics from Critics," *New York Dramatic Mirror*, March 4, 1914.

15. Thomas Dickinson, *The Insurgent Theatre* (1917; reprint, New York: Benjamin Blom, 1972), 129, 63, 15–16, 81.

16. Krows, "Burns Mantle."

17. Ibid.

18. *The Best Plays of 1925–26*, ed. Burns Mantle (1926; reprint, New York: Dodd, Mead, 1947), vi.

19. *The Best Plays of 1919–1920*, ed. Burns Mantle (Boston: Small, Maynard, 1920), iv.

20. *The Best Plays of 1921–1922*, ed. Burns Mantle (Boston: Small, Maynard, 1922), iii.

21. Ibid., iii, 11. Milne's play is about a ninety-year-old poet whose family learns on his deathbed that the work whose profits they have all enjoyed was not that of their paterfamilias but of a colleague who died young many years earlier.

22. *The Best Plays of 1922–1923*, ed. Burns Mantle (Boston: Small, Maynard, 1923), x.

23. *The Best Plays of 1923–1924*, ed. Burns Mantle (Boston: Small, Maynard, 1924), 8; *The Best Plays of 1930–31*, ed. Burns Mantle (New York: Dodd, Mead, 1931), vi.

24. *The Best Plays of 1929–30*, ed. Burns Mantle (New York: Dodd, Mead, 1930), 237.

25. *The Best Plays of 1934–35*, ed. Burns Mantle (New York: Dodd, Mead, 1935), 325.

26. *The Old Maid*, made into a 1939 film starring Bette Davis, is the story of a spirited young woman in antebellum New York City who gives up her illegitimate daughter to her sister so that the girl will grow up with social privilege. To protect and cover her own feelings, the main character is strict and cold to the girl, enduring heartache but keeping her secret. *Both Your Houses* features an idealistic young congressman willing to fight a construction project to be federally funded in his state when he learns of the hidden costs and backroom bargains that have gone into the bill.

27. *The Best Plays of 1934–35*, 144; *The Best Plays of 1932–33*, ed. Burns Mantle (New York: Dodd, Mead, 1933), 5.

28. *The Best Plays of 1936–1937*, ed. Burns Mantle (New York: Dodd, Mead, 1937), vi.

29. *The Best Plays of 1924–1925*, ed. Burns Mantle (Boston: Small, Maynard, 1925), 5; *The Best Plays of 1927–28*, ed. Burns Mantle (New York: Dodd, Mead, 1928), xi.

30. *The Best Plays of 1924–1925*, viii.

31. *The Best Plays of 1932–33*, 61.

32. *The Best Plays of 1951–1952*, ed. John Chapman (New York and Toronto: Dodd, Mead, 1952), 4.

33. *The Best Plays of 1933–34*, ed. Burns Mantle (New York: Dodd, Mead, 1934, reprinted 1948), v, vi. Henry Bial observes in *Acting Jewish: Negotiating Ethnicity on the American Stage and Film* (Ann Arbor: University of Michigan Press, 2005) that in the twentieth and twenty-first centuries "The Jewish audience for Broadway theater, by accounts both statistical and anecdotal, is disproportionate even to the Jewish numerical representation in the population of the New York metropolitan area" (18).

34. Recent volumes of the series under the sixth (current, at the time of this publication) editor, Jeffrey Eric Jenkins, include plays that have neither necessarily played on Broadway nor have wide, popular appeal.

35. Mantle himself was once quoted in a brief profile as having "two basic tests in judging dramas. Does he believe them? Does he want to believe them?" (Skolsky, "Tintypes"). Frustratingly, the quote leaves unclear whether he is talking about drama qua literature or qua theatre, a distinction he discussed with readers (and surely with himself) in several of the *Best Plays* introductory essays.

36. *The Best Plays of 1950–1951*, ed. John Chapman (New York and Toronto: Dodd, Mead, 1951), 5.

37. *The Best Plays of 1924–1925*, ix.

38. For a superb description of the sort of theatre Mantle (and most Americans) would have taken for granted in the last two decades of the nineteenth and first few years of the twentieth century, see David Mayer's *Stagestruck Filmmaker: D. W. Griffith and the American Theatre* (Iowa City: University of Iowa Press, 2009), esp. chapter 1, "The Mobile Theatre." Among other things, variety turns (musical, dance, and comic numbers) worked into and between the scenes of what we might prefer to think of as "straight" plays (because they had scripts but not musical scores) were ordinary and expected. Mantle was born just as the "combination" touring company (what we would now call road shows) took over in the United States, creating elaborate networks or touring routes that served much of the United States outside of New York. Mayer notes that not only did combination companies bring such plays (with variety turns in them) across the nation, but also that many companies toured with *two* groups of performers: actors for the play proper and a whole other group of vaudevillian-type performers for the interpolated numbers. My point is not that Mantle missed such theatre, saw it as "correct," mourned its passing, resisted the new, or anything else of the sort. It is that he was able to see evolution and overlap in both the sorts of works offered on the American stage and in the audience members who would, by virtue of their age, see differing things as "ordinary" or as "new."

39. Paul DiMaggio, "Social Structure, Institutions, and Cultural Goods: The Case of the United States," in *The Politics of Culture: Policy Perspectives for Individuals, Institutions, and Communities*, ed. Gigi Bradford, Michael Garen, and Glenn Wallach (New York: The New Press, 2000), 38.

40. Alice Goldfarb Marquis, *Art Lessons: Learning from the Rise and Fall of Public Arts Funding* (New York: Basic Books, 1995), 99.

41. Berman quoted in ibid., 139.

42. David Savran takes up the constituting of an audience to support serious theatre in the 1920s in *HighBrow/Lowdown: Theater, Jazz, and the Making of the New Middle Class*

(Ann Arbor: University of Michigan Press, 2009). In a chapter titled "Pandering to the 'Intelligent Minority,'" Savran offers a collaged portrait of middle- and upper-middle-class theatregoers ranging from intellectuals and aspiring artists to white-collar workers anxious about distancing themselves from a laboring or immigrant hoi polloi, to wealthier patrons less concerned with "respectability" but eager to see and be seen. Savran also points out that the portion of the audience who sat downstairs—those with whom Mantle would have rubbed shoulders—had more money and possibly less earnest intellectualism than many who saved in order to be able to sit in the balcony.

43. Ethan Mordden, *All That Glittered: The Golden Age of Drama on Broadway, 1919–1959* (New York: St. Martin's, 2007).

44. See Neil Postman, *Amusing Ourselves to Death: Public Discourse in the Age of Show Business* (New York: Penguin, 1985).

45. Maurice Browne, "The Temple of a Living Art" (Chicago Little Theatre, 1914), 10, 13 (pamphlet independently published by the Chicago Little Theatre). It is admittedly possible to read this list as clearly marked aspirers to middlebrow respectability. Neither Mrs. Lake Avenue nor the laborers who work in the factory her husband presumably owns are on the list.

46. DiMaggio, "Social Structure," 53.

47. Ibid.

48. In 1988 I wrote an article about regional theatre productions of *A Christmas Carol* as educational/outreach endeavors. I asked each education director with whom I spoke whether research was done to track the long-term effects of free, "outreach" theatregoing ventures. In other words, did attending theatre as a young student for free or at a discount and under the guidance of a teacher result in becoming a theatre supporter as an adult? No education director had ever undertaken to find out (in terms of his or her own theatre—and I looked at theatres with long-standing outreach programs), nor had any ever heard of such a study being done. See Dorothy Chansky, "A Tale of Two Carols," *InTheater Magazine*, December 18, 1998.

49. Patrick Healy, "In Broadway Lights: No Vacancy," *New York Times*, April 28, 2010, http://www.nytimes.com/2010/05/02/theater/02stages.html?pagewanted=1&ref=theater.

50. *The Best Plays of 1934–1935*, vii.

Weeki Wachee Girls and Buccaneer Boys

The Evolution of Mermaids, Gender, and "Man versus Nature" Tourism

—JENNIFER A. KOKAI

In 1956, science writer Horace Loftin worked to dispel the myth of the mermaid in the *Science News-Letter:* "Instead of being petite and curvaceous," he wrote, "the mermaid of actuality is tub-like, and weighs from 600 to 2000 pounds."[1] Mermaids, he believed, were based upon the sea cow, or manatee, as the American variant is most commonly known. Even in 1956, Loftin wrote worriedly about the hunting and extinction of manatees, using their ties to mermaids to advocate for their preservation. He stressed their "inoffensiveness" and their similarities to human mothers: "to nurse, the mother sits up with her head and shoulders above water, holding a baby to her breast between her flippers."[2] Loftin's scientific analysis is that "mermaids," usually imagined as women, are based upon sightings of these female manatees, with breasts bared above water, nurturing children.

The last time I saw a manatee up close was in the mid-1980s; it had found itself in a lake at the Florida tourist attraction Weeki Wachee, "the city of the mermaids." The lake, fed by spring water, lay between the old-fashioned theme park portion, with bird shows, glass-bottom boats, nature trails, and, most importantly, an underwater show featuring "real, live mermaids," and the newly adjacent water park Buccaneer Bay. This visiting manatee, who may have represented the origins of the concept of mermaid, served as a visual link between two kinds of mermaids, the graceful women of the park's history, who tamed the water, and the swimmers racing by on slides made by domesticating the water.

This article is about three kinds of mermaids and mermaid performances as tourism. Specifically, it is about Weeki Wachee's underwater theatre and how it has changed from when it opened on October 12, 1947, to today. During this time, the park evolved from a site popular for water-based performances emphasizing femininity, heterosexuality, and passive spectatorship to participatory performances predicated on active, aggressive, and athletic displays at a newer water park. Mirroring this, the idea of "mermaid" in popular culture has expanded from the idea of attractive, unobtainable women with long, flowing hair and physically hybrid bodies to include world-champion swimmers who rip through the water like fish. Over time, the appeal of the park and its performances have changed. Despite these changes, the social concerns of what constitutes "family friendly" tourism in the United States, as demonstrated by newspapers, documentaries, short films, and other participants in the larger cultural discourse, have remained remarkably the same, largely centering on the spectacle of contained, white, heterosexual female bodies for a presumed male audience. In charting the evolutions of the park, I demonstrate how tourism uses performance to perpetuate certain notions of gender and identity. These often subtle methods are frequently shrugged off as "good clean fun," yet these performances reach more people and have a potentially far greater impact than the traditional theatre ever could.

Mermaids: The Beginnings of the Tail

The figure of the mermaid seems to intrinsically draw upon novelty and kitsch, something that is certainly true of Weeki Wachee. The park's most famous predecessor, for example, is probably the 1842 display of the Feejee Mermaid by legendary showman P. T. Barnum in his American museum. The mermaid was originally created by a Japanese fisherman, who sold it to an American sea captain, and it eventually found its way to The American Museum in New York.[3] With typical panache, Barnum created an elaborate press campaign complete with fake naturalists, bogus lectures, and illustrated pamphlets of petite, curvaceous beauties. According to Barnum's autobiography, the "mermaid" was actually made of a monkey's body attached to a shark's tail. Whatever it was, drawings and reconstructions make clear that it was hideous, nothing at all like the graceful pictures in the ads promised, and although curiosity initially brought audiences in, the display had no longevity. As folklorist Steven Levi recounts,

"Barnum's monthly profits more than doubled the first month that the mermaid was on exhibit. After its debut in the American Museum, the Feejee Mermaid dropped from sight."[4]

Like Barnum's mermaid, who lured spectators in with promises of beauty but was actually hideous, mermaids have long held complex and contradictory associations in mythology, but they are almost always female. They are often conflated or used interchangeably with sirens, the Greek mythological figures that lured sailors to death with their beautiful singing. Author Francesca Sautman records that in the Middle Ages they were often depicted with a mirror and a comb, accessories still used in some Weeki Wachee publicity photos, which carried associations with "Christian moral and didactic messages (vanity as a mortal sin, a dangerous temptation for the soul) and to a broader mythical content (the mirror as soul-gazing instrument, the connection to death through looking behind)."[5] Besides these associations, the contemporary U.S. depiction of mermaids often owes a great deal to the Hans Christian Andersen story "The Little Mermaid," a tale about a mermaid who wants a soul and the love of a prince. In Andersen's version, the prince ultimately marries someone else and the titular mermaid commits suicide. She becomes an air spirit and is promised a soul through good deeds.

But before Disney's retelling of the Andersen story made this the dominant mermaid image in popular culture, there was another, much more famous underwater beauty. In 1941 the image of the mermaid in America became synonymous with one person, Esther Williams. Excellently summarizing Fredric Jameson's arguments on postmodernism and multinational capital, sociologist Steven J. Fjelmen writes that "the culture of late capitalism has seen the spread of commodification into perhaps the last two available domains—the unconscious (pornography, psychotherapy, fantasy) and nature (wilderness parks, zoos, and anthropology)."[6] Esther Williams, or "The Million Dollar Mermaid," was the perfect marriage of these two commodities. Williams was a champion swimmer who missed the opportunity to swim at the Olympic level because of World War II. Instead she was scouted by Hollywood producer Billy Rose to join the Aquacade at the San Francisco World's Fair in 1940 with Johnny Weismuller, the actor famous for playing Tarzan. There she learned to "swim pretty" instead of fast, with her head and face above water.[7] When the fair closed, she became a major movie star specializing in "aqua musicals," that is, movies with extended choreographed routines and synchronized swimming in enormous pools.

Williams was considered a rarity in Hollywood pictures, not only because of her very specific fame as a "mermaid" but also because "long before strong women were in vogue in Hollywood, Williams packed a combination of youth,

Figure 1. Mermaid viewing herself in a mirror, 1969. Image courtesy of the State Archives of Florida.

beauty, and athleticism . . . often schlepping her leading men through the water."[8] She was five foot eight and had the athletic thighs and arms of a swimmer. Williams's emergence as a star and the rage for her (and only her) aqua musicals indicates a specific need that her novelty films filled in the early 1940s. This need was somehow tied to the water and Williams's beauty, because as studio head Lewis Mayer famously said, "Wet, she's a star. Dry, she ain't."[9]

The fact that Williams's movies, and this new genre, appeared at the commencement of World War II was likely no coincidence. During the war, women were asked to step up and take on male roles, famously becoming riveters and pilots, and easily completing athletic tasks like repetitive manual labor and lifting heavy materials. Yet, at the same time, the world seemed unstable and unfriendly, and studios attempted to shore up traditional gender roles with beautiful white women who initially challenged those roles by behaving in "tomboy" ways.[10] Regardless of these female characters' occupations at the beginning of the film, they almost always ended up happily acquiescing to heterosexual marriage and relinquishing their prior non-feminine behaviors by the end.[11] Williams's film roles fulfilled the studio-desired balancing act, focusing on her traditional beauty in a framework of heterosexual romance, with her athletic body remaining in the frame enhanced by revealing bathing suits, unremarked upon, allowing space for women to see themselves as physically capable of carrying men if needed. Although subsequent iterations of mermaids in U.S. popular culture have differed, they have always been variations on this theme and thus offered something for men and women.

The Original Mermaids of Weeki Wachee

We're not like other women fighting traffic on the shore
Tired of going shopping
Living lives that are a bore.
Don't have to do the cooking, hardly ever catch a cold.
Don't know how to clean an oven and we never will grow old.
We've got the world by the tail.
OPENING SONG FROM "THE LITTLE MERMAID" AT WEEKI WACHEE, 2005

When Weeki Wachee opened in 1947, the mermaids picked up the threads of novelty, female beauty, athleticism, and domestication that the Feejee Mermaid and Esther Williams had perpetuated. The attraction was the brainchild of former Hollywood stuntman Newt Perry, who was known as "the human fish" due to his appearance in hundreds of newsreels performing tricks underwater, including eating bananas and wrestling alligators.[12] He was good friends with Weismuller, and, perhaps inspired by the Aquacade, he latched on to the Florida development boom by planning a water-based attraction. Perry decided to merge his famous connections and know-how with the spectacle of attractive women, and in 1947 he built an eighteen-seat underwater theatre in a formerly trash-filled spring on the Florida Gulf about thirty-five miles north of Tampa.[13]

The first theatre was essentially a tank submerged mostly below the water. The top was open to the air and covered with a canvas awning. The theatre was held down with sandbags (and the weight of spectators), and large plate glass windows separated the watery "stage" from the audience's space.[14] The term "mermaid" was at first used interchangeably with "Aquabelle" (which

Perry seems to have borrowed from the Aquacade), and the performers didn't wear tails; they did, however, perform the entire forty-minute show underwater without coming up for air, using Perry's system of sucking air from a compressed air hose as needed, a trick he learned as a navy diving instructor. During their routines, the swimmers performed tricks such as drinking soda, doing ballet, and eating bananas. Originally, there was no narrative or music to accompany the performance, leaving only the noise of the audience and their conversations.

Although there were male performers in the beginning, Perry quickly realized that the spectacle of idealized 1940s white female beauty was one of the major draws of the show and phased the men out.[15] His Hollywood connections helped Weeki Wachee's fame grow, and Universal-International decided to use the location in 1948 to film *Mr. Peabody and the Mermaid,* further cementing the notion that Weeki Wachee featured female performers. As part of the promotion for the film and the park, Perry held a "Florida Mermaid Queen" beauty pageant. After its initial success, he would repeat this pageant several times, solidifying the public notion that the park featured women performers and that what made a mermaid a mermaid was first and foremost her beauty. This is echoed by former mermaid Ginger Stanley Hallowell, who told scholar Lu Vickers in an interview, "He said, 'I'm looking for mermaids, for girls to be swimmers who don't look like swimmers,' whatever that means."[16] Since Hallowell had just won a beauty competition, what that likely means is he wanted women who could "swim pretty," like Williams. That is, Perry wanted women who looked more feminine and beautiful than athletic, even if the job required they be both.[17] Perry was also looking only for white performers and white audiences in the still racially segregated South.

The elimination of men from the performance was audience driven and not Perry's original intent. The women sold more tickets and attracted more publicity, and so men involved in the show became land-based, assuming the role of announcers. But why were women performers more attractive than men? As the movie recast the Weeki Wachee swimmers from "Aquabelles" to "Mermaids," one reason likely has to do with the mythological history of mermaids as primarily female, as women in Western culture have historically been considered aligned with nature, emotional and animalistic, as opposed to rational and scientific.[18] In our cultural mythology, perhaps the women simply seemed more at home in the landscape.

In addition, just as mythical mermaids are unusual, but natural, sea creatures, Florida itself was also characterized in terms of exotic ecology. Florida had long been advertised to those in more urban areas as a vacation paradise, attractive for its warm climate and extensive beaches. During the Great Depression, however, Florida was hit hard and "came to be seen as dangerous, a playland that had lost much of its charm."[19] The 1940s brought with it the development of an interstate, military factories, and air-conditioning, and this led to an enormous influx of permanent population, an increase of 46 percent. But Florida still retained its image in the popular imagination as exotic, home to natural splendor, wildlife, and "strangely" named locales like Weeki Wachee. Accordingly, the park was advertised as a nature-based attraction. While the springs, and the mermaids in them, could be seen as "tamed," they were a naturally occurring water source and not a domesticated water source delivered through pipes created by men. Male swimmers such as Perry, with his overtly athletic figure, naval background, and Tarzan connections, would more likely have been read as "conquering" the water as opposed to being part of its natural ecology.

Women performing in this natural "tamed" water source, not quite a domesticated water environment, also contributed to a family-safe yet chastely erotic spectacle. Geographer Erik Swyngedouw chronicles how by the late nineteenth century, "the increasingly commodified domestication of water announced the withdrawal of the urban elite body and bodily hygiene from the public or semi-public sphere and its retreat into the privacy and intimacy of the bathroom and the toilet. Nudity and exposing the naked body to the 'elements' became improper and uncivilized."[20] He further argues that because of this, images of people, women in particular, pouring domesticated water on themselves became eroticized, gesturing to the intimacy and secrets of private bathing.[21] If the audience was presumed to be seeing through the male gaze of the show's creator, the women in the audience wanting to be like the mermaids and the men wanting to be with the mermaids, the swimmers onstage were in a semi-private location, separated from the audience by glass, and this gave the audience the frisson of being voyeurs. At the same time, however, the spring was a natural spring, and the swimmers were positioned as mermaids, natural creatures. This made their act not quite the private act of bathing, but something different. Using women performers located this spectacle as both natural and unnatural, public and private, civilized and uncivilized, sexual and chaste. In short, women mermaids gave white tourists from more urbanized areas visiting Florida the idealized, eroticized version of nature they expected and wanted. The male visitors and male announcers were placed in the role of urbanization and progress, located inside the comfortable theatre.

In 1959 the American Broadcasting Company (ABC) purchased the park through its Leisure Division. ABC built a new, extremely expensive underwater theatre that sat five hundred patrons and developed an underwater loudspeaker system that let the mermaids hear both commands and music, allowing for dance choreography. By 1964 the mermaids were performing full-length plays, the first being *Alice in Wonderland,* wearing mermaid tails and visiting with celebrities like Elvis Presley, Don Knotts, and Esther Williams herself.[22] According to an article from the *St. Petersburg Times* on August 12, 1961, "Mermaids' Curves Foil Dragon," ABC also added statuary of concrete topless mermaids that surrounded the park and a robotic dragon to the water show named Wily Willie that made "horrifying passes at the mermaids" but was foiled by their "curves," a pun on both the mermaids' swimming abilities and their appearances.

In addition, in 1974, ABC built an Indian Village, an unoccupied replica of a thatched-roof Seminole village.[23] Constructed after Disney began building Walt Disney World, this offered guests an experiential attraction the mermaid show did not. However, actual Native American bodies were absented, as the village was conceived of as a "ghost town." Ironically, this allowed the white tourists to stand in for the absent Native Americans much as white settlers had displaced the Native Americans in Florida history. Given that their black employees were behind the scenes and that there had been only one non-white mermaid in the park's history (a Japanese woman who performed for four months in 1969),[24] ABC kept the underlying notion of white female bodies on display as "family friendly," and the empty "Indian village" was the only "diversity" evident in the park's performances.[25] The fabrication of this village, in a "nature" based park, could also work to connect Native Americans (or their societies) more closely with nature—in opposition to the "civilization" of the white tourists.

Does a Mermaid Have a Vagina?

Cultural representations of mermaids in the United States have often wavered between overtly sexual and the stuff of children's stories, and managing this dichotomy was one of the key concerns for Weeki Wachee as well. As I discuss in more detail below, those responsible for the show see only female mermaids as sexually acceptable, and yet the resulting female-only space leads to inferences of more inappropriate sexuality that must be contained. In her analysis of the Disney movie *The Little Mermaid,* scholar Laura Sells writes, "The human world can be aligned with the white male system and the water world situated outside that system."[26] While the world on land is rational and orderly (and, in the movie, white), the world under the sea is mysterious, full of animal "others,"

Figure 2. Unidentified mermaid drinking a soda, 1950. Image courtesy of the State Archives of Florida.

and removed from the need for economic labor. Sells argues that this mimics the way "first world" residents characterize the "third world."[27]

By deciding to feature only mermaids and no mermen, the fantasy world constructed for the mermaids at Weeki Wachee could also be seen as a female space apart from the patriarchal world on land, even potentially a queer space. As the mermaids teasingly sing, they're "not like other women on the shore," they don't do domestic labor, and they don't age. The potential for queerness is especially evident in early productions of *The Wizard of Oz, Cinderella,* and *Alice in Wonderland,* where all parts were played by women. A photo from a 1970 production of *Cinderella* shows an incredibly feminine and beautiful "Prince" tenderly holding "Cinderella's" calf and gazing at her foot.

The potential for this space is mitigated, however, by the glass windows and presence of the audience, which make the mermaids' sexuality much more about attracting the male gaze of the family patriarchs, who as "heads of the household" in the pre-second-wave feminist era had presumably selected or acquiesced to this vacation destination. This is supported by publicity photos that exist from the early periods, which are repetitive in nature and fairly overtly work to sexualize the mermaids and keep them in a heterosexual framework.[28] The mermaids are frequently posed with some kind of phallic imagery, eyes closed rapturously drinking from a glass soda bottle, consuming banana after banana, and in one case pretending to eat a giant hotdog. Pop culture scholar Laurie Essig, writing about the "Mermaid Parade" at Coney Island, argues that the omnipresence of the phallus is necessary to keep mermaids from being perceived as monsters (or lesbians, whom U.S. culture has often conflated with monsters).[29] She writes of mermaids in contemporary popular culture as having "their desires . . . firmly located within the only truly legitimate sexual practices in our culture, the desire for heterosexual intercourse, for the insertion of a penis into a vagina, even if that vagina belongs to a fish."[30] The props used in the show create the simulated heterosexual sex necessary.[31]

However, at the same time, this heterosexual framework is handily contained by the mermaids' anatomy. No matter how alluring, mermaids are forever chaste because they live in the water and their fish tail negates the possibility they could have genitalia. Ailene Goodman writes of a mermaid's anatomy: "Paradoxically, she is the fish-tailed enchantress, yet despite the desire she arouses, she cannot possibly fulfill her promise as a sex symbol in any way, shape or form."[32] Even though what is being highlighted in the Weeki Wachee show is a heightened sexuality and femininity, the fact that mermaids are impossible to copulate with means the show stays family fare; their threatening sexuality is contained within the frame of heteronormativity. Just as their inaccessibility keeps them appropriate for family audiences, their visual use of the phallus and their hyperfemininity and whiteness, the last of which avoids cultural notions of women of color's sexuality, also work to keep them beautiful "women" practicing heterosexuality, although not engaging in it—a perfect role model for young girls in our patriarchal society.

The potential for a connection between the Weeki Wachee mermaids and lesbianism that the park works so hard to contain has been made explicit at least twice, although in very different ways, by those outside the park. One example is in a 2000 short film made by Kim Cummings called *Weeki Wachee Girls*.[33] The film, set in 1979, centers on two teenage friends, Katie and Maura, who live near Weeki Wachee and dream of being mermaids. Their friendship is challenged when Katie discovers Maura is in a lesbian relationship. In the film, the water does echo Sells's claim of a space apart from the white male world. Katie's backyard pool is where the two girls have their deepest discussions and where they have created a world with only the two of them. Outside the water, threats of religious censure, parental abandonment, and other worldly concerns intrude. The film ends on a positive note with the three girls—Katie, Maura, and Maura's girlfriend—practicing mermaid tricks underwater while a male voice sings over the closing credits, "Hey, let's stay, together. We can be OK, together."[34]

Although this film connects the underwater world of Weeki Wachee mermaids and lesbianism in a positive way, it was not made in conjunction with the park, and the girls just aspire to be mermaids. They are not actually allowed access to the park or the theatre. In a 2004 episode of *The Simple Life: Road Trip,* a reality show on Fox that featured socialites Nicole Richie and Paris Hilton traveling about the country undertaking a variety of odd jobs, like catching crayfish and working as maids at a nudist resort, the second episode showed the two visiting Weeki Wachee to perform as mermaids. In a scene not aired on television but available as a DVD extra and online, Richie pitches ideas to the mermaids on how to "improve" the show. In response to the question, "So what did you all come up with?" Richie responds, "What if we did Mermaid on Mermaid. Like a little, you know, lesbian action? You guys, sex sells. OK, it's 2004. You've got to admit." The Weeki Wachee employee responds, "But this is a family park."[35] Note that the end of the most popular show, "The Little Mermaid," featuring a "fifteen-year-old" emerging from the water to dance and form a romantic connection with an adult prince, does not violate the standards for a "family park." What Richie suggests is taking what the mermaid shows have long implied, faux lesbianism for the male gaze, and making it explicit, which is quickly rejected by the park employees. Family-friendly must equal conventional narratives of monogamous heterosexuality.

The repeated use of phallic props (presumably they could have eaten fruit other than all those bananas, and Vickers notes they did switch to apples for a while in the 1950s to avoid just that sexual connection) and the rejection of anything explicitly homoerotic makes it clear that these mermaids are heterosexual and performing for the male gaze.[36] The lascivious props are stand-in men demonstrating heteronormativity.[37] Eventually, in the later shows, the park did introduce men, like the prince in *The Little Mermaid,* potentially to make even more inarguable the heterosexual nature of the show. But importantly, these men never wear tails, and they are not called mermen. In a 2007 Web film made by comedian Thomas J. Kelly documenting his attempt to become the park's first "merman" and thus somehow save Weeki Wachee from closure, the unseen camera person (presumably Thomas) solicits opinions from existing mermaids and staff about the notion of a "merman." Their responses include:

Well the guys that we have here, who play our princes, never would they ever put on a mermaid tail. Never ever, ever. You couldn't pay them enough money to do it.

To find a man that wants to dress up like a girl, and not, kind of, like, it'd be like drag a little bit, I suppose. It would make you question their masculinity.[38]

For those at Weeki Wachee, and perhaps in the larger dominant culture, the mermaid is always female, and the mermaid tail inherently signifies female. For a man to wear it would be to perform in "drag," or even be coded as potentially queer; it could only be acceptable as "family fare" if explicitly comedic in the way drag is often used by straight men in popular culture.[39] I argue that this is because of the cultural signification of mermaids in general, their dual role as seductress of male sailors and as chaste, childlike women who can never actually engage in heterosexual penetration. There is no space for men in this myth, except for the prince the mermaid longs to be with or be like. In a heteronormative culture that considers drag to be either dangerously queer or comically grotesque, a merman can only be a joke or a monster.[40]

Not Just Pretty Swimmers: Mermaids as Athletes

Although it gets lost in the carefully constructed framework of beauty, femininity, and heterosexuality built around the Weeki Wachee mermaids, it is important to remember that these performers are athletes. Being a mermaid is a demanding job. Mermaids need to be able to hold their breath underwater for extended times (forty-five seconds is a minimum), to do complicated flips and turns gracefully, and to endure the pressure of the cold spring water on their bodies. In early shows, one mermaid also performed a deep dive, down to four hundred feet, adding additional tension by letting go of her air hose and staying out of sight for an extended time. Vickers argues, "Jacques Cousteau hadn't popularized human ventures into the undersea world yet. People still gazed at Florida's deep springs with as much wonder as had their nineteenth-century counterparts. The announcer played on the aquaphobia of the audience, often wondering out loud: "Where's the mermaid? Can you hold your breath with her?"[41] Since the mermaids could hold their breath for more than two minutes, no, the audience could not.

Ultimately, the mermaids' graceful shows were not just about femininity; they were also about the taming of nature, the ability for certain special kinds of humans to survive and thrive in an inhospitable environment and for it to look "natural." The show implied that the mermaids' stunts could put them in harm's way, and yet as a family tourist destination the expectation was that the mermaids would always be fine. In actuality, several mermaids were hospitalized for various mishaps.[42] The dangers to the mermaids were not just related to drowning. Multiple newspaper articles recount the predatory wildlife that could easily infiltrate the spring. A January 12, 1989, article from the *St. Petersburg Times* discusses the discovery of an eleven-foot alligator in the park on Christmas Day. Luckily, because of the gator's timing, no visitor or mermaid actually encountered the animal, which was "destroyed."[43] Still, the author writes, "it is a graphic demonstration of what can happen when man ventures into Mother Nature's playground." The alligator represents a fearful possibility that has recurred throughout the park's existence, and any new appearance of an alligator is heavily documented. Alligators have been found in public swimming holes,[44] and even lurking in a castle set piece in the underwater theatre.[45]

Despite the ever-present natural threats, in the heyday of the park the mermaid show and the mermaids were novel for their ease in the water. Although they performed ballet, the true draw of their performance was that it was entirely underwater. In interviews, mermaids note that people often accused them of faking the performances. Bonnie Georgiadis, a mermaid from the 1960s, recalled, "they'd think the theatre windows were aquariums with little fish in them and that we were suspended out there on strings and there were big fans blowing out our hair."[46] The spectators' assumptions of trickery indicate that the mermaids were doing what the audience could not do (or even possibly believe), that they were somehow different than human, or superhuman.

Modern Mermaids and Nostalgic Yearning for the Past

In 2008, photographer Annie Leibovitz was asked by the Disney Company to recreate the visuals of their movie *The Little Mermaid* in a photo shoot. To represent the titian-haired main character, Ariel, Leibovitz placed actress Julianne Moore (renowned for her red hair) in the center of the frame, stationary on a rock. Surrounding her are mermaids and men swimming gracefully. In a departure from the Weeki Wachee's conception of tails as drag, perhaps not surprisingly, Leibovitz chose to feature Olympic champion Michael Phelps as the largest visible merman. In the 2008 Olympics in Beijing, Phelps won eight gold medals, an all-time record in swimming. At this date, he has sixteen Olympic medals in total, as well as seven world records. Phelps is now synonymous in popular culture with water. The other mermaids and mermen were depicted by other famous swimmers: Janet Evans, Rowdy Gaines, Brendan Hansen, and Cullen Jones.[47] Notably, the press releases specified that Phelps and the other swimmers were actually shot underwater, in a movie studio tank, while Moore, an actress, was shot on land and digitally inserted into the final picture. The swimmers were comfortable and at home enough in the water to be able to pose for attractive photographs.

Describing Olympic and other high-level swimmers as "mermaids" has become a common rhetorical trope in newspaper articles. An article by Henry Samuel from the April 24, 2008, edition of the British paper the *Telegraph* reports that French swimmer Laure Manaudou, known as the "French Mermaid," would not be participating in the Olympics. Ironically, given the "sexy, temptress" connotations that often accompany "mermaid," Manaudou fell apart in competition after nude photographs of her were put on the Internet.[48] An article from the *Washington Post*'s July 7, 2008, issue refers to forty-one-year-old female swimmer (and mother of a toddler) Dara Torres as "Mermaid Mom."[49] These are not the graceful mermaids Newt Perry sought, who were swimmers who didn't look like swimmers. These are women with incredibly defined muscled bodies. These are not women who do ballet in the water; these are women who tear through the water faster than others can move on land. The modern mermaid could kick an Aquabelle's tail.

If the tricks the mermaids performed were astonishing to audiences who had not yet seen Jacques Cousteau's documentaries, or who perhaps had grown up without a neighborhood swimming pool and swim teams, it makes sense that expectations for what impressed audiences vis-à-vis man's domination of water would increase. In fact, this relationship was paralleled by Weeki Wachee itself. In 1979, faced with dwindling attendance and revenues, ABC announced that they were going to build a new water park next to the original section. Known as Buccaneer Bay, this park had the requisite thrilling waterslides, areas for kids and parents, and snack bars that compose the modern Florida water-based tourist attraction.[50] This was a switch from a nature-based park, which *tamed* the water, to an artificial construction of pipes and tubes that *domesticated* the spring.

The mermaids and other Weeki Wachee employees attributed their drop in attendance to the rise of Disney World as a Florida tourist destination. Perhaps that didn't help, but it is my contention that even without Disney World, attendance at Weeki Wachee and the mermaid show would have begun to dwindle, just as interest in the Feejee Mermaid and Esther Williams had long ago. Both Disney and Weeki Wachee creator Newt Perry had movie backgrounds, but the approach they chose for their tourist destinations differed a great deal. Perry

Figure 3. Buccaneer Bay, 1987. Image courtesy of the State Archives of Florida. Photo by Jurgen Vogt.

chose to create an inactive attraction, similar to the experience of watching a movie. In the two big attractions, the bird show, where the audience sat and watched exotic birds perform tricks and work with trainers, and the mermaid show, visitors to the park were usually in a passive spectating position. At Disney World, even in the traditional "dark rides," spectators moved through the show experience. They were active participants in the park's experiences.

At Weeki Wachee, the novelty and joy of the mermaid show came from the audience's inability to do what the mermaids could do. They could not stay that long underwater; they could not swim as well. But at Disney World the reverse was true. In a traditional "dark ride" like Peter Pan's Flight (built in 1971 for the park's opening), spectators could fly just like the characters in Peter Pan. The audience was given the ability to put themselves in the place of the story's hero or heroine; they could experience new things, new thrills, new sights, and new worlds that they did not have access to in their normal lives. As performance scholar Richard Schechner writes in his analysis of the theme park Colonial Williamsburg, "the domain of the performance surrounds and includes the spectator. Looking at becomes harder, being in, easier. There is no house, and spectators are thrown back on their own resources for whatever assistance they need to maintain who and where they are."[51] Schechner wrote about this in relation to living history museums, but I believe his argument holds true for amusement parks as well. The environment dictates a more involved personal experience than the traditional theatre structure of the mermaid performances.

The water park that ABC built in 1982 was thus a natural evolution of the mermaids' function as vicarious tourism for previous generations. It was a reconfiguration of the experience of humanity triumphing over water, but one based on active spectators: instead of watching beautiful women perform impossible tasks, audience members could become modern mermaids. A waterslide provides tourists with the pretense of engaging in a dangerous water experience with the safety of knowing there is a lifeguard at the base of the ride should they actually encounter trouble. These lifeguards, in fact, comprised of local teenagers who everyone knows have passed a certification test, actually more closely represent the modern notion of merpersons like Phelps. Unlike the mermaids, who need to be strong swimmers but look feminine, lifeguards can be of either gender, and the public's greatest awareness of them is their strong swimming abilities. As sixteen-year-old, newly minted Buccaneer Bay employee Glen Badonsky confessed in a July 11, 1988, article in the *St. Petersburg Times,* "The prestige of being a lifeguard is nice, but mainly I like dealing with the kids here."[52] The lifeguard's feeling that his job commands a mixture of admiration, prestige, and public relations duties is not unlike the description a mermaid might have given of her job in the past.

The switch was not just from passive to active tourism with the addition of Buccaneer Bay to the original park. This switch was gendered as well, as evident in the name of the new park and the increased presence of male lifeguards. If the prior discussion demonstrates that the mermaid is considered essentially female by virtue of her tail and social mythological function, then a "buccaneer" is inevitably male, and labeling the park for buccaneers continues the unspoken conception of the ideal park visitor as masculine. Derived from a term for French hunting men in St. Domingo, *buccaneer* came to be synonymous with "pirate" when that same group of men began raiding excursions on the Spanish coasts of America.[53] Pirates are almost always depicted as men, and they are active and aggressive, known for looting, killing, and raping women.[54] The names of the waterslides and attractions in Buccaneer Bay support the image of aggression and violence: "Pirate's Revenge," "Double Revenge," "Devil's Ladder," and "Swashbuckler."[55] Men working as lifeguards at these attractions do not have to worry about perceived effeminacy in the same way that men working in the mermaid show might. Although audiences previously wanted female mermaids who seemed part of the local ecology, they now seemed more interested in an experience of personally conquering water—which has traditionally been characterized as a masculine activity.

Perhaps appropriately for a park named after pirates, Buccaneer Bay began to draw criticism for its apparent habit of overlooking lecherous guest behavior and the availability of alcohol. In a June 2, 2003, issue of the *St. Petersburg Times,* Robert King editorialized about the scandalous behavior that ruined his trip to the park with his children: "alcohol on the beach and dirty dancing on the dock—makes me wonder how much longer Weeki Wachee and Buccaneer Bay will remain a water hole you want to take your kids to."[56] In particular he is complaining about the addition of a "tiki bar" that serves alcohol to adult patrons, and teenage girls dancing in a way "that would make Britney Spears blush" to a song by pop singer Justin Timberlake that includes the line, "Can I have you naked by the end of this song?"[57] The author attributes the girls' style of dancing to the lascivious suggestions of the male singer.

Given the park's emphasis on masculinity, perhaps this is where female bodies are now located: the "dirty dancing" teenage girls. They now take up the mantle for the same concerns and policing of women's bodies as Weeki Wachee's mermaid show did long ago. Again, a "family" attraction depends upon controlling young women's sexuality, walking the line between maintaining clear heterosexuality (although the writer describes the teenage girls "bumping and grinding" on an isolated dock, he asserts they were simply following the command of a male singer rather than performing any kind of homosexual or homosensual act) and sexual purity (he is appalled to see his three-year-old daughter mimicking the dance moves of the older girls). The frustrations the author of the article expresses are not with the employees of the park, however, but the guests, and even though he offers the complaints, he is not really sure whom to complain to; his solution is to just stop going there. King also makes it clear that he is contrasting this new, lewd and out-of-control female sexuality with the Weeki Wachee of old, in which the mermaids represented a safe, domesticated femininity and sexuality.

King expresses nostalgia in his article, for a Weeki Wachee "safe" for families, and, in fact, by 2003 the mermaid show and the original park trafficked almost entirely in nostalgia. As Florida historic preservationist Phil Wernli told me in a 2009 phone call, for the past decade or so the water park had accounted for 60 to 70 percent of the combined parks' revenue. In fact, beginning in 1997 Weeki Wachee became "endangered." The current owners, Florida Leisure Acquisition, closed all park attractions other than the mermaid show and allowed the facilities to begin to fall into disrepair and crumble while they focused on Buccaneer Bay. Faced with the potential closure of the park, old park employees and mermaids decided to draw attention to the park's plight by putting on a monthly "alumni" show: "Merlinnium, Tails of Yesteryear."

As mermaid Barbara Wynns, who became one of the lead activists for pre-serving the park, declared in a 2004 issue of *National Geographic Magazine,* "Wrinkles, cellulite, chubby, whatever—we're ready to go."[58] Given the dependency of the original theme park on the spectacle of female beauty, it is questionable why the mermaids believed that their alumni performances of older mermaids (their ages ranging from forties to mid-seventies) would attract more ticket-paying individuals and help revitalize the park. And, in fact, while the publicity brought in "nostalgia and a timely flood of donations" that helped stave off closing for a time, there was no noticeable uptick in paying visitors and the park continued to suffer financial difficulties, teetering constantly on the brink of closing.[59]

In a 2003 article in the *New York Times,* Wynns offered the following suggestions for revitalizing the park: "Why not put on bathing-suit fashion shows in the mermaid tank, bus tourists the 88 miles from Disney World, even have a mermaid circulate through the park, like Mickey, Minnie and Goofy?"[60] The article brushes off her suggestions as wistful and outmoded, gestures to the glory days of the park. Another *St. Petersburg Times* editorial, this one from September 30, 2003, urges people in its very title to "Visit Weeki Wachee Out of Respect." The author, Sheila Stolls, asks plaintively, "Doesn't anyone understand the value of kitsch?" and argues that "there is a quieter, gentler, more natural aspect of Florida that is being lost."[61] This last suggestion, that by ignoring Weeki Wachee something "natural" is at stake, is patently ironic. The mermaids who were created by Hollywood show people and who were once so novel as to be suspected of fraud were now considered "natural."

As to whether or not Florida citizens recognized the value of kitsch and the nostalgia that is always intertwined with it, one unkind letter to the editor in the *St. Petersburg Times* noted on November 12, 2002, "Sorry, senior citizens, but people do not go to Weeki Wachee to see elderly mermaids!"[62] But given letters like Stolls's and other editorials such as park employee John Athanason's argument in *Hernando Today*—"Whether it's the allure of the mermaids or the magnificent natural beauty of the spring itself, there is little doubt Weeki Wachee Springs exudes a sense of nostalgia and charm that has kept it alive for the past 61 years"—it is clear that the people who did attend Weeki Wachee did so to see elderly mermaids and to reminisce about the past.[63] In the early 2000s, the park was transitioning from a tourist attraction to a kind of museum, and the mermaid "alumni" were unwittingly reinforcing that idea. Ultimately that is exactly what the park became, when after a long series of legal battles with its landlord, the Southwest Florida Water Management District (or Swiftmud) proved conclusively the park could not safely maintain its infrastructure; on

November 1, 2008, Weeki Wachee became a Florida state park. Future plans for the park potentially include "more cultural resources, preserving the history of the mermaid attraction, environmental issues and expanding the attraction to include interpretive programming."[64] These suggestions dovetail with what Florida preservationist Wernli told me when he mentioned plans for the park to emphasize its history, first and foremost.

In a jubilant article from February 17, 2008, former mermaid Vicki Smith celebrated the park's absorption by the state by telling reporter Tony Holt that "the end result of the SWIFTMUD feud reminds her of when the park was in its heyday. Now it can be seen as a reliable attraction for local families. 'To me, it's come full circle,' she said."[65] But Smith is remembering incorrectly, substituting nostalgia for the park for its actual journey. In truth, the park's journey has not been circular, but rather linear, a parallel in the developing nature of humanity's relationship to water.

Once mermaids were manatees, mysterious creatures who were both humanlike and not, and whose home was the sea. Barnum brought them to land, combining promises of beauty with the body of a horrifying monster. Hollywood stuntman Newt Perry then transformed the fish monster to human women, who seemed the embodiment of femininity, rendering the space below land as safe, domestic, white, and heterosexual, as the United States in the 1950s and 1960s was idealized to be. The mermaids were also superhumanly odd, however, more comfortable in the water than any average human could conceive. Eventually, as the world underwater grew as familiar and quotidian as the land above, the hyperfeminine mermaids transformed to masculine buccaneers, fake danger and adrenaline replacing graceful ballet, and active replacing passive spectatorship. Now the role that mermaids and Weeki Wachee offer is nostalgia for a time when water was mysterious and in and of itself a spectacle worth seeing, and for a safe, passive, white heterosexual femininity that is continuously eroding for those on dry land, a dry land where women are more often characterized these days, as Disney's Little Mermaid, Ariel, sings, as "bright young women, sick of swimmin', ready to stand."[66]

Notes

Many thanks to Phil Wernli and Lindsey Harrington at the State Archives of Florida for their assistance with information and obtaining images.

1. Horace Loftin, "Nature Ramblings: Mermaids," *Science News-Letter* 69, no. 22 (1956): 350.
2. Ibid.

3. Steven C. Levi, "P. T. Barnum and the Feejee Mermaid," *Western Folklore* 36, no. 2 (1977): 149–54.

4. Ibid., 151.

5. Francesca Sautman, "Mermaid," in *Encyclopedia of Sex and Gender: Culture Society History*, vol. 3, ed. Fedwa Malti-Douglas (Detroit: Macmillan Reference USA, 2007), 1005.

6. Stephen M. Fjellman, *Vinyl Leaves: Walt Disney World and America* (San Francisco: Westview Press, 1992), 6.

7. Esther Williams, *The Million Dollar Mermaid* (New York: Simon and Schuster, 1999), 44.

8. David Fantle and Tom Johnson, *Reel to Real: 25 Years of Celebrity Interviews* (New York: Badger Books, 2003), 99.

9. Scott Eyman, *Lion of Hollywood: The Life and Legend of Lewis B. Mayer* (New York: Simon and Schuster, 2005), 421.

10. Michelle Ann Abate, *Tomboys: A Literary and Cultural History* (Philadelphia: Temple University Press, 2008), 147.

11. For more on this see Robert L. McLaughlin and Sally E. Perry, *We'll Always Have the Movies: American Cinema during World War II* (Lexington: University Press of Kentucky, 2006), 218–19.

12. Lu Vickers, *Weeki Wachee: City of Mermaids* (Gainesville: University of Florida Press, 2007), 20.

13. Maryan Pelland, *Weeki Wachee Springs* (Charleston: Arcadia Publishing, 2006), 7.

14. "Underwater Theatres State's Latest Promotion to Lure Visitors' Dollars," *St. Petersburg Times*, October 19, 1947, 11.

15. Tim Hollis, *Glass Bottom Boats and Mermaids Tails* (Mechanicsburg, Pa.: Stackpole Books, 2006), 99.

16. Vickers, *Weeki Wachee*, 110.

17. The job also required they be "sinkable"—meaning they didn't shoot to the surface when submerged underwater—and able to ignore the many fish nibbling on them. Vickers, *Weeki Wachee*, 139.

18. Val Plumwood, *Feminism and The Mastery of Nature* (New York: Routledge, 1993), 19.

19. Tina Bucuvalas, Peggy A. Bulger, and Stetson Kennedy, *South Florida Folklife* (Jackson: University of Mississippi Press, 1994), 207.

20. Erik Swyngedouw, *Social Power and the Urbanization of Water: Flows of Power* (New York: Oxford University Press, 2004), 37.

21. Ibid.

22. From about.com's Florida travel site, http://goflorida.about.com/od/attractionsaz/a/weekiwachee.htm (accessed April 2, 2010).

23. Tim Hollis, *Dixie before Disney: 100 Years of Roadside Fun* (Jackson: University Press of Mississippi, 1999), 152.

24. Vickers, *Weeki Wachee*, 187.

25. Weeki Wachee continues to have issues with representing Native Americans. In the 1990s they introduced a new show, "Pocahontas Meets the Little Mermaid." A transcript found on the internet (http://www.roadsideamerica.com/story/2069) includes the lyrics: "INDIAN CHORUS: PO-CA-HONTAS NOW, TEACHING LIT-TULL MERMAID, SHE WILL SHOW HER HOW . . . TO BE AN IN-DEE-UN!"

POCAHONTAS:
If you're an Indian you have to try
To make it rain from clear blue sky!
So put yourself in an Indian trance,
And your moccasins will make a little Indian dance
EVERYONE: Yi Yi Yi! Yi Yi Yi!

26. Laura Sells, "Where Do the Mermaids Stand?" in *From Mouse to Mermaid: The Politics of Film, Gender and Culture,* ed. Elizabeth Sells, Lynda Haas, and Laura Sells (Bloomington: Indiana University Press, 1995), 177.

27. Ibid., 178.

28. The majority of archival materials that remain are in the private collection of the women who performed as the mermaids. The archivists at Disney informed me there are no archives prior to ABC's purchase by Disney. Lu Vickers has collected and published many of the mermaids' materials in her book and mentions that when the park was purchased in 1989 by the Florida Leisure Acquisition group, "box after box of publicity photos was burned" (*Weeki Wachee,* 221). This was corroborated by Phil Wernli at the Florida State Archive, who mentioned that the remaining materials are primarily film and video left to decay in file cabinets at the park. Due to this, Vickers's project relies on images from the two Weeki Wachee books, private photos and video belonging to the author, and footage and photos put online by other tourists. There are extensive videos of many of the performances, dating back to the early 1950s, on youtube.com.

29. For more on this conflation and its history in popular culture see Bonnie Zimmerman, "What Has Never Been: An Overview of Lesbian Feminist Criticism," in *Making a Difference: Feminist Literary Criticism,* ed. Gayle Greene and Coppelia Kahn (New York: Routledge, 1985), 194.

30. Laurie Essig, "The Mermaid and the Heterosexual Imagination," in *Thinking Straight: The Power, the Promise, and the Paradox of Heterosexuality,* ed. Chrys Ingraham (New York: Routledge, 2005), 151.

31. At some point a statue of a man was also introduced to the water "stage," which, in *The Little Mermaid,* Ariel caresses and cuddles, providing further masculine stand-ins.

32. Ailene S. Goodman, "The Extraordinary Being: Death and the Mermaid in Baroque Literature," *Journal of Popular Culture* 17, no. 3 (1983): 32.

33. Cummings is currently attempting to raise funds to produce a feature-film version.

34. *Weeki Wachee Girls,* directed by Kim Cummings (DVD, 2000). The film was available on youtube.com but has since been removed.

35. Transcription made by author from youtube.com. watch?v=vP2kiPhMXL4 (viewed June 2, 2009). Although presumably in jest, Richie also suggests diversifying the mermaids, hiring a bunch of black mermaids, and staging a riot like the Los Angeles riots for which Richie (who is of mixed-race origins, black and white) comes in and settles the dispute. The mermaids also laugh at this.

36. In *Visual Pleasure and Narrative Cinema,* film theorist Laura Mulvey argues that in film women are constructed as passive and men as active: "The determining male gaze projects its fantasy on to the female figure which is styled accordingly. In their traditional exhibitionist role women are simultaneously looked at and displayed, with their appear-

ance coded for strong visual and erotic impact so that they can be said to connote to-be-looked-at-ness." Quoted in *Film Theory and Criticism,* ed. Leo Braudy and Marshall Cohen, 6th ed. (New York: Oxford University Press, 2004), 841.

37. Vickers, *Weeki Wachee,* 242.

38. Quotations from *Little Merman: Episode 2,* found at www.littlemerman.com (accessed June 3, 2009).

39. For more on this see Alison Shaw, *Changing Sex and Bending Gender* (New York: Berghahn Books, 2005), 113.

40. It is perhaps worth noting here that as I revised this article the cover of the July 2010 issue of the popular culture magazine *Entertainment Weekly* featured comedian Will Ferrell with a digitally imposed tail being "fished" out of the ocean by actor Mark Wahlberg, famous for action movies and portraying aggressive behavior. In this instance, the tail is again being played for humor and ridiculousness, and nothing sexual between the two men is suggested.

41. Vickers, *Weeki Wachee,* 110.

42. For more on mermaid mishaps see ibid., 174.

43. Ken Zapinksi, "Man vs. Nature." *St. Petersburg Times,* July 12, 1989, 3, http://news.google .com/newspapers?id=QtMNAAAAIBAJ&sjid=K3cDAAAAIBAJ&pg=6482,4137150&dq =buccaneer-bay (accessed June 3, 2009).

44. Ibid.

45. Bethia Cafrey, "Go Underwater for a Career," *Evening Independent,* WHAT CITY IS THIS PAPER FROM? April 23, 1974, B1, http://news.google.com/newspapers?id= OILAAAAIBAJ&sjid=IVgDAAAAIBAJ&pg=6592,2306621&dq=weeki+wachee+alligators (accessed June 5, 2009).

46. Vickers, *Weeki Wachee,* 153.

47. Disney press release, http://thedisneyblog.com/2008/04/25/julianne-moore-michael-phelps -are-latest-annie-leibovitz-dream-photo-subjects (accessed June 3, 2009).

48. http://archive.gulfnews.com/indepth/olympics08/sports/10207957.html (accessed June 10, 2009).

49. http://www.washingtontimes.com/news/2008/jul/07/guilty-of-a-comeback (accessed June 10, 2009).

50. Despite the pirate-themed names, the park is not overtly decorated in a "pirate theme." In fact, it retains, for a water park, a rustic environment. The slides are constructed out of wood, it is heavily treed, and a man-made beach abuts an unadorned lake.

51. Richard Schechner, "Collective Reflexivity: Restoration of Behavior," in *A Crack in the Mirror: Reflexive Perspectives in Anthropology,* ed. Jay Ruby (Philadelphia: University of Philadelphia Press, 1982), 65.

52. Lisa Peeples, "Summer Soldiers," *St. Petersburg Times,* July 11, 1988, 3, http://news.google .com/newspapers?id=PLwMAAAAIBAJ&sjid=WWYDAAAAIBAJ&dq=buccaneer-bay &pg=4568%2C3840219 (accessed June 10, 2009).

53. *Oxford English Dictionary,* 2nd ed., 1989, online (accessed 6/10/09).

54. With the advent of the popular *Pirates of the Caribbean* movie series, pirates have experienced liberal feminism and now include women looting, killing, and taking sexual liberties with others.

55. "Spiral Water Flume to Open at Park," *St. Petersburg Times,* March 21, 1983, 3, http://news

.google.com/newspapers?id=hB4MAAAAIBAJ&sjid=xloDAAAAIBAJ&dq=buccaneer
-bay&pg=5171%2C6775236 (accessed June 10, 2009).

56. Robert King, "Dirty Moves, Beach Booze Jeopardize Idyllic Park," *St. Petersburg Times*, June 2, 2003, http://news.google.com/newspapers?id=6bcMAAAAIBAJ&sjid=VV4DAAAAIBAJ&dq=buccaneer-bay%20dirty%20moves&pg=5848%2C2729212 (accessed June 10, 2009).

57. Ironically, this song, "Rock Your Body," is the same song involved in the Super Bowl fracas with Janet Jackson's exposed breast that ended in massive fees for the network CBS in 2004, which led to a nationwide referendum on a woman of color's body.

58. Kimberly Ayers and Boyd Matson, "'Mermaids' Fight to Save Florida Roadside Attraction," March 22, 2004, *National Geographic*, http://news.nationalgeographic.com/news/2004/03/0322_040322_TVmermaid_2.html (accessed January 14, 2011).

59. Mitch Stacy, "Florida's Weeki Wachee Springs, Home of the Live Mermaids, Still Struggling," *USA Today*, March 20, 2007, http://www.usatoday.com/travel/destinations/2007–03-20-weeki-watchee-florida_n.htm (accessed June 15, 2009).

60. Abby Goodnough, "Sad Days for Mermaids of the Sequined Sort," *New York Times*, August 12, 2003, A1, http://www.nytimes.com/2003/08/12/us/sad-days-for-mermaids-of-the-sequined-sort.html (accessed June 10, 2009).

61. Sheila Stoll, "Visit Weeki Wachee Out of Respect," *St. Petersburg Times*, September 30, 2003, G6, http://news.google.com/ newspapers?id=QdQNAAAAIBAJ&sjid=qHgDAAAAIBAJ&pg=4391,6492741&dq=weeki+wachee (accessed June 10, 2009).

62. Vilmar Tavares, "If Weeki Wachee Can't Support Itself, Let It Fail," *St. Petersburg Times*, November 12, 2002, 2, http://news.google.com/ newspapers?id=3CAMAAAAIBAJ&sjid=LF4DAAAAIBAJ&dq=weeki%20wachee&pg=6673%2C1357024 (accessed June 10, 2009).

63. John Athanason, "Weeki Wachee Springs Embarks on a New Era," *Hernando Today*, January 8, 2009.

64. Ibid.

65. Tony Holt, "Former Weeki Wachee Mermaids Swim Happy," *Hernando Today*, February 17, 2008, http://www2.hernandotoday.com/content/2008/feb/17/former-weeki-wachee-mermaids-swim-happy/ (accessed June 15, 2009).

66. Ron Clements and John Musker, lyrics from "Part of Your World," *The Little Mermaid*, directed by Ron Clements and John Musker (DVD, 1989).

Julia Marlowe's Imogen

Modern Identity, Victorian Style

—PATTY S. DERRICK

On October 2, 1923, at Jolson's Fifty-ninth Street Theatre, Julia Marlowe and E. H. Sothern staged an expensive, visually beautiful production of *Cymbeline*. After spending sixty thousand dollars to mount the play with specially designed costumes from London and simple but beautiful set designs, they withdrew it from their season's repertory after only one week, and at the end of the season, Marlowe, a wealthy and established star, retired from acting.[1] Marlowe had first staged *Cymbeline* early in her career, in 1892–93, and yearned to return to the role of Imogen, but by 1923 much had changed in the American theatre. Even though the play had not been seen in New York since 1906 and would have seemed like a new play to audiences, Marlowe and Sothern's production failed soundly. *Cymbeline* had never been an easy play to stage and certainly had never attained the popularity of *As You Like It, Twelfth Night,* or *Merchant of Venice,* but several well-known nineteenth-century stars in the United States and in England staged it. Despite the play's odd incongruities of time and place, its occasional inconsistencies of plot, and its nearly endless conclusion crammed with startling revelations, the character of Imogen appealed to many actresses: Helen Faucit, Helena Modjeska, Adelaide Neilson, Ellen Terry, and Viola Allen, along with Julia Marlowe. While Faucit viewed Imogen as the "woman of women," she readily admitted the difficulty of the role: "she taxed largely my powers of impersonation."[2] Indeed, the character of Imogen is a complex one, with several facets to her identity and several distinct roles to play within her world. As she was preparing to play Imogen in 1896, George Bernard Shaw commented to Ellen Terry that the heroine is two entirely different people: a real woman and "an idiotic paragon of virtue."[3] Of course, Shaw's feminism prevented his joining

Figure 1. Julia Marlowe as Imogen in *Cymbeline,* 1892, by permission of the Folger Shakespeare Library.

the nineteenth-century cult of Imogen with its idealized conception of womanhood, yet he astutely pointed to the same problem Faucit suggested: How does an actress portray this woman of women, this universal type of womanliness, when Shakespeare's text produces a character of seemingly irregular subjectivities? Reviewers of Julia Marlowe's 1892–93 Imogen noted her shortcomings in portraying "strong, even violent emotions," suggesting that the role required a more textured and less essentialist conception.[4] However, by 1923 Marlowe had studied the role for thirty additional years, preparing several acting versions, and her final promptbook reveals that she was comfortable with portraying the conflicting facets of Imogen's identity, refusing to eliminate through textual cutting what could be called shifting or unconnected subjectivities. While her choice of play and increasingly outdated vocal style failed to appeal to the particular tastes of many audiences and critics in 1923, her own interpretive practices were more progressive than her detractors realized.

In order to understand Marlowe's 1923 approach to portraying Imogen's complexities, it is necessary first to examine Imogen's reception by nineteenth-century commentators. Throughout the century, critics celebrated Imogen as the epitome of idealized womanhood, the "perfection of woman,"[5] or, as a *Boston Daily Advertiser* reviewer asked, "What element in woman is there that is worth the having, which she does not possess?"[6] Henry Austin Clapp called her "the most wifely of wives,"[7] suggesting that Imogen's behavior exemplified that vague cultural ideal of womanliness, what Anne E. Russell described as consisting of "modesty, innocence, self-restraint, refinement and respect for hierarchy," with an emphasis on restraint.[8] William Winter, echoing the conventional view of Imogen, wrote, "she resents no injury, harbours no resentment, feels no spite, murmurs at no misfortune."[9] Perceiving in Imogen endless patience and restraint, Winter elsewhere chronicled his view of her with such descriptors as "sweetness of temperament; purity of life; the dignity of virtue; the noble passion of vilified honor; . . . wistful, childlike, winning simplicity."[10] David E. Shi writes that among the nineteenth-century genteel elite and the emerging middle class, females were assumed to possess a higher moral sensibility than males and that such "pedestaled notions of women" nourished a powerful "cult of domesticity" in which women were "self-denying angels ministering to a male-dominated world." Such images were depicted in hundreds of sentimental romances, written largely by women for women.[11] While literary critics denigrated this type of literature as too predictable and too domestic, its underlying presumptions about women clearly influenced both theatre commentators and performers in their reading of Imogen, a character who presented what Mrs. Anna Jameson called a "variety of tints . . . mingled together in such perfect harmony."[12] The "variety of tints" that Jameson noted as the key to understanding Imogen points precisely to the shifting interiorities that have troubled actresses in their attempts to find that ever-elusive "perfect harmony."

In 1892–93, Julia Marlowe beautifully portrayed the tender, loving parts of Imogen but could not accommodate the character's strong, less ideally feminine passions and behaviors: anger, forceful self-assertion, independent action, spirited scorn and indignation, unrestrained grief. Thirty years later, however, an experienced and mature Marlowe found a way to portray Imogen's "variety of tints"—vocally and physically—without reducing the character to a universal type of nineteenth-century womanliness. Rather than having too little subjectivity for a *dramatis persona*, Imogen has a bit too much, creating problems for any actress who seeks to essentialize her.[13] In 1923, Marlowe portrayed an identity that contradicted the notion of a harmonious display of idealized womanhood. Her Imogen was self-assured, fearless, somewhat domineering, outspoken, independent in thought and action, and unconcerned with hierarchy, while simultaneously valuing her identity as a wife—loyal and loving. Marlowe seemed to recognize that Shakespeare did not create a stable, unbroken interiority in Imogen; nineteenth-century cultural assumptions created that character. While Marlowe held on to the vocal stylings of her Victorian past, she broke with tradition in 1923 by presenting an Imogen who could be warm and beautiful but also aggressive and complicated, an Imogen who could show control at one moment and recklessness the next.

Marlowe's Early Imogen

In 1892 and again in 1893, a young Julia Marlowe performed Imogen in Boston, with an acting version of the play that she had prepared herself. Her prompt-book is no longer extant, but contemporaneous commentaries provide a hint to the strengths and weaknesses of her production, and her own comments reveal that, despite her careful, independent study of the role, she too was influenced by the nineteenth-century critical tendency to idealize Imogen: "Imogen as a woman seems to me to possess every quality which makes woman adorable—youth, beauty, purity, femininity in its finest sense, and a touching, never-swerving loyalty."[14] The admirable qualities Marlowe lists here and no doubt displayed in her stage portrayal impressed most of the Boston reviewers. Henry Clapp found her production's early scenes more effective than later ones, especially Imogen's farewell to her husband, which Clapp declared had "the profundity and thrill of a most womanly tenderness," and he viewed her repulse of Iachimo with its shifting emotions as "exceedingly fine and beautiful."[15] However, beginning with the major interview with Pisanio (3.4), Marlowe "ceased to be satisfying," according to Clapp, who stated further, "The softer part of the young wife's grief was indeed touchingly displayed; but of the more violent passion, of the fierce yet tender anguish of her sense of outrage at her lord's cruel injustice and monstrous and blind suspicion, Miss Marlowe's speech and action scarcely afforded a trace."[16] The *Boston Evening Transcript* review of the 1892 performance likewise noted that Marlowe fell "short of showing the character in a very strong light," since her skills "for the expression of the stronger . . . more violent emotions are as yet slight."[17] Wingate too observed that she "did not succeed in making all that the character merits. The earlier scenes were acted to acceptance; the cave scene fell beneath its rightful strength."[18] William Winter believed Marlowe's Imogen was "handsome and pleasing" because she comprehended "the essential quality of the character—innocent, lovely, confiding, faithful womanhood," but Marlowe nevertheless "did not evince deep sympathy with it, nor was her execution facile."[19] While the *Boston Globe* reviewer suggested that the fault of her 1893 production lay both in the character and in the actress ("The character of Imogen lacks some of the advantages for an actress of Miss Marlowe's temperament"),[20] Edward Fuller attributed Marlowe's shortcomings to her lack of maturity: "It remains a sketch rather than a completed portrait."[21]

Most critics of the 1892 production faulted Marlowe's portrayal of Imogen's time in the forest through her return to her father as weak and ineffective in the expression of strong emotion, especially over the headless corpse, but Mrs. Sutherland of the *Boston Evening Transcript* saw something else: "Imogen's utter physical and moral weariness; nothing could be more finely conceived nor carried out than the listless, almost automatic part she takes in the further proceedings of the play, up to the moment when she recognizes Posthumus in his peasant's dress before Cymbeline and the wounded Iachimo; then for the first time the blood begins to course through her veins once more."[22] Sutherland's interpretation may be accurate, suggesting that Marlowe had a precise plan for Imogen and the rest of the critics simply failed to perceive it. In the absence of an 1892–93 promptbook with Marlowe's holographic stage directions, we can never know, although evidence from the 1923 reviews and promptbook points to the accuracy of Sutherland's assessment. The ironies contained within the criticism of Marlowe's early Imogen present interesting testimony to the difficulty of performing this role. While the critics extolled Imogen as epitomizing the nineteenth-century womanly ideal, they simultaneously censured Marlowe for failing to show a less womanly side of the heroine. If Imogen is, in fact, so modest and refined that she feels and shows no resentment or spite when injured, how could she also express fierce passion without violating the moral and social restraint expected of women? If the womanly ideal consisted of youthfulness, naive purity and innocence, and physical attractiveness, then an Imogen who spoke and acted too boldly or angrily or assertively would cease to be beautiful and childlike; however, these are all facets of this complex character, creating difficulties for the actress attuned to her audience's cultural expectations.

Cymbeline's Failure in 1923

Despite its occasional inconsistencies, the romanticized character criticism popular in the nineteenth century fueled the cult of Imogen and made her an attractive vehicle for actresses, especially for Marlowe, who wished to play only women who do not fall when tempted.[23] The nineteenth-century star system with its actor-managers, a system in which the independent Marlowe flourished, gave some actresses the opportunity to choose the type of role they wished to play, one in which they could dominate a production; however, by 1923 an idealized portrayal of Imogen could no longer satisfy most post–World War I audience members, and, furthermore, the star system had largely died, Marlowe and Sothern being two of its last proponents. In the early years of the twentieth century, the Theatrical Syndicate was tightening its grip on theaters and bookings, so a production of a nonstandard play like *Cymbeline* represented a financial risk, a risk that Marlowe and Sothern had to assume themselves. By the late 1920s, great American actors made excursions into Shakespeare, popular Shakespeare, but none built a repertory of his plays.[24] The 1923 failure of *Cymbeline* seems to mark, then, the last gasp of the old star system and the end of a long theatrical tradition (that is, solely Shakespearean repertories) perpetuated by the actor-managers.

The new plays being written and performed in the twentieth century also contributed to the 1923 failure of *Cymbeline* because, by contrast, Shakespeare's romance seemed old-fashioned. Ibsen's rejection of melodramatic characters and situations, Strindberg's movement toward expressionism, Chekhov's subtle plot constructions, Shaw's and O'Neill's exposition of forbidden topics—all these forces influenced post–World War I critics, who, in turn, influenced audiences. Although H. H. Furness Jr. praised the 1923 *Cymbeline* as the best of his generation and Marlowe's Imogen as "her masterpiece," other voices prevailed.[25] John Corbin of the *New York Times* declared, "Now at last they have produced a really bad play by Shakespeare."[26] *Cymbeline*, with its conventional devices, startling discoveries and climaxes, and potentially idealized heroine, bore too many similarities to the popular melodrama that serious critics had come to denounce as unrealistic. The cult of Imogen could no longer carry the play; in fact, the "exalted poetic sentiment" of Imogen fell so out-of-step with 1920s dramatic tastes that she appeared foolish to many, as Marlowe herself explained: "A great wave of cynicism and materialism following the war changed the theatrical standards and tastes of many persons that did not know they were being neatly reformed. A period wherein the pornographic drama went so far that the police had to be called in must contain a considerable element to whom the idyllic beauty of Imogen could appear but foolishness."[27] At the beginning of Marlowe's career, Imogen had been called "the angel of light whose lovely presence pervades and animates the whole piece,"[28] but at the end of her career—a career she hoped to crown with a masterful, carefully prepared portrayal of this heroine—she felt that critics, critics who had been negatively influenced, no doubt, by the nineteenth-century idealization of Imogen, saw Imogen as merely silly. Marlowe and Sothern withdrew *Cymbeline* and completed the 1923–24 season with well-established crowd-pleasers: *Romeo and Juliet, Merchant of Venice, Hamlet,* and *Twelfth Night.*

While the play's structure and fanciful plot no doubt contributed to its 1923 failure, Marlowe's acting style also received harsh criticism. Although in the 1890s and early 1900s her acting methods seemed new because she refused to play for points and struggled to create psychologically truthful impersonations, by the 1920s some critics considered her style, with its clear and musical enunciation, too romantic and artificial. Heywood Broun and J. Ranken Towse had always loved Marlowe's vocal style, but they deplored its excesses in *Cymbeline.* Twentieth-century critics agreed with their predecessors that the character of Imogen was "the virtue and salvation of *Cymbeline*," a part "well worth the acting."[29] However, Broun, writing for the *World,* expressed disappointment with Marlowe's version, focusing on her vocal style: "She finds parting with every phrase sweet sorrow. Each word is welcomed and asked to sit down. . . . This retarded pace is all but ruinous." Broun theorized that Marlowe had fallen victim to the crime of great actors who possess vocal richness and then are betrayed by it, "hypnotized into listening to the tones which they create."[30] The *Evening Post*'s reviewer, J. Ranken Towse, admired Marlowe's handling of the pre-Milford-Haven scenes but targeted for criticism her "excessive and disillusionizing elaboration" in the later scenes.[31] Burns Mantle called the production a "picturesque failure," which "the Shakespearean dears read to death."[32]

John Corbin had always admired Marlowe's acting, but he described her style in *Cymbeline* as "too labored" with overwrought mannerisms and "extreme deliberation in utterance further retarded by fake pauses," robbing her portrayal of spontaneity and passion.[33] His assessment suggests that her acting style was outdated in contrast to a new verbal style of psychological naturalism championed by younger actresses in contemporary plays. Of course, Marlowe's production ran four hours, even with 1,277 lines (approximately 39 percent) cut from the text's 3,278 lines. Although Towse blamed some of the four-hour-long tedium on the "dead weight of the plot,"[34] Corbin stated that most of the time "was consumed by ungracious silences," referring to Marlowe's and Sothern's vocal habit of pausing.[35] Unlike his contemporaries, Alexander Woollcott of the *Herald* continued to admire Marlowe's voice and style, although he admitted that she occasionally abused her vocal beauty by blowing up every word; nevertheless, he maintained, "it is a tremendous force, her voice," one of magnificence unimpaired by time.[36] Marlowe had spent decades preparing an acting text and rehearsing Imogen's lines, as if they were musical measures, in order to reveal the heroine's poetic temperament.[37] However, the vocal emphases marked in her

1923 promptbook suggest that the critics correctly designated the predominant weakness in this production. Many of Marlowe's speeches, especially those beginning in act 3, scene 4 when Imogen arrives in Milford-Haven and reads her husband's letter, contain heavy markings for emphasis and numerous pauses. Marlowe believed that the poetry of Imogen should be emphasized, and some critics denounced this very quality as unnatural, artificial, untruthful. In other ways, Marlowe's style was very much like that of her contemporary, the more modern Mrs. Fiske, with its emphasis on psychological truthfulness and its concentration on inner feeling and repressed external action.[38] Marlowe had many times spoken and written about her own technique in these terms. Marlowe insisted that Imogen be the center of this play, cutting only 34 of Imogen's 529 lines, and critics in 1923 endorsed this view, with even John Corbin saying, "All that there is of poetry, of genuine pathos and romance, centres in her scenes."[39] Lines that traditionally had been cut in order to essentialize Imogen remained in Marlowe's version; however, Marlowe's spotlighting of Imogen's poetry with a vocal style that called attention to the heroine's poetic soul only further marked Marlowe as old-fashioned and further doomed an already unpopular play. Her romantic, musical delivery could be forgiven, even applauded, in popular roles—Juliet, Portia, Ophelia—but not in *Cymbeline*, not even for Imogen.

Marlowe's 1923 Imogen

While Marlowe sought to unify her 1923 portrayal of Imogen through an emphasis on poetic delivery, her multifaceted representation alternated among womanly tenderness, intimidating anger and scorn, even childlike fear, each emotion exhibiting another aspect of Imogen's complexity, sometimes within a single scene. Certainly, Marlowe's production intended to spotlight the character of Imogen and her shifting interiorities, since her acting text condenses Shakespeare's twenty-six scenes to seventeen, with Imogen dominating ten of them: 1, 2, 4, 5, 7, 9, 11, 13, 14, and 17. (This analysis omits Marlowe's scenes 2, 5, and 9, Shakespeare's 1.3, 2.2, and 3.2.)

Scene 1

Imogen was never offstage for very long. The production's first scene (Shakespeare's 1.1 combined with 1.5) demonstrates well that Marlowe aspired to portray Imogen in all her complexity and "variety of tints," rather than reduce the character to a universal type or to one dominant trait (as Ellen Terry had done, under the advice of Shaw, by emphasizing Imogen's impulsiveness as the key-note of her nature).[40]

Marlowe's Imogen first enters guarded by the Queen, but the young princess quickly breaks from her stepmother's hold and rushes to her husband's side, resting her head on Posthumus's chest, revealing not only her scorn for the Queen but also tender sympathy for her husband.[41] Once left alone, the couple embrace and sit, but Marlowe's Imogen looks around as she cautions, "I something fear my father's wrath" (1.1.86). She begins to weep on his shoulder, creating a lovely stage picture of wifely love and loyalty further enhanced when she kisses his hand as he kneels before her (at l. 96); however, her body language changes when the Queen reenters, and she ceases to be the soft, apparently dependent, submissive wife, becoming again the princess, unaccustomed to being turned away. Sothern's Posthumus starts to leave when Marlowe's Imogen physically pulls him back to her, and not content merely to offer him her diamond ring ("take it, heart" at l. 112), she places the ring on his finger, a decisive act that considerably mitigates her next line, "But keep it till you woo another wife" (l. 113), a statement often criticized as unrealistic for a young bride. Marlowe's nonverbal self-assurance emboldens Posthumus, who places his bracelet upon her arm. They are embracing and kissing when Cymbeline reenters, and Posthumus now takes the assertive stance, stepping in front of and shielding Imogen from her father's wrath (at l. 124). As Cymbeline threatens death if Posthumus returns, Marlowe's Imogen breaks from her husband and rushes to her father, who roughly throws her to the ground and shouts, "away / Thou'rt poison to my blood" (ll. 127–28). No frightened, fragile girl, this Imogen is willing to risk even physical violence in defense of her love. Posthumus helps her up, takes her in his arms one last time, and then exits, leaving Imogen alone with her angry father.

Marlowe sits as Cymbeline crosses with a big sweep, and with his back to the audience, she verbally defies him, "I am senseless to your wrath" (l. 135), causing him to approach her in what must be interpreted as a threatening manner after his previous roughness with her. Yet she does not wilt even when he commandingly expresses, "That mightst have had the sole son of my queen" (l. 138); instead of shrinking from her father's physical intimidation, this Imogen stands to oppose him eye to eye, "O *blessed* that I might *not*! I chose an *eagle* / And did avoid a *puttock*" (ll. 139–40). Marlowe's vocal emphasis (marked in italics) along with her standing posture here suggests a strong, self-assured passion, especially with her emphasis on "I." Marlowe's Imogen continues to stand and defend her husband's worth until Cymbeline again approaches her and shouts, "What, art thou mad" (l. 147), causing her to fall back on a bench as he rushes toward her. But she does not weep; instead, she ignores her father's wrath and begins to dream of another life, a different identity, a much simpler one than that to which she was born: "Would I were / A neat-herd's daughter, and my Leonatus / Our neighbor shepherd's son" (ll. 148–50). Imogen occasionally contemplates an alternate identity in the play but not always the sweet, pastoral one of a neat-herd's daughter, as she demonstrates less than fifteen lines later (in Marlowe's text) as she again dreams of a new identity, this time a much more aggressive one: "I would they were in *Afric* both together; / Myself by with a *needle*, that I might *prick* / The goer-back" (ll. 167–69). Marlowe's Imogen is sitting as she begins this speech, and she rises firmly as she imagines herself jabbing the more cowardly of the two men, no doubt Cloten. Marlowe takes the papers that Posthumus has sent through Pisanio and sweeps in front of the Queen to exit, without a thought that she is supposedly a prisoner, indeed ignoring the Queen and issuing strict commands to Pisanio.

Imogen's many facets in this opening scene complicate any actress's attempt to essentialize this heroine. Whereas Marlowe in 1892–93 endeavored to blend Imogen's many "tints" in the first scene and elicited favorable criticism for her prettiness and womanliness, her 1923 portrayal had deepened with more texture and emotional coloring. Allowing Imogen's complexities to emerge without reshaping them to a cultural standard of feminine restraint and submission, Marlowe drew an enthusiastic response from H. H. Furness Jr., who saw in the opening scene an Imogen who was both "lovely" and "sure of herself."[42]

Scene 4

The same sort of shift from loveliness to bold self-assurance occurs in Marlowe's scene 4, the meeting between Imogen and Iachimo (Shakespeare's 1.6); however, the 1923 promptbook reveals that Marlowe added sharper edges to her portrayal than had been noticed in her 1892–93 productions. Actresses had always favored this scene, and critics often noted it. In this scene of heightened emotion, some critics described Helen Faucit's Imogen as "too vehement" and "too unfeminine,"[43] while commentators felt that Adelaide Neilson's 1880 portrayal showed "the finest judgment, not going into a frenzy when she discovers his baseness, but repulsing him with infinite courage."[44] Ellen Terry in 1896 startled Iachimo and her audience with the suddenness of her anger, but since the hallmark of her portrayal was impulsiveness, the anger quickly passed when Iachimo adopted his new posture; Terry's Imogen eagerly interjected "Yes! Yes!"

as Iachimo switched to praising Posthumus.[45] Viola Allen in 1906 emphasized Imogen's perplexity throughout the scene, even during her outburst of anger.[46] Julia Marlowe, therefore, had a strong and varied tradition from which to draw both in 1892–93 and in 1923. One reviewer in 1892 perceived her succession of emotions—from reserve to misery of heart to strong loathing and indignation to mistrust—as all depicting "wifely and womanly reserve."[47] Mrs. Sutherland in 1893 saw a similar emotional progression from initial reserve to "quick, contemptuous abhorrence" to cordial dislike, all "shown forth with perfect freedom from effort and with unfailing, swift dramatic effect."[48] Charles E. Russell, Marlowe's business manager and biographer, remembered this scene from her early production: "To Iachimo's insinuated detraction of her lord she listened with staring eyes of a childlike and innocent wonder; and she told with the lowering pitch of her voice as much as with her contracting brows and lightening eyes the slow growth of perception in her of the vileness of his thought. The explosion of her wrath ('Away! I do condemn mine ears') was a wild cry of a desperately wounded and indignant heart."[49] Russell's description of Marlowe here clearly resonates with the nineteenth-century nomenclature of the ideal woman: childlike but also womanly, innocent but also profound and deep.

Marlowe carried over certain features of her early portrayal to her 1923 production, especially in the first part of the scene. The 1923 promptbook indicates that the scene opens with Imogen discovered center, seated on a sofa, lost in a reverie of her currently miserable life and her fantasy of having been "thief-stolen / As my two brothers, happy" (1.6.5–6). She greets Pisanio, who announces Iachimo's arrival and hands her a letter from her husband. Imogen rises to read the letter aloud and motions for Iachimo to sit as she resumes her seat on the sofa. Marlowe's Imogen is entirely relaxed and unsuspecting of Iachimo's motives, partially because Marlowe excised some of his unseemly lines with their references to "apes and monkeys" and "Sluttery" (cuts include 1.6.39b–41a, 42–43a, 44–46). However, Iachimo (played by Frederick Lewis) fails to disturb this Imogen even with his reference to the "cloy'd will" longing "for the garbage" (ll. 47–50a), so he must pretend his own words make him ill, placing his hand over his eyes, causing her to inquire, "Are you well?" (l. 51).

Imogen changes the subject to Posthumus, opening the door for Iachimo's next strategy: describing the jollity of her husband as he supposedly berated a friend in love and women in general. Although Marlowe's Imogen remains seated, her voice reveals her shift from relaxed self-confidence to disbelief as she asks, "Will *my lord* say so?" (l. 73). Charles Russell recalled from her 1893 production the vocal effect Marlowe created with this short line when she slowly and emphatically uttered "my lord," revealing "pain, amazement, and a touch of incredulity" and "a peculiar rising circumflex on 'so' that signaled something of her own purity as well as doubt of her husband's falling off."[50] Her composure cracks only slightly at this point, and Marlowe vocally creates a sense of impatience in Imogen as she listens to Iachimo's tale: "*What* do you pity, sir?" and "*Why* do you *pity* me?" (ll. 82, 89). When Iachimo more directly details Posthumus's revolt at line 99, he rises and moves toward Imogen; her pain and disappointment are apparent as she pauses, rises, and crosses slowly to the table and drops the letter before speaking, "My lord, I fear, / Has forgot Britain" (ll. 112–13), with no vocal emphases marked in either Marlowe's preliminary or final promptbook. Seeing his first opening with her, Iachimo quickly responds, "And himself" (l. 113), causing Marlowe's Imogen to turn her head quickly and look at him. As he continues his speech, he slowly moves close to her, but on the verge of tears, she commands, "Let me hear no more" (l. 117). Iachimo then passes in front of her and leans toward her over the table with his suggestion, "Be reveng'd" (l. 126). Here Iachimo begins a physical encroachment on a saddened, confused Imogen, who asks, "How should I be reveng'd?" (l. 132); before responding, he moves behind the table until he is beside her, kneels, and offers himself for her "sweet pleasure" (l. 136). Imogen immediately rises as Iachimo attempts to embrace her. As Iachimo has physically intimidated her, now Imogen reveals a similar capability. Marlowe's Imogen shrieks as Iachimo tries to touch her, and she demands, "Away!" (l. 141), followed by a long pause. Her standing posture and sudden outburst cause him to "retire abashed" (final promptbook). She then begins an angry speech, whose vocal emphases punctuate her movement on stage, movement that clearly surprises and intimidates Iachimo:

> I do *condemn* mine ears that have
> So *long* attended thee. If thou wert *honorable,*
> Thou wouldst have told this tale for *virtue,* not
> For such an end *thou* seek'st, as *base as strange.*
> Thou *wrong'st* a gentleman who is as far
> From *thy* report as *thou* from *honor,* and
> Solicits here a lady that disdains
> Thee and the *devil alike.* (ll. 141–48)

While she speaks, she moves toward Iachimo, and he quickly backs away, keeping his eyes fixed on her until he puts some distance between them. Her nonverbal message is clear to an ashamed, uncomfortable Iachimo.

    J. Ranken Towse admired Marlowe's "notable vitality" in this episode and saw in it a "fine outburst of indignant loathing" that "overwhelmed him [Iachimo] when she realized the full drift of his overtures."[51] H. H. Furness Jr. likewise described the extent of her passion as "flood gates . . . let loose upon him," and further commented that her rage was "almost uncontrollable."[52] Marlowe's voice, demeanor, and movement all produced an effect that revealed a development beyond her culturally restricted and very restrained 1890's portrayal, in which a "glimpse" of her anger, noted only in her voice, "awed" Iachimo.[53] By 1923, Marlowe's Imogen overwhelmed him with unrestrained wrath, her physical advances forcing him to back away from her. Although able to forgive, this Imogen indeed resents injury and feels spite, contrary to William Winter's character analysis earlier in the century.[54] She uses the same intimidating body language that her father had previously used with her in scene 1, except that her target, unlike Cymbeline's, backs away showing humiliated submission and perhaps even fear.

Marlowe's Imogen cools down only when Iachimo falls to his knees and raises his arms to heaven, praising Posthumus and begging her pardon, his final deceptive strategy. She apparently forgives Iachimo (Furness thought too quickly) but remains somewhat distracted for the remainder of the scene, returning her focus to her husband's letter. Marlowe agrees to safeguard Iachimo's trunk but walks to the table to retrieve the letter, the letter in which Posthumus affirms that Iachimo is "of noblest note" (l. 22), a reassurance that she seeks at this moment. Iachimo again kneels to her and kisses her hand as she exits, rereading the letter silently. Originally, Marlowe intended that Imogen would again read the letter aloud, with the curtain falling as she finishes and kisses it, but Marlowe crossed out those stage directions in the final promptbook, no doubt a time-saving measure but one that forces the audience to remember the letter's contents. Her complete trust in Posthumus, whom she has no reason to doubt, outweighs her misgivings about this stranger. Marlowe's Imogen graciously forgives, but her return to the letter suggests she feels a tentative forgiveness that seeks a sort of secondary validation; in other words, she doubts the legitimacy of her own feminine sweetness, an indication that she knows she is more than a simple paragon of virtue. Marlowe's scene-ending action reveals the character's depth, her cognitive self-awareness; in other words, the audience watches her thinking about and analyzing her own thoughts.

Scene 7

In Marlowe's scene 7, the next morning's encounter between Imogen and Cloten (Shakespeare's 2.3.66–158), her Imogen remains strong and independent. In Shakespeare's text, Imogen's vehement rejection of Cloten is easily understood since in 1.2 and 2.1 he was established as the laughingstock of even his own courtiers; however, the only derisive comment about Cloten prior to Marlowe's scene 7 comes from Imogen herself in scene 1, when she calls him a "puttock" (1.1.140) and implies that she perceives Cloten as an opportunist, not as a buffoon, and as an ugly, potential threat, not a comical fool. Both Cymbeline and Cloten are attempting to force an identity upon her—that of an unmarried, obedient girl—and their presumptions offend her, precipitating her immediate impatience with the wooing Cloten.

Quickly Marlowe's Imogen enters to the awaiting Cloten, who kneels and tries to reach out and kiss her hand, but she sweeps by him on her way to the table, where she sits. Moving to the table and leaning on it in front of her, Cloten (played by France Bendtsen) demands a respectable answer to his vow of love, and Marlowe's Imogen warns him that if he persists, she "shall unfold equal discourtesy / To your best kindness" (2.3.98–99). His standing posture while leaning toward her over the table sends a physically intrusive message, meant to intimidate, but she responds by picking up her embroidery and beginning to work. Previously in the production, Marlowe's Imogen had not weakened in the face of physical intimidation, and her encounter with Cloten sustains this pattern of fearlessness, now through her ironic use of the traditionally feminine activity of embroidery. Undeterred, Cloten moves closer, sitting next to her on the bench and suggesting that she is insane. Not one to abide his verbal intimidation, this Imogen stands and, according to H. H. Furness Jr., "bursts forth in indignant anger at his insolence":[55] "I am much sorry, sir / You put me to forget a lady's manners, / By being so verbal: . . . I care not for you" (ll. 106–8, 110). The intensity of her verbal and nonverbal stance causes a now-standing Cloten to sink back onto the bench. While her outburst and her words no doubt upset him, her dismissive nonchalance (picking up a book to read) infuriates him. Cloten leaps up and crosses to her, pounding on the table with both hands as he shouts, "You sin against / Obedience, which you owe your father" (ll. 113–14). With Marlowe staring at him, Cloten begins to malign Posthumus and to dishonor her marriage contract, to which she merely averts her gaze. Her apparent disregard causes him again to lean over the table and pound on it as he further vilifies Posthumus as a "base slave" (l. 124). Once again, Marlowe's Imogen stands and explodes, "Profane fellow" (l. 126), causing Cloten to back away as she pauses in silence, gathering herself before describing how much lower he is in her worldview as compared to her husband. Cloten approaches the table and thumps on it before speaking, "The south-fog rot him" (l. 133), and Marlowe's Imogen intends to end their dialogue with her scornful reference to her husband's "meanest garment" being dearer to her than thousands of Clotens, but she abruptly stops her retreat when she discovers that the bracelet is gone. As he begins to bluster, she "hardly seems to hear Cloten's words," according to Furness, until she "turns upon him like a tigress" with "I am sprited with a fool; / Frighted, and anger'd worse" (ll. 141–42), a line that Marlowe screams;[56] however, her attention quickly shifts away from Cloten, and she remains agitated— sitting, standing, pacing—for the rest of the scene until she disdainfully exits, "So, I leave you, sir, / To the worst of discontent" (ll. 156–57). He starts to follow her as he shouts, "I'll be reveng'd" (l. 157), but thinks better of the idea and returns to center stage, where he begins smashing the furniture and repeating "his meanest garment" over and over as the curtain falls. Cloten is left angry and baffled, not comprehending that Imogen's self-conception is deeper and more complex than his masculine conception of her.

Scene 11

While delineating the shifting interiorities in Imogen, shifting because no one around her accepts the identity she has chosen for herself, Marlowe simultaneously pulls a thread of self-confidence through all her varied scenes and emotional responses. As long as Marlowe's Imogen retains the dream of recovering and living her desired identity, she can exhibit strong, dominating passions alongside softer, gentler emotions; the fullness of her being emerges in every scene; however, once Imogen is stripped of her goal and dream in scene 11, Marlowe strips from her much of the complexity established in the production's first half. In 1892–93, Marlowe had been criticized harshly for her performance in the play's second half, and in 1923 she apparently partially re-employed her earlier interpretation. Marlowe's scene 11 (Shakespeare's 3.4) contains Imogen and Pisanio's arrival in Milford-Haven and Imogen's discovery of her husband's betrayal and intended treachery. H. H. Furness Jr. considered it "the most important scene of the play" for its dramatic interest.[57] Indeed, the scene offers actresses many spectacular moments from Imogen's reading of the letter to her wish to die to her agreement to don a page's disguise and flee to Rome. Helen Faucit described her own portrayal as Imogen reads the letter: "As the last word drops from her lips, her head bows in silence over the writing, and her body sinks as if some mighty rock had crushed her with its weight. These few words have sufficed to blight, to blacken, and to wither her whole life. The wonder is, that she ever rises. I used to feel tied to the earth."[58]

Adelaide Neilson imitated Faucit's swoon and followed that moment with, as Henry Clapp noted, "honest indignation, outraged affection and pure anguish . . . without rant or affectation."[59] Ellen Terry reacted to the letter quietly, reading it as a soliloquy, and then impulsively began tearing her husband's letters from her bosom. She noted in her promptbook that her response should be "Mighty. The Ocean. Electrical—or—nothing at all."[60] Marlowe's original performance of the scene was recalled by Charles Russell: "When the full horror and monstrosity of this treachery had by slow degrees won its way into her reluctant consciousness she went like one in a dream. Her voice took on that curious, strained, throaty, unreal, tonic quality that a somnabulist's voice has, and she seemed to hear not a word that Pisanio was saying. Only her figure stood there; her mind was far away dwelling on something unseen, and when she said 'my heart . . . 'tis empty of all things but grief,' she had one of those great and rare moments in the theater when every soul there hangs, all else forgotten, on the word that follows word."[61]

In 1892–93, Marlowe assumed a soulful lethargy in this scene and carried it through until the play's final scene, and apparently she used pieces of this interpretation in her 1923 portrayal, because J. Ranken Towse praised Imogen's "stony horror upon her realization of the charge against her" and "the despairing resolution with which she offered herself to the sword"; however "moving and impressive" the scene was in 1923, Towse commented much like his 1892–93 predecessors, "But from this point the dramatic interest of Miss Marlowe's performance declined."[62] Furness disagreed with Towse's assessment that the performance declined after this scene, echoing the same sort of disagreement Mrs. Sutherland had with her fellow critics in 1893. Furness saw in scene 11 the beginnings of Marlowe's careful and astute interpretation of Imogen. After her "stunned consternation at the monstrous charge of infidelity," Imogen's "mind and imagination go on weaving images, but her heart, as she says, is empty 'of all things but grief'; even Posthumus is no longer there." Furness perceived an artistically valid purpose thereafter for Marlowe's use of pauses and vocal deliberation, since Imogen "suddenly finds her whole house of life fallen in ruins; the very foundations uprooted and reason almost dethroned."[63] Marlowe clearly perceived Imogen as building her chosen identity on her marriage to Posthumus. Although Marlowe had revealed several of Imogen's interiorities in the first half, the character was always reacting to obstacles in her process of self-definition, a process she continues to pursue in Milford-Haven. Once Imogen believes Posthumus has rejected her, the very foundation of her self-image is withdrawn, and she must either return home to become that unmarried girl her father had tried to make her or move ahead and become someone else. Without the identity she self-assuredly chose for herself, Marlowe's Imogen becomes numb, a distinctively new portrayal in 1923. However, the final promptbook reveals that Marlowe modulated the listlessness noticed by all critics with non-verbal hints of the earlier Imogen.

This pivotal scene opens with Marlowe's Imogen wearily looking at Pisanio then crossing to sit on a rock. Furness noted that Marlowe was "petulant" in her reproach of Pisanio for their fruitless journey.[64] As she begins to speak to him, the promptbook specifies that he looks at her apprehensively, until she rises and approaches him on "Pisanio! man! / Where is Posthumus?" (3.4.3–4), at which he turns his face away and sighs. No doubt slightly alarmed by his demeanor but also tired of it, Marlowe's Imogen commands, "put thyself / Into a havior of less fear, ere wildness / Vanquish my staider senses" (ll. 8–10), and while she speaks she takes his arm and shakes it, holding on to it until she questions, "What's the matter?" (l. 10), and pulls him around to face her. Still the Imogen the audience has seen before, Marlowe conveys self-assurance and even impatience, but when Pisanio silently offers her a letter, Marlowe backs up a step or two. For the first time in the production, she shows fear as she worries that her husband might be "at some hard point" (l. 16). Imogen sits to read the letter aloud as Pisanio, kneeling beside her, buries his face in his hands but turns his head to look at her midway through her reading; he begins to look wild and desperate as she completes the letter and starts up immediately as she begins to collapse, first falling on one knee before fully fainting. Pisanio kneels at her head, chafes her hand, and then lifts her, resting her head on his knee. After a lengthy pause, Marlowe's Imogen looks up at him and slowly pleads, "What is it to be false?" (l. 41), before being helped back up to her seat on the rock. Pisanio, standing behind her, reaches out to touch her but does not as she ruminates, "Poor I am stale, a garment out of fashion" (l. 52), and beginning at this point, as Furness states, "her words fall from her lips as from one in a dream. She does not even hear Pisanio's reiterated appeals."[65]

At times, Marlowe breaks this trance-like state, which Furness describes with bursts of emotional action, with glimpses of the earlier Imogen. She rises on "Come, fellow, be thou honest" (l. 65), grasping Pisanio and drawing him to her before startling him with "A little witness my obedience: look!" (l. 67) when she draws his sword, causing him to raise his hand and shrink back in horror. She then sinks back into herself as she realizes her heart is "empty of all things but grief" (l. 70) but again unnerves him when she thrusts the sword into his hand and commands, "strike" (l. 72). Pisanio immediately throws the sword away, crossing away from her and sitting on a rock with his head in his hands. Marlowe shifts back into her dreamlike state as she ponders the necessity of dying and the prohibition "against self-slaughter" (l. 77). Then, quickly, she kneels before him and physically forces him to look at her at "Come, here's my heart" (l. 79), but just as quickly discovers the letters tucked into her bodice and sinks back on her heels, dropping the letters on "The scriptures of the loyal Leonatus / All turn'd to heresy?" (l. 83). She remains resting on her heels as she quietly contemplates the pain of Posthumus's betrayal and the sacrifices she has made for her husband; however, her passion resurfaces as she thinks of his remembering her after he satisfies his appetite with another woman, a notion that causes her to beat her head and chest and turn quickly to Pisanio, grabbing him by the arm, "Prithee, dispatch / Where's thy knife?" (ll. 98–99). The apparent treachery of Posthumus is bad enough, but the thought that he has denied her identity and given it to another woman rouses Marlowe's Imogen to passionate emotion. Rising and stooping over her, Pisanio assures her that he has not slept since receiving the letter, but Marlowe, on her knees, clutches Pisanio around his knees and urges him, "Do't, and to bed then" (l. 102). When he assures her that he would never harm her, she sits back on her heels again and wearily questions him about the purpose of this tiresome journey, hearing little of his responses until he mentions that Posthumus has certainly been duped by some villain, at which point Marlowe is sitting next to a rock, leaning lethargically over it. His mention of a villain causes her to rise with "Some Roman courtesan" (l. 125), again sparking her jealousy momentarily, but she listlessly sinks back down on the rock as Pisanio begins to spin his plan of deceiving the world that she is dead. Marlowe's Imogen questions him but with little emotion, "What shall I do the while? where bide? how live?" (l. 130). She turns her head to inform him that she refuses to return to her father's court, then rising and showing more decisiveness as she rejects any plan that would send her back to Cloten, "whose love-suit hath been to me / As fearful as a siege" (ll. 135–36). Coordinated with Marlowe's decisive posture, these particular words as suggest that the actress saw Cymbeline and Cloten's previous attempt to usurp Imogen's identity for their own purposes as a crux in the formation of the heroine's self-awareness.

Marlowe again sinks back onto her rocky seat to utter, "There's livers out of Britain" (l. 142), a weary declaration never to return home, when Pisanio turns in his tracks to face her and offer another plan: a disguise that would allow her to travel safely and view her husband's residence. Marlowe's Imogen leaps to her feet and eagerly presses Pisanio for more details, "Nay be brief: / I see into thy end, and am almost / A man already" (ll. 167–69). Interestingly, the lines in which Pisanio describes her necessary masculine behavior ("waggish courage," "saucy" and "quarrelous") have been cut from this production, and his primary instructions are that she "must forget to be a woman; change / Command into obedience" (ll. 156–57). Marlowe probably elected to retain these lines because they hit upon the essence of her Imogen, a woman whose chief desire is to be Posthumus's wife but who is self-determined, purposeful, and quick to command others. In disguise as a page boy, she must attempt to perform a subjectivity entirely contrary to her own—masculine but also obedient—a difficult task for one who has resisted performing externally mandated roles and identities. Pisanio hands her the new clothing, and she puts her hands on his shoulders at "Thou'rt all the comfort / The gods will diet me with" (ll. 181–82), her gesture again connoting empathy as well as dominance. Her words thank him for his comfort, but her action comforts him. Pisanio gives her the box containing the Queen's apparent stomach restorative, then kneels before her with hands up to heaven until she says, "Amen, I thank thee" (l. 195). Marlowe's Imogen seems careless of the risks she assumes, an attitude she has exhibited from the play's beginning, but Pisanio clearly fears the worst as he collects the letters from the ground, handing them to her. As the curtain falls, he looks upward and sobs as she exits.

Scene 13

Early in the play, Imogen had dreamed of alternate identities: a neat-herd's daughter, a girl kidnapped with her brothers, a barbaric torturer of cowards. When she defines herself, whether in fantasy or reality, Imogen does not think about restrictions such as social class, and in act 3, scene 4 she is willing to reject most gender restrictions as well. She eagerly assumes her masculine disguise and agrees to perform a different subjectivity (the submission and obedience of a servant boy) for one purpose: to reclaim the identity that is drifting farther and farther away from her. This is no Rosalind, who revels in the liberation of her disguise. Marlowe's Imogen, always the fearless, self-assured one, simply does what she must do and performs the identity dictated by her disguise, beginning in scene 13 (Shakespeare's 3.6), the cave scene.

As noted earlier, critics often condemned Marlowe's 1892–93 performances of this scene for lacking "the variety of coloring equal to the great demands of the occasions," her portrayal being admired for sweetness but criticized for monotony.[66] In 1923, Marlowe added a great deal to break the much-criticized monotony, but John Ranken Towse still noted that the cave scene (and subsequent scenes in Wales) suffered from excessive histrionics, perhaps used by Marlowe "to vitalize the dead weight of the plot."[67] Marlowe seemed to be less concerned with giving her audience a fetching, tantalizing image of the feminine boy than with offering a thoroughly developed interpretation of a character who at this moment in the play seriously attempts to perform a secondary identity, one fundamentally foreign to her. In the first half of the production, Marlowe's Imogen saw herself as a bold, self-assured but loyal and loving wife, while in the second half she has been instructed to "forget to be a woman" and to "change / Command into obedience" (3.4.156–57) if she is to succeed with her disguise and carry out her long-range goals. The result of denying her self-defined image is at times humorous in Marlowe's hands, especially when she encounters her boisterous brothers, an indication that she had infused the scene with much more variety and coloring than her original production revealed.

When Marlowe as Fidele appears before the cave, alone, exhausted, starving, she does not shrink from the sound of her own voice, as Faucit had done, or employ comical touches with the sword, as Terry had done; instead, Marlowe grasps her sword and goes inside the cave fairly quickly. Belarius and her brothers enter the stage, with Belarius (played by Albert Howson) looking inside the darkened cave and warning the brothers of some creature, perhaps a fairy, eating their food. As they tiptoe away, Marlowe's Fidele appears with a wooden platter in one hand and a drinking horn in the other. Upon seeing the strangers in the fading light, Marlowe falls to her knees, dropping the platter and cup, "Good masters, harm me not" (l. 45), assuming the identity of a submissive servant boy. Sitting back on her heels to relate her history as Fidele, she mentions her hunger, then collapses. After Belarius helps her up, a raucous Guiderius (played by Murray Kinnell) rushes to Imogen, putting his hand on her shoulder, shaking her, and saying, "Were you a woman, youth, / I should woo hard but be your groom" (ll. 68–69). He then shakes hands with her with a slap of palms, causing Marlowe's Imogen to look away and wince in pain. The exchange is clearly meant to be played for laughter, because no sooner does Marlowe recover from the hand-slapping than Arviragus (played by H. Fisher White) leaps to her side and slaps her on the back with "I'll make't my comfort / He is a man" (ll. 70–71), welcoming the boy as another brother with a robust hug that causes her again to look away in pain. The preliminary promptbook from the 1923 production shows that the hug is played for comedy, an effect achieved partially by its physicality but also by the awkwardness of Imogen's performative identity. Clearly, she is performing an unfamiliar role here—submissive, tentative, fearful. Marlowe's performance in this scene was never well accepted (in 1892–93 or 1923), but she sustained a portrayal of Fidele that was consistent with the character and the text that she shaped: an ordinarily self-assured, outspoken woman who is constrained by physical hunger and fatigue and by the secondary identity that she must believably perform in order to survive.

After the farcical byplay, the men go inside the cave and Imogen sits and daydreams of a simpler identity; had these three boys been her brothers, then she would have been the least valued of Cymbeline's children and therefore on more equal social footing with Posthumus, a fantasy Marlowe verbalizes while wringing her hands. Imogen imagines a life in which her identity is restricted and devalued, allowing her the ironic freedom to define herself as she pleases. Julia Marlowe chose to underplay the scene, to follow the line she had created in reshaping the text, although most critics found the scene disappointing after the explosive passions she had exhibited in the production's first half.

Scene 14

After cutting a short Roman scene (3.7) and Cloten's imagined beheading of Posthumus and rape of Imogen (4.1), Marlowe moves to Shakespeare's 4.2, her scene 14, the morning after Imogen's arrival at the cave, scene 13. After Imogen takes the medicine that Pisanio gave her and her new companions conduct a burial, placing Fidele's body next to Cloten's headless body, Imogen wakes and believes the dead body next to her is her husband's. Marlowe slowly wakes, rolling on her side and sitting up before noticing the corpse on "O gods and goddesses" (l. 295). She rises to her knees as she tries to remember what happened to her but falls back with "'Twas but a bolt of nothing, shot at nothing, / Which the brain makes of fumes" (ll. 300–301). Imogen's habit of dreaming an alternate reality fails to help her as she moves nearer the body, reaches down, and touches the blood. At this point, Marlowe eliminates the catalog of body parts (leg, hand, foot, thigh, muscles, face, as had been done in Macready's production with Helen Faucit) and acknowledges only, "A headless man? The garments of Posthumus?" (l. 308). Bending over the body on one knee, Marlowe deduces that Pisanio and Cloten conspired to kill both Posthumus and her. Having cut Imogen's maddened outcry ("Where is thy head? Where's that? Ay me, where's that?" [l. 321]) as well as her smearing of blood on her cheek, Marlowe simply throws herself over the body, remaining there silently as trumpets and drums sound to announce the entrance of Lucius, two captains, and six soldiers. Since the Soothsayer has been cut from the play, the soldiers quickly notice the bodies on the ground, Lucius being the first to investigate, "Soft, ho, what man is here?" (l. 353), with Marlowe substituting "man" for Shakespeare's "trunk." Lucius picks up a bit of drapery and sees the decapitated head, shrinking back in horror and ordering a captain to check the page boy's condition. The captain kneels and takes Imogen's head in his lap when suddenly she throws her head back and gasps, almost as if she had been in a detached, trancelike state, which is completely understandable considering she has lost her home, her father, her identity, and now, she believes, her husband.

Marlowe again underplays this episode, unlike Adelaide Neilson, who went into a frenzy over the supposed death of Posthumus.[68] But Marlowe continues to portray Imogen as she previously had: as one who has been physically ill and then poisoned, now facing the destruction of the goal toward which she has resolutely worked. As she creates a new identity, servant to a slain Briton, she stumbles a couple of times, breaks down and sobs over the body, then stands. Lucius puts his hands on her shoulders, a gesture of dominance and protection, and assures Fidele that his men will bury the body; Lucius supports the servant boy as they follow the soldiers carrying the body offstage, with Marlowe weeping as trumpets and drums sound again. Marlowe was criticized for lacking strong passion in this scene, but her textual omissions preclude such a display. Her Imogen shows quiet sadness, quiet because she is ill, because she plays a servant boy's role, and because she is generating and beginning to perform a variation of that masculine identity for the next phase of her physical and psychic journey. She moves forward as self-assuredly as she always has, not stumbling from uncertainty but rather from physical infirmity.

Scene 17

Marlowe cut and reshaped the play's conclusion with its battle scenes and many revelations so that Shakespeare's seven scenes (4.3 through 5.5) become three, scenes 15–17, and Imogen appears primarily in scene 17. Combining lines from various scenes and eliminating long stretches of dialogue, Marlowe seemingly hastened the denouement; however, she and Sothern choreographed a very elaborate battle scene of clamorous chaos, spanning scenes 15 and 16. Posthumus's scene in which he encounters the British lord (5.3) has been cut except for fifteen lines in which he decides to be taken prisoner as a Roman and to cease fighting. Furthermore, the entire jail scene with the dream vision and the descent of Jupiter is excised, a stage tradition since David Garrick.

Marlowe's final scene (Shakespeare's 5.5) opens with the knighting of the brothers and their supposed father, after which Cymbeline watches the entrance of the Roman prisoners: Lucius, Iachimo, Posthumus, and Imogen at the rear. The king notices the last prisoner, but the moment of recognition passes because Marlowe's Imogen does not respond, but rather, with self-confidence, continues to perform her latest identity. No longer weak or ill, Marlowe's heroine stands firmly, even supporting the wounded Iachimo, who leans on her arm.

She glances down and sees her ring on his hand, and, according to the prompt-book, "In her face is seen 'He is Posthumus's murderer!'" This bit of business occurs at the same moment Lucius begs Cymbeline to spare the life of the young page boy, although Marlowe's Imogen/Fidele pays no attention and keeps her back to the king as she continues staring at Iachimo, who sinks to his knees. At Lucius's request, Cymbeline rises and calls out, "Boy / Thou hast look'd thy-self into my grace" (5.5.93–94), to which Marlowe turns her head momentarily to him then turns her attention back to Iachimo's ring. As Cymbeline speaks to the servant boy whose back is turned, Marlowe nonverbally conveys that an idea has occurred to her by looking quickly at the king, then just as quickly back at Iachimo, and finally back to the king as he offers to grant a boon. She kneels where she stands and still intent upon Iachimo softly says, "I humbly thank your highness" (l. 100), spoken, according to the promptbook, primarily with gesture. Marlowe continues her focus on Iachimo, motivating Cymbeline to rise, approach her, and ask, "Know'st him thou look'st on? speak, / Wilt have him live?" (ll. 110–11), at which he touches her and pulls her around to face him. Resting his hand on her shoulder, a gesture of confidence and superiority that Imogen knows well, Cymbeline agrees to hear the boy's story privately; after Marlowe takes his hand and rises, they cross to the throne area, where she whis-pers to the king while still watching Iachimo, then stepping up on the throne platform next to Cymbeline. From this moment until the end of the play, she exhibits the body language of one who is again self-assured even though she maintains her secondary, and supposedly submissive, identity for a while longer, unaware that she will soon reclaim her primary one.

Placing his hand on the page boy, Cymbeline encourages him to address Iachimo, and Marlowe reaches from the platform and seizes Iachimo's ringed hand, demanding to know "Of whom he had this ring" (l. 136). As Iachimo be-gins to tell his tale, Posthumus, still disguised and guarded as a Roman, twice tries to rise and is forced back to the ground by the guards. Nearly fainting and held up by guards, Iachimo asks the king, "Wilt thou hear more, my lord?" (l. 146), and Marlowe's Imogen gestures 'yes' to Cymbeline, who moves closer to Iachimo and encourages him to continue his story, even giving him wine when he weakens on "Give me leave; I faint" (l. 149). While Iachimo describes his wa-ger with Posthumus and his villainy towards Imogen, large portions of which Marlowe has cut, he turns and sees Posthumus glaring at him, causing him to straighten in terror. Marlowe follows Iachimo's gaze, sees her husband, and steps forward, moving away from Cymbeline's side. Posthumus springs from his knees and seizes Iachimo by the throat, hurling him to the ground, while Imogen stands amazed, listening to her husband shout, "O, give me cord, or knife, or poison / Some upright justicer" (ll. 213–14). Marlowe drops to her knees as Sothern's Posthumus confesses his own villainy in having Imogen killed, during which she rises and moves behind him, stopping to kiss his hair gently before he drops down on his right hip, crying, "My queen, my life, my wife! O Imogen, / Imogen, Imogen" (ll. 226–27). He falls face down on the ground, and Marlowe bends over him with "Peace, my lord" (l. 227), but he turns his head away even though Marlowe's Fidele lifts him to his feet and stands in front of him. Posthumus resents the page's intrusion and violently grabs Imogen, jerking her in front of him first and then throwing her to the ground behind him. Pisanio reveals all by rushing to Imogen with "O, my lord Posthumus, / You ne'er kill'd Imogen till now" (ll. 230–31).

With the help of Pisanio, Marlowe's Imogen rises and faces her husband, asking, "Why did you throw your wedded lady from you?" (l. 261; lines between 236 and 259 have been excised), but she does not run to him or throw her arms around his neck. Instead, Marlowe stands still, extending her arms and waiting for Posthumus to run to her, which he does before placing his head on her shoulder. Audiences might have expected the opposite stage image of the couple's reunion, a traditional image of Imogen throwing herself into Posthumus' arms and hanging smilingly upon his breast, as Helen Faucit had played the moment.[69] But Marlowe's design for this moment reveals the self-assurance and dominance that have controlled this heroine's subjectivity from the start of the play. Once her performative identity is stripped away, she reaffirms her own identity. Imogen's next lines to Posthumus, "Think you are upon a rock; and now / Throw me again" (ll. 262–63), have a much less subservient tone when her body language conveys a message of self-possession and control. In fact, Posthumus's demeanor, not Imogen's, communicates a childlike quality, rushing into her arms and resting his head on her shoulder before her arms close around him in a masterly and motherly way. Cymbeline interrupts the moment by asking for her attention; Marlowe's Imogen looks first at Posthumus and then at Cymbeline, and half laughing and half crying for joy, she kneels before her father, "Your blessing, sir" (l. 266). Father and husband together lift her up, and the play moves swiftly, with many cuts, as Imogen defends her brothers and Belarius, after which their identities are revealed, and Marlowe's Imogen returns to her husband's side. Once Cymbeline takes his sons in his arms, Marlowe steps forward, embraces Belarius, and assures the king that she feels no loss of the kingdom but rather, "I've got two worlds by't" (l. 374). Again, Marlowe stands firm, extends her arms, and her brothers go to her and receive her embrace, each separately. Cymbeline turns his attention back to the Roman prisoners, and Imogen speaks her final line to Lucius, "My good master, / I will yet do you service" (ll. 403–4), causing him to kneel to her before she turns back to her husband. Iachimo then offers the ring and the bracelet to Posthumus, who springs forward to retrieve them and returns to Imogen's side. Marlowe clasps her arm around him for an instant, according to the promptbook, and Posthumus puts the bracelet and the ring on her, followed by Cymbeline's announcement, "Pardon's the word to all" (l. 422). Since the Soothsayer was cut from the production, the play concludes immediately with all prisoners released from shackles, a general outburst of rejoicing, and Cymbeline's announcement of Roman and British peace. Joyful trumpets sound as an exit procession begins.

The final scene of Marlowe and Sothern's production is trimmed from 485 lines to 281½ lines, a substantial reduction that cuts the story of the Queen's evil plans prior to her death (only the death is announced), the character of Cornelius along with his explanation of the potion Imogen had taken, Belarius's description of the kidnapping, the Soothsayer's interpretation of the prophecy bestowed on Posthumus in his dream vision, and all evidence (mantle and neck mole) proving the legitimacy of Guiderius and Arviragus as Cymbeline's sons. The focus is squarely on Imogen's reunion with husband, father, brothers, and friends. Indeed, Marlowe prepared a text and staged a production in which Imogen dominated, with a stage presence in over half the scenes and close to 25 percent of the production's lines (as opposed to around 16 percent in Shakespeare's text). Marlowe offered a carefully conceived interpretation of Imogen's sometimes contradictory subjectivities, and her nonverbal language conveyed a strong, self-confident heroine that should have appealed to post–World War I modernists; however, with one foot in the past, Marlowe retained her elaborately poetic vocal style, preventing her from bridging the gap between Victorian and modern tastes.

Conclusion

As early as 1908, Walter Prichard Eaton was calling for more realism on the American stage, declaring that the modern naturalistic drama appeals to the playgoer, while the "blank verse drama seems to him archaic, outworn, false, a thing now for the closet, not the stage," and "to our modern ears nothing but lifelike speech will be tolerated from the players."[70] However, other voices of the day recognized the unique art and poetry of *Cymbeline*. H. Granville-Barker noted the play's deficiencies but also asserted that despite the unlikely tale Shakespeare tells, "in its unlikelihood lies not only its charm, but largely its very being; reduce it to reason, you would wreck it altogether," which suggested the necessity of rendering a poeticized version on the stage, as Marlowe intended.[71] In 1923, others attempted productions of *Cymbeline* in England, one a modern-dress version that drew "a rather bewildered response."[72] The other production offered a more traditional setting with a text divided into two parts, as Marlowe also did, and a simple stage design using curtains and an inner stage to keep the narration continuous, a design very similar to Marlowe's. The production starred Sybil Thorndike, who brought too much "nervous modernity" to Imogen, according to James Agate, and "swallowed the character at one gulp" then looked "round the stage for something about which to be effective."[73] More modern touches—whether in acting style or with period transfer—did little to improve the play's success. H. H. Furness Jr., admittedly a devoted fan of Julia Marlowe, affirmed that "no manager yet has made a success of the play of *Cymbeline,* but we may now say that, at least in our generation, no actors other than Julia Marlowe and E. H. Sothern have done as much toward accomplishing such a feat."[74] Indeed, the Marlowe-Sothern production was, according to Alexander Woollcott, handsomely mounted, especially attractive in the mountain scenes, while it also achieved "excellent fluidity in the march of the play."[75] John Corbin praised the text Marlowe prepared and found the scenic design to be extremely beautiful.[76] Despite their occasional tributes to the production, neither could see past Marlowe's vocal embroidery to appreciate her progressive, textured interpretation of Imogen, the complex heart of the play.

Marlowe's preliminary promptbook is a Temple edition (1916) pasted in a workbook, held at the New York Public Library (NCP.280791B), Shattuck CYM #36. The final promptbook consists of three typescripts, held at the Museum of the City of New York (MCNY 43.430.631 A, B, C), Shattuck CYM #37. All act, scene, and line numbers correspond to *The Riverside Shakespeare,* ed. G. Blakemore Evans (Boston: Houghton Mifflin, 1974).

Notes

1. Charles Edward Russell, *Julia Marlowe: Her Life and Art* (New York: D. Appleton, 1926), 527, 530.

2. Helen Faucit (Lady Martin), *On Some of Shakespeare's Female Characters* (1893; reprint, New York: AMS, 1970), 158.

3. Bernard Shaw quoted in Alan Hughes, *Henry Irving, Shakespearean* (Cambridge: Cambridge University Press, 1981), 206.

4. "Hollis Street Theatre: *Cymbeline,*" *Boston Evening Transcript,* February 19, 1892, 5.

5. Mrs. M. Leigh Elliott, *Shakespeare's Garden of Girls* (London: Remington, 1885), 26.

6. Henry Austin Clapp, "Madame Modjeska as Imogen," *Boston Daily Advertiser*, March 29, 1884, 4.

7. Henry Austin Clapp, "Miss Neilson as Imogen," *Boston Daily Advertiser*, February 24, 1880, 1.

8. Anne E. Russell, "'History and Real Life': Anna Jameson, *Shakespeare's Heroines* and Victorian Women," *Victorian Review* 17, no. 2 (1991): 37.

9. William Winter, *Shadows of the Stage* (Boston: Joseph Wright, 1892), 52–53.

10. William Winter, *Shakespeare on the Stage*, series 3 (New York: Moffatt, Yard, 1916), 148.

11. David Shi, *Facing Facts: Realism in American Thought and Culture, 1850–1920* (New York: Oxford University Press, 1995), 17–18.

12. Mrs. Anna Jameson, *Shakespeare's Heroines: Characteristics of Women Moral, Poetical, and Historical* (1832; reprint, New York: A. L. Burt, n.d.), 201–2.

13. This theory of developing or shifting subjectivities is explained in Alan Sinfield, *Faultlines: Cultural Materialism and the Politics of Dissident Reading* (Berkeley: University of California Press, 1992), 62–63.

14. Marlowe qtd. in Charles E. L. Wingate, *Shakespeare's Heroines on the Stage* (New York: Thomas Y. Crowell, 1895), 113.

15. Henry Austin Clapp, "Marlowe's Imogene: Her Revival of Shakespeare's *Cymbeline*," *Boston Daily Advertiser*, February 19, 1892, 5.

16. Ibid.

17. "Hollis Street Theatre," *Boston Evening Transcript*, February 19, 1892, 5.

18. Wingate, *Shakespeare's Heroines*, 113.

19. William Winter, *Shakespeare on the Stage*, series 2 (New York: Moffatt, Yard, 1915), 136.

20. "As Imogen: Miss Marlowe in Classic Drama at the Hollis Street," *Boston Globe*, March 16, 1893, 6.

21. Edward Fuller, "Julia Marlowe-Taber," in *Famous American Actors of Today*, ed. Edward McKay and Charles E. L. Wingate (New York: Thomas Y. Crowell, 1896), 166.

22. Mrs. Sutherland, "Hollis Street Theatre: *Cymbeline*," *Boston Evening Transcript*, March 16, 1893, 10.

23. C. E. Russell, *Julia Marlowe*, 365.

24. Lloyd Morris, *Curtain Time: The Story of the American Theater* (New York: Random House, 1953), 324.

25. Horace Howard Furness Jr., "A Review of *Cymbeline*," *The Drama: A Monthly Review* 14, no. 3 (1923): 87–88.

26. John Corbin, "The Play," *New York Times*, October 3, 1923, 12.

27. C. E. Russell, *Julia Marlowe*, 528.

28. Jameson, *Shakespeare's Heroines*, 201.

29. "Miss Marlowe Reproached," *Boston Evening Transcript*, October 8, 1923, 12.

30. Ibid., 9.

31. J. Ranken Towse, "Shakespeare's *Cymbeline*," *New York Evening Post*, October 3, 1923.

32. Burns Mantle, ed., *The Best Plays of 1923–24* (Boston: Small, Maynard, 1924), 5.

33. Corbin, "The Play," 12.

34. Towse, "Shakespeare's *Cymbeline*."

35. Corbin, "The Play," 12.

36. Alexander Woollcott, "The Return of Imogen—Sothern and Marlowe Again," *New York Herald*, October 3, 1923, 16.

37. C. E. Russell, *Julia Marlowe*, 171.
38. Garff B. Wilson, *Three Hundred Years of American Drama and Theatre*, 2nd ed. (Englewood Cliff, N.J.: Prentice-Hall, 1982), 202.
39. Corbin, "The Play," 12.
40. Hughes, *Henry Irving*, 217.
41. All stage directions are taken from Marlowe's final promptbook.
42. Furness, "Review of *Cymbeline*," 87.
43. Carol J. Carlisle, "Macready's Production of *Cymbeline*," in *Shakespeare and the Victorian Stage*, ed. Richard Foulkes (Cambridge: Cambridge University Press, 1986), 144. Also, Carol Jones Carlisle, *Fire and Ice: Helen Faucit on the Victorian Stage* (London: The Society for Theatre Research, 2000), 96.
44. Clapp, "Neilson as Imogen," 1.
45. Hughes, *Henry Irving*, 67.
46. "Miss Allen's Imogen; Actress at Her Best," *New York Times*, October 23, 1906, sec. 9, p. 1.
47. Clapp, "Marlowe's Imogen," 5.
48. Sutherland, "Hollis Street Theatre: *Cymbeline*," 10.
49. C. E. Russell, *Julia Marlowe*, 197–98.
50. Ibid., 197.
51. Towse, "Shakespeare's *Cymbeline*."
52. Furness, "Review of *Cymbeline*," 87.
53. C. E. Russell, *Julia Marlowe*, 198.
54. Winter, *Shadows*, 52–53.
55. Furness, "Review of *Cymbeline*," 87.
56. Ibid.
57. Ibid.
58. Faucit, 190.
59. Clapp, "Neilson as Imogen," 1.
60. Ellen Terry quoted in Hughes, *Henry Irving*, 221.
61. C. E. Russell, *Julia Marlowe*, 199.
62. Towse, "Shakespeare's *Cymbeline*."
63. Furness, "Review of *Cymbeline*," 87.
64. Ibid.
65. Ibid.
66. Clapp, "Marlowe's Imogen," 5.
67. Towse, "Shakespeare's *Cymbeline*."
68. Winter, *Shadows*, 54.
69. Faucit, *Shakespeare's Female Characters*, 218–20.
70. Walter Prichard Eaton, *The American Stage of To-Day* (Boston: Small, Maynard, 1908), 61, 63.
71. Harley Granville-Barker, "Cymbeline," in *Prefaces to Shakespeare*, vol. 1 (1927; reprint, Princeton: Princeton University Press, 1978), 466–67.
72. Barry Jackson, "Producing the Comedies," *Shakespeare Survey* 8 (1955): 79.
73. James Agate, *Brief Chronicles* (New York: Benjamin Blom, 1943), 187.
74. Furness, "Review of *Cymbeline*," 88.
75. Woollcott, "Return of Imogen," 16.
76. Corbin, "The Play," 12.

BOOK REVIEWS

Slavery and Sentiment on the American Stage, 1787–1861: Lifting the Veil of Black.
By Heather S. Nathans. New York: Cambridge University Press, 2009. xi + 249 pp. $99.00 cloth.

It is surprising to realize that, despite an outpouring of scholarship in the last twenty years about minstrelsy and performances by and of blacks during the first half of the nineteenth century, excepting studies of *Uncle Tom's Cabin,* Heather Nathans's is the first book to focus on the theatrical portrayal of slaves and slavery during the period. Nathans examines these subjects through the lens of antebellum sentiment, that mix of piety and moral commitment that expressed itself in emotional language and impassioned deed. Because so many representatives of slaves on nineteenth-century stages were white, sentiment is a slippery slope for contemporary students of antebellum performances of blackness. Who felt what about whom in this exchange?

Nathans approaches her subject topically via six chapters that explore legal issues respecting slavery during and after the Revolutionary War, the compromise rhetoric of patriotic fervor mixed with abolitionism, colonization and the search for Africa, Yankees and Sambos, the tension between violence and abolitionism/sentiment and brutality, and the theatre as a mirror of real-time events. A rich body of dramatic and performative material supports and clarifies each topic across the antebellum period and landscape.

(Private) sentiment was a useful antislavery tool only if it produced (public) action. Chapter 2 of *Slavery and Sentiment* is exemplary of Nathans's skill at following a historical map and illustrating it with dramatic landmarks. Here, her map is that of the post-1800 movement through presidential administrations and laws that shift focus from the individual trauma slavery represented, reflective of a politics centered on "the way in which the well-being of the state was embodied by the individual," to "works focused on white characters negotiating the complex relationships that would preserve the nation" (64). In the era's plays, marriage became the metaphor for union.

As laws careened from the 1820 Missouri Compromise to the Fugitive Slave Act of 1850, Nathans demonstrates how the sentimental republican body of the early national period failed, how the sentimental appeal to the unified body of the earlier nineteenth century failed, and how the sentimental appeal of the 1850s to the slave body as national redeemer also failed. In the process, the black slave body was displaced from its own tragedy and the white political body became central to the drama of slavery and sentiment.

Following a chapter concerning dramatizations of Africa that does much both to clarify antebellum projections of its land and people and efforts to "colonize" free blacks and slaves to Africa during the antebellum era, Nathans moves to the cultural ground of American "Yankees" and "Sambos." Here, students of staged Yankees and Negroes connect not only with the dominant repertory but also with lesser known works, such as John Townsend Trowbridge's *Neighbor Jackwood* (1857). Nathans weaves the discussion of staged Yankees and Negroes around the career of abolitionist Parker Pillsbury, who very well understood how to use rhetoric and dramatizations of slavery narratives to bind passion and compassion in the Yankee figure with a sentimentalized staged Negro who clearly merited both pity and action. Nathans documents the shift from an earlier, listless abolitionist stance that appealed to Enlightenment rhetoric and the rights of man to one infused with a call to action against both fugitive slave laws and denials of the right to petition Congress for redress of grievances. She connects plays to the humanizing (sentimental) rhetoric of abolitionists like Pillsbury and the desegregation of abolitionist organizations, concluding that, by the 1850s, "not only had the stage Yankee begun to realize his potential as a moral champion, his black [stage Negro] protégé had become 'worthy' of his protection" (162). The result was an emotional amalgamation exemplified in the dramatized version of *Neighbor Jackwood*, where, Nathans argues, "Yankee" and "Negro" merge.

Abolitionists had many strategies for drawing support to their cause. As conditions deteriorated after the 1830s, slave narratives became more pathetic, descriptions more violent, and embodiments of them more performative. In addition to visual images of beseeching slaves and white liberators, antislavery fairs raised funds through music, dancing, and plays as well as through the sale of handicrafts and other goods. Henry Ward Beecher staged "slave auctions" in his Brooklyn church, a "ritualized performance of emancipation" (193), with the white purchaser/liberator at the center of the exchange. Events outside theatres were quickly brought into them: the Nat Turner rebellion metamorphosed into the Roman play *The Gladiator* (1831); the deliberate burning of the anti-slavery Pennsylvania Hall in Philadelphia in 1838, three days after it opened, is deftly linked by Nathans to Forrest's productions of *Othello;* the Bowery Theatre's *The Black Schooner* (1839) was a hugely successful dramatization of the Amistad case; and *Ossawattomie Brown* (1859) provided a resiliently stage-worthy dramatization of John Brown's raid on Harpers Ferry.

Clearly, sentiment was reaching its limits as a way to arouse support for ending slavery, as liberating whites repeatedly claimed center stage from the enslaved blacks who were the subject of the abolition drama, disempowering them by sentimentalizing slaves as objects of pity. *Slavery and Sentiment* concludes with a chapter devoted to temperance and similar strategies to establish the legal, social, and cultural parity that equality, post-slavery, would require. Here, Nathans offers several plays, including Harry Seymour's *Aunt Dinah's Pledge* (c. 1850), a staged Negro version of the novel's much more dignified, independent, temperate, and compassionate characters.

As the tie between alcohol and the violence of slavery sounded its last and strongest sentimental notes in *Uncle Tom's Cabin* (although more resonantly in the novel than in dramatizations of it), free blacks took up other cultural issues, from establishing alternate theatre venues, such as Boston's black Histrionic Club (1857), to the reaffirmation in court (1853) of integration at the Howard Athenaeum and other Boston theatres. To be sure, such victories were not universal, but they did herald the end of the slavery drama. What lay beyond Appomattox was the long and brutal struggle for equality and a rhetoric of feeling and action that could keep the nation's eyes on the prize.

A topical organization serves Nathans's project in that it allows her to redistribute evidence and examine the same plays from different angles. It serves *Slavery and Sentiment* less well in that sentiment, both as a political and as an analytical strategy, unfolds itself temporally, in response to cultural and historical events occurring between 1787 and 1861. Enlightenment appeals seem cold in comparison to romantic sentiments, which seem fulsome and personal in comparison to the sentiment fueling public action at midcentury. Abolitionist strategies in this regard responded to earlier strategies that had played themselves out. Similarly, in the same way that one may feel unanchored in time while "lifting the veil of black" in this book, so there are certain landmarks on this journey that demand to be observed while passing—*Uncle Tom's Cabin* and *The Octoroon*, for example, mentioned in reference to several topics, but never fully explored.

Despite antecedent sentiments and absent monuments, however, Nathans's book clearly succeeds in illuminating "how the debate over black participation in American society translated into the vernacular of the popular stage" (1). The great strength of this work is to reinsert theatre into culture and culture into theatre so as to make clear the intimate connection between historical events, social organizations, and cultural activity. This contextualization characterizes the best work of recent theorized history, Heather S. Nathans's *Slavery and Sentiment* among them.

—ROSEMARIE K. BANK
Kent State University

Acting Wilde: Victorian Sexuality, Theatre, and Oscar Wilde. By Kerry Powell. London: Cambridge University Press, 2009. 204 pp. $90.00 cloth.

In *Acting Wilde: Victorian Sexuality, Theatre, and Oscar Wilde,* Kerry Powell infuses vigorous new meaning into Shakespeare's legendary dictum that the world is but a stage and all mortals merely actors. Powell builds on this concept in examining Oscar Wilde's struggle to determine whether people could write their own scripts and fashion their own images and performances, challenges that haunted Wilde throughout his life. As Powell notes, Wilde's "visionary theatricality" *literally* discerned life as "a continuum of performance," an observation that "lies at the core of his importance" in both theatre and thought (1). Drawing extensively upon newly discovered or reinterpreted materials—particularly Wilde's courtroom transcripts—Powell discusses how Wilde's gendered identity was formulated and even textualized through the historical framework of Victorian values that made impossible a distinction between "the 'performed' and the 'real.'" Furthermore, Powell argues that Wilde's place in charting modern drama has been seriously underrated, noting he "altered the course of drama by strategically abandoning" its traditional mimetic basis and sought "to create new worlds and perform new selves" (171).

Powell frames his short but richly textured book within the framework of Wilde's fame, beginning with his renowned American tour and ending with the prison term that left him a shell of a man. Throughout six chapters, Powell charts the various poses that Wilde adopted or was forced to assume: "his attempt, perhaps doomed at the outset, to create himself anew, on his own terms, while inhabiting a character in a script written by someone else with very different motives" (17). One of the most potent illustrations of this stylization is the iconic photograph of Wilde by celebrity photographer Napoleon Sarony depicting the author as a "gorgeously clad, dreamy-eyed figure" (24). Powell's incisive discussion strikes at the heart of his central theme—whether Wilde assumed his own pose or whether Sarony controlled and thus "invented" him—and is underscored by the ensuing landmark litigation concerning the ownership of this pose. Powell further locates this issue of identity ownership in Wilde's subsequent works, such as the title character in *The Picture of Dorian Gray,* who "seizes control of the portrait he sat for" (37).

Powell also examines the concepts of identity and performativity in Wilde's five most prominent plays: *Lady Windemere's Fan, Salomé, A Woman of No Importance, An Ideal Husband,* and *The Importance of Being Earnest.* Powell views these works as "the acting out of the author's conflict and to a high degree his compromise with an increasingly powerful variety of late-Victorian feminism" that demanded the standards of feminine purity be applied to men as well as women—an admirable undertaking but one that would ironically help bring about Wilde's downfall (41). Powell scrupulously examines the textual evolution of these plays, incorporating the importance of social and feminist influences on Wilde's revisions and exploring the "new if fitful recognition" concerning gender conceptions as "regulatory fictions" rather than universal truths of identity (43). In the process, Powell leads readers through the tangled Victorian ideals of purity, drawing upon contemporary factual and fictional references and noting the changing influence of these forces on Wilde's own works.

For example, Powell cites the chasm between the first and rarely cited draft of *Lady Windemere's Fan* and the final version, which presents a considerably more sympathetic view of the "Puritan" woman, a "softening" that Powell argues "would become the paradigm of Wilde's social comedies," as though he were negotiating radical feminist views with his own "deep hostility towards them" (55). Similarly, Powell argues that *Salomé,* despite its often "bold defiance of Victorian dramatic practice," also exposes Wilde's anxiety over the struggle between female purity and mainstream male heterosexuality (59), while *A Woman of No Importance* evolves from an ideological engagement with feminism to a reasoned amalgamation of gender identity. While an autobiographical strain clearly informs all of Wilde's work, Powell finds it particularly striking in *An Ideal Husband,* which portrays an eminent man "on the brink of exposure" who is saved—unlike Wilde—in the play's comic if contrived resolution (99).

In Powell's estimation, Wilde's most popular play, *The Importance of Being Earnest,* clarified for the author the issue of self-performance and provided "a turning point in Victorian thinking about subjectivity" by serving as "a textual crossroads where performativity and history meet" (101). Rejecting G. B. Shaw's famous condemnation of the play as lacking in humanity and thus authenticity, Powell argues that this very criticism reflects the play's blurring of masquerade and identity, a central theme of Powell's book as well as an ongoing crisis throughout Wilde's life. If the self is indeed defined by performance, then this play unflinchingly confronts the potential contradiction—or hypocrisy—between authentic and staged identity.

In his penultimate chapter, Powell confronts the most notorious and—for Wilde—the most tragic episode of the writer's life: his trials on charges of "gross indecency." Powell examines the ongoing difficulty of defining this slippery and flexible term, while citing its application in other trials as well. More importantly, though, Powell argues that this criminal clause "is less historically important than we have been led to believe," and he takes to task the widely accepted notion that Wilde's trials crystallized for the first time the cultural identity of the gay man, "the site where homosexuality was invented" (126). While acknowledging that he is not the first scholar to cast shadows over this mythical view, Powell argues that the Victorian public was quite familiar with the concept of homosexuality through the many signifying factors associated with such a lifestyle, although it was a term that dare not speak its name. Furthermore, the reticence of Victorian newspapers to report any specific, sordid details kept the concept of sex out of Wilde's trials, allowing the true nature of Wilde's "crimes" to be conveniently glossed over. But the recent discovery of a transcript of Wilde's first trial has seriously undermined these long-held beliefs, making clear "for the first time the centrality of sexual behavior to the libel trial" (142). Housed in the British Library and donated by an anonymous source, this transcript clearly asserts, writes Powell, that Wilde was charged with specific sexual transgressions, thus "inevitably and fundamentally" altering how "we understand Wilde and his trials" (134).

In his final chapter, Powell brings his central theme of performativity full circle by poignantly describing how, in prison, Wilde viewed himself as an unwilling actor in a scripted performance, "a puppet worked by some secret and unseen hand to bring terrible events to an issue" (160). Still, having been stripped of everything, he perceived the possibility of reconceiving himself "in the wreckage of his life," of rewriting himself on this clean slate, a task that demanded he examine his past and take upon himself "the burden of his doom" (162). Drawing upon Christ as a model for such performativity, "Wilde learned that disgrace, imprisonment, and sorrow need not embitter or destroy him, but could be the means to self-enlargement" (164). But in the end, as so acutely expressed in *De Profundis,* Wilde resigned himself to the role into which society had cast him: "a sorrowful clown, a puppet, the failed hero of a tragedy" (168). Finally, in his epilogue, Powell proclaims Wilde a precursor of modern drama, "not by putting visible reality on stage, but by undermining it with a yearning to discover through performance a humanity that . . . could not be realized" in the alienating venue of naturalist theatre or, for that matter, in any life (174).

Through a close examination of Wilde's textual revisions of his plays, viewed in the context of the author's private life as well as contemporary political complexities, along with an overarching view of the influence and significance of the changing concepts of gender identity, Powell provides in *Acting Wilde: Victorian Sexuality, Theatre, and Oscar Wilde* an important contribution not only to the body of Wilde scholarship but also to the ever-expanding studies of gender identity and performativity as a means to self-identity.

—**KAREN C. BLANSFIELD**
Dramaturg, Deep Dish Theater
Chapel Hill, NC
http://www.deepdishtheater.org/

❦

Highbrow/Lowdown: Theater, Jazz, and the Making of the New Middle Class. By David Savran. Ann Arbor: University of Michigan Press, 2009. viii + 326 pp. $35.00 cloth.

In an essay tracing major changes in twentieth-century American theatre, Paul DiMaggio observes that film killed the theatrical "road," simultaneously capturing most of its audiences and creating a vast new public for dramatic entertainment. "Without competition from commercial producers," he notes, "those who would elevate theater to art inherited the stage by default" ("Cultural Boundaries and Structural Change: The Extension of the High Culture Model to Theater, Opera, and the Dance, 1900–1940," in *Cultivating Differences: Symbolic Boundaries and the Making of Inequality,* ed. Michele Lamont and Marcel Fournier [Chicago: University of Chicago Press, 1992], 29). Those practitioners, critics, and audiences keen on such "elevation" are the heart of David Savran's stunningly smart new book. At first blush, this project might seem straightforward enough. The genteel reader of the nineteenth century morphs into the serious modernist of the twentieth; the Little Theatre births a taste for experimental work and the need for it to be difficult enough to require university study on both sides of the footlights; modern dramatic literature claims its rightful place among other serious art work, and Eugene O'Neill's quick succession Pulitzer Prizes seal the deal.

But wait. The biggest theatre phenomenon to germinate in the 1920s was the so-called integrated musical, and no theatre historian—whatever his or her aesthetic preferences—could deny that musicals were then and are now the major live theatre draw. How can these two arcs be reconciled? Savran's answer is jazz, but jazz, just like live theatre, was a contested sphere in the 1920s, and one of the major achievements of *Highbrow/Lowdown* is its refusal to simplify complicated rubrics.

"Jazz," writes Savran, "given its many manifestations, guises, contexts, and performance venues . . . represented the most significant form of cross-mediated performance in the 1920s: a form that undermined the autonomy of dance and concert music, cabaret, social dancing, vaudeville, revue, and narrative theater. It was, in short, less a discrete style than a musical and social energy linking all these performance practices" (16). Jazz as music had, to be sure, certain formal properties, which Savran outlines, and as music it was associated with African Americans, although its influences were also Latin American. So ubiquitous were jazz's "many manifestations" that "all the debates in the 1920s about American modernism (musical or otherwise) seemed to pivot around jazz" and a preoccupation "with questions about the character of national tradition" (69). Broadly speaking, these questions were whether American meant "negroid," whether a machine ethic now damned the masses to being cogs on an assembly line, and whether there was any way to maintain a difference between high and low arts.

Savran's answers to all the above questions are "yes and no." While white America may have preferred the "sweet" (white) jazz of Irving Berlin, Paul Whiteman, and George Gershwin to the "hot" jazz created by blacks for blacks, Savran notes the impossibility of ascertaining "racial provenance" (28). Gershwin's *Tip Toes* and *Lady, Be Good* (the latter featuring "Fascinating Rhythm") are one syncopated step away from being vaudeville revues, but Gershwin's "classical" bona fides had been assured with the composition of *Rhapsody in Blue,* which made critics take the musicals seriously, if in some cases nervously. What to make of the jazz rhythms that both enabled and normalized sophisticated lyrics while freely indulging in hybrid, promiscuous borrowing? "Is *Porgy and Bess* opera when performed at the Metropolitan but a musical when presented on Broadway?" asks Savran (66).

The latter question points to a central theme in *Highbrow/Lowdown,* namely, audience and critical anxiety. The truly highbrow and the genuinely lowbrow had never been part of a theatre equation. New immigrants who did not (yet) speak English preferred movies because of both price and the absence of a language barrier. This left an "intelligent minority," the phrase used "to describe the audience at which the new commercial art theater aimed its appeal" (105).

Savran uses Pierre Bourdieu's theories as an optic and combs the work of major 1920s drama critics to assess who signed up for a new kind of theatre meriting the name "jazz" even when it overtly eschewed the term. Savran's assessment of the emerging audience is mostly about class, which he points out is less a matter of dollars per se than it is an attitude toward self that is reified and shored up by activities that confirm one's worth. Even Emily Post advocated theatregoing as the entertainment of choice for the "smart set" (132), although fans also included "bohemians," or people who really liked literature and art, or who vaguely understood these as "worthwhile" (itself indicating a kind of anxiety).

How this audience actually related to machine-age theatre that wanted to be seen as serious art is unpacked in Savran's terrific reading of Elmer Rice's *The Adding Machine*. The play is a perfect case study in how evolving audiences were fascinated by lower- or lower-middle-class "others" as victims of the dehumanizing assembly line that was also discomfiting the more privileged, but with different effects. While Rice's lowly bookkeeper can't understand life outside of repetitive work, kneejerk morals, and cheap entertainments, the audience imagined itself able to escape into a world of aesthetics and ideas via acquired culture (including theatre) that "endeavored to fulfill the middlebrow dream by reconciling the competing claims of art and commerce" (148). In other words, consume this product (which had better be worth the price) in order to escape the tawdry and debilitating realm of getting and spending. Savran locates this audience's representative neither in the lowbrow Mr. Zero nor in the boss who represents capital, but in the unseen inhabitants of the afterlife who understand purposeful leisure. That the contours of this leisure depend on someone else's labor is the unmentioned elephant in the "intelligent minority" room.

No discussion of the "elevation" of American theatre in the 1920s would be possible without including Eugene O'Neill, whom Savran saves for his final chapter. Here the topic is not literature but the close embrace of critics and playwright in constructing O'Neill as "a holy man of art—one part saint, one part messiah—whose agonies redeemed the American theater from the tyranny of dreck" (246). O'Neill's acknowledged influences were all European, which ironically enabled American critics in search of an American art, and themselves looking for credibility, to use these putative bona fides to support an unexamined credo that art somehow "must transcend the social" (259). This flattering notion undergirds how "upper-middlebrow drama help[s] to maintain Broadway's distance from Hollywood, on the one hand . . . and [today] more risky Off Broadway drama, on the other" (267). Anxiety about our own "most dearly held assumptions and prejudices" still underwrites the plays that achieve commercial success as O'Neill's legatees.

I have two small quibbles with this otherwise superb book. I wish there were actual snippets of music on the page to illustrate Savran's clear and sophisticated parsing of composition and scoring. Such quotes function the same way as pictures and excerpts from plays and surely belong in a study that investigates them with such nuance. Second, I wished Savran had situated himself and his readers in the audience population (or rather its direct descendants) he constructs. Surely it is not possible to shed one's "most dearly held assumptions," which here may still be that there is a kind of theatre (off-Broadway? off-off-Broadway?) that eschews the close embrace of uplift and commerce.

No matter. The fact that this book neither pulls punches nor flattens the terrain in mapping the heady route from old to "new middle class" in the American theatre makes it unique and indispensable.

—DOROTHY CHANSKY
Texas Tech University

⌇

Shakespeare and the American Musical. By Irene G. Dash. Bloomington: Indiana University Press, 2010. 248 pp. $65.00 cloth, $24.95 paper.

In the opening paragraphs of her introduction to *Shakespeare and the American Musical,* Irene G. Dash suggests that "Sometimes Shakespeare scared people, especially those writing about the American musical. . . . Despite Shakespeare's texts being in the forefront of the development of the organic musical and being popular, these adaptations were basically overlooked. But they shouldn't have been. Right from the start, from the time that Richard Rodgers and Lorenz Hart decided to turn to a Shakespeare play rather than write their own story, his works were central" (1). With this statement, Dash begins to address what she sees as a "gap" in musical theatre scholarship by arguing for the centrality of five important musical productions adapted from Shakespeare between 1938 and 1971 to the development of the American "organic" or "integrated" musical form. These works are *The Boys from Syracuse (The Comedy of Errors), Kiss Me, Kate (Taming of the Shrew), West Side Story (Romeo and Juliet), Your Own Thing (Twelfth Night),* and *Two Gentlemen of Verona* (a rock musical adaptation). As revealed in the quote above, Dash makes several assumptions about musical theatre history and scholarship that contribute to the breakdown of her primary argument (the first being that these works have been "ignored" by musical theatre scholarship—an interesting case to make in the light of the published scholarship on her first three examples, very little of which can be found in Dash's bibliography). Dash's secondary goal is to demonstrate "how American culture transmuted these Renaissance plays into a vibrant new experience in the modern theater" (9), and this objective is accomplished with some success. The book is divided into an introduction, five chapters (each looking at one of the musical adaptations indicated above), and a brief coda.

In order to demonstrate her example productions' centrality to the development of the "organic" or "integrated" American musical form, Dash attempts to position musical Shakespeare adaptations as a series of innovations, many times as "firsts" in musical theatre history, which create trends in musical theatre history and form development. Unfortunately, Dash provides little evidence for these kinds of claims, nor does she reference contemporary productions or other scholars' work that would challenge her ideas. For example, she tries to position *The Boys from Syracuse* as the first "organic" musical without reference to other possible claimants (except for a brief mention of Rodgers and Hart's *On Your Toes,* which she dismisses based on a quote by Ethan Mordden stating that the production's ballet did not move the plot forward; however, Mordden, in *Sing for Your Supper* [which Dash cites in the same paragraph] argues *for* the musical's "integrated" status). Further, Dash positions many of her examples as pioneering innovative voices for "political and social change in the twentieth century" (186). For example, she claims that the rock musical adaptation of *Two Gentlemen of Verona* (1971) was the first "completely racially mixed cast," but her explanation of this statement (that the casting reflected the racial mix of the city) is simplistic and poorly defined, leading readers to wonder if this truly was the "first" innovation of this kind. These failings may be attributed to the fact that Dash cites very few critical musical theatre sources, and the general histories of musical theatre she references are, in some cases, outdated.

Additionally, as her primary argument deals with a specific theatrical form, confusion could have been avoided if Dash had thoroughly defined that form. She uses "organic" or "integrated" interchangeably throughout the text, taking for granted that her readers share the same understandings of these terms, and without discussing any criteria for designating a musical as "integrated." Another troubling point is that her descriptions of "organic" or "integrated" form change between chapters to serve the particular needs of the argument. In her chapter on *The Boys from Syracuse* she focuses almost exclusively on the integration of dance to the narrative frame to argue for the production's "integrated" form, while ignoring other aspects of integration, such as the music itself (which she admits she knows very little about, reducing her discussion of the music to personal observations such as "strong background beat" [174]).

However, in her chapter on *Your Own Thing* she seems to minimize the centrality of dance in "integrated" musicals, conceding that dance in this particular example "interrupt[ed] the progress of the plot" (144), while still arguing for its integrated status.

The book's most persuasive points concern how American culture and musical theatre served to adapt Shakespeare's plays into a "dynamic new experience" in contemporary theatre. The research contained within each chapter is more relevant to Shakespeare's adaptability within the confines of a particular vernacular culture than to its impact on the development of distinct forms of musical theatre. Within each chapter, Dash discusses the plot (extensively), essential themes and characters within Shakespeare's plays, and where each set of adapters departed from Shakespeare's original. She then attempts to make an argument for each set of differences based upon the specific time and culture of the adaptation. Dash focuses primarily on pairing the adaptation with the original Shakespeare and providing an inside view into the adapter's choices (composers, librettists, directors, choreographers, designers) through her extensive research of the adapter's papers, drafts, and personal interviews (even if the discussion is at times filled with her own assumptions on what the adapters must have been thinking about current events). Further, each chapter provides insight on Shakespearean gender roles and relationships (the subject of many of Dash's prior books) and how gender roles change from their Shakespearean originals within each adaptation.

Particularly helpful to readers are her discussions in chapter 1 *(The Boys from Syracuse)* about the particular influence of George Abbott and George Balanchine on the integrated creation of the production; and her observations in chapter 2 about the incorporation of Shakespearean "double vision" into *Kiss Me, Kate,* the contribution of choreographer Hanya Holm, the production's connections to the 1935 Alfred Lunt-Lynn Fontanne production of *The Taming of the Shrew,* as well as its subsequent performances and translations around the globe. While much has been written about the form and significance of *West Side Story* in musical theatre history, Dash gives a particularly helpful discussion in chapter 3 of the development of the story line from Shakespeare's original work to its first incarnation, *East Side Story,* and the further crafting of the narrative (with its focus on dance storytelling) into *West Side Story.* Chapter 4, discussing *Your Own Thing,* and chapter 5, discussing *Two Gentlemen of Verona,* are perhaps the weakest chapters in terms of Dash's primary argument, as she cannot provide evidence that either of these musicals served to change or nuance the development of the integrated musical form.

While it is clear that Dash enjoys and values musical theatre, the imbalance between her rather general knowledge of musical theatre history and form and her expert knowledge of Shakespeare undermines her overarching argument. That being said, much of the information presented in her five chapters on the process and mechanics of adaptation will be of interest to students, scholars, and theatre professionals.

—TRACEY ELAINE CHESSUM
University of Maryland, College Park

Albee in Performance. By Rakesh H. Solomon. Bloomington: Indiana University Press, 2010. 296 pp. $24.95 paper.

Edward Albee (The Later Plays). By Anne Paolucci. Middle Village, N.Y.: Griffon House, 2010. 165 pp. $20.00 paper.

In the world of Albee scholarship, it is always exciting to welcome new studies exploring a subject who has himself continued to grow and change both in terms of his playwriting and in his directing—of both his own and others' plays. These two volumes represent two traditions in Albee scholarship, the exploration of Albee as a working theatre artist and the study of Albee's plays as literature. As an Albee scholar and director, and someone who has worked with Albee personally for over fifteen years (including watching him offer suggestions to actors on how to play *The Zoo Story*), I was completely absorbed by Rakesh Solomon's detailed and nuanced exploration of Albee's direction of his own work. The study is the culmination of over thirty years of documentation, starting in 1978, of Albee directing Albee, including countless hours of interviews with not only Albee but also several of his most famous and long-serving collaborators, including director Alan Schneider, actor Wyman Pendleton, and stage manager Mark Wright. Solomon documents Albee's productions of his plays *The American Dream, The Zoo Story, Box, Quotations from Chairman Mao Tse-Tung, Fam & Yam, The Sandbox, Who's Afraid of Virginia Woolf?, The Marriage Play,* and *Three Tall Women,* giving a chapter to each production. The book eventually moves beyond Albee directing Albee, and the last chapter, "Albee and His Collaborators on Staging Albee," is a collection of interviews with other directors who have directed Albee's work. This chapter is filled with wonderful details from some of Albee's most recent productions, including Lawrence Sacharow's *Three Tall Women* and David Esbjornson's stagings of *The Goat, or, Who Is Sylvia?*, *The Play about the Baby*, and *Who's Afraid of Virginia Woolf?*

The revelations that come with Solomon's documentation are quite stunning at times—including a jaw-dropping moment when Albee reveals that the Young Man in Albee's absurdist farce *The American Dream* has actually come to kill Mommy and Daddy rather than to serve as a kind of cynical present from Grandma. The importance of Solomon's work lies in the fact that it is clear from Albee's directorial choices not only that many directors have misinterpreted his plays but also that major scholars may have significantly veered from authorial intention (at least as Albee himself would have it). Another surprise, at least for some readers, might be the extent to which Albee teases out the humor and comedy in his plays—even in scripts as apparently serious as *The Zoo Story* and *Who's Afraid of Virginia Woolf?*

At the heart of what may be jarring to some who consider Albee's work to be the quintessence of absurdism is Albee's utterly naturalistic approach to directing his own plays and his insistence that actors play the characters as human beings. According to Solomon, this approach is tied to director Alan Schneider's influence as a mentor for Albee's directing—Schneider, a devotee of Lee Strasberg's acting technique, directed most if not all of the premieres of Albee's plays from the 1960s through the 1980s.

Solomon notes that during a production of *The American Dream*, a play that may be considered Albee's most successful attempt to create an absurdist Ionesco-like farce, Albee instructs his actors to "see and believe in yourselves as actual, physical, realistic, naturalistic persons—not stylized characters" (40). Having worked with Albee myself on this play, I can confirm this rather confounding advice: he gave me this same instruction, to have the actors in *The American Dream* play it "utterly naturally." Solomon also notes Albee's detailed process in casting, his generosity working with actors, and his willingness to sit through massive cattle calls making time, if only a moment, to connect with each actor auditioning for his play. This too seems to go against Albee's apocryphal reputation for being a rather intimidating figure in the professional theatre—the actors in these case studies are devoted to him and admire his directing skills.

Solomon solidifies his conclusions by reaching back into theatre history and carefully examining Albee's directorial work in the light of other playwrights who directed their own work, including George Bernard Shaw, Bertoldt Brecht, and Samuel Beckett, among others. The author's extraordinary thirty-

year documentation of Albee's plays in production, both directed by the author and by others, is a major gift to directors, actors, designers, and others
who are interested in considering the author's intent in theatrical production.
Although Solomon himself invokes Wimsatt and Beardsley's famous "The In-
tentional Fallacy," challenging the notion that the author's intent is knowable,
Albee scholars, in particular, would ignore this new study at their peril. It will
prove an indispensable source and catalyst for future Albee scholarship and
a highly influential creative guide to understanding one of America's greatest
and, perhaps, most mysterious playwrights.

With *Edward Albee (The Later Plays)*, Anne Paolucci picks up the task of examining Albee's plays through the lens of Pirandello, which she began with
her much earlier work, *From Tension to Tonic: the Plays of Edward Albee* (1972).
Paolucci's Pirandellian approach to Albee has certainly been explored by other
writers, but not with the depth of her knowledge of Pirandello, and certainly
not with the cohesiveness of technique that she brings to the task. One might
argue against the parochialism of this approach, but since Albee himself has
regularly cited the influence of Pirandello on his own work, this seems a sen-
sible line of attack. Notably, in Albee's published interviews, Pirandello often
rises to the top as a major influence, even though Albee tends to avoid citing
specific writers as influences, preferring to provide a list of many playwrights
whose work made an impression on him.

In this volume, Paolucci explores the plays that Albee has written since the
1980s, both individually (each is given its own chapter) and then in comparison.
For example, she explores the notion of loss of innocence in *Fragments* and *The
Play about the Baby;* the standpoint of marriage and the inevitable "fall from
bliss" in *Marriage Play, The Goat or, Who is Sylvia?,* and *Counting the Ways;* the
thematic concerns of mortality and death in *The Lady from Dubuque* and *Three
Tall Women;* the inherent metatheatricality of *Finding the Sun* and *Listening;*
and Albee's new explorations of form and content in *At Home at the Zoo* and
Occupant. The volume ends with Paolucci's distillation of her own technique of
analysis, crediting T. S. Eliot, A. C. Bradley, Dorothy Sayers, and Hegel. Indeed,
Paolucci admits a strong debt to Hegel's critical dialectic as interpreted through
T. S. Eliot, which Paolucci takes great pains to explore. At the heart of her exploration of Albee and Pirandello as chief proponents of the theatre of the absurd
are two ideas. The first of these is that of "*art transcending itself* in the modern
world," which, Paolucci argues, has produced the theatre of the absurd. And the
second idea, which she feels "follows naturally from Hegel," is Hegel's notion of

an "evolution of the spirit," an idea that Paolucci believes to provide a cohesive structure to understanding Albee's work (163).

She strengthens her analysis with her second chapter, "A New Theatre," which builds the comparison between Albee and Pirandello, providing background on both writers, focusing mostly on Albee's journey from an unknown to the leading playwright of his generation. She references Robert Brustein quite often, and one wonders if she has looked at more recent volumes on Albee's work, such as Stephen Bottoms's collection in the *Cambridge Companion to Edward Albee*. At the heart of this chapter, however, is the strong argument for a connection between Albee's and Pirandello's techniques, quoting Brustein's notion that in each case there is a "perfect fusing of the *process* and the *product*" (19). In particular, she clearly demonstrates how both playwrights work with realism through a metadramatic lens—and by the end of the chapter it is clear that although Paolucci hopes realism will "exit gracefully into the wings of history" (23), what she is really after is an acceptance on the part of theatre critics of Albee's non-realistic, non-linear technique. The irony here, if we accept Solomon's research on Albee directing Albee, is that Albee insists on a totally naturalistic approach to staging and performing his plays.

Because of Paolucci's fascination with Hegel, her exploration of Albee takes a decidedly romantic approach. Throughout each of the following chapters, Paolucci focuses on this notion of a "scrim" of realism hiding a much deeper absurdist approach to all of Albee's work—using, strangely enough, a romantic lens. She attempts to build a case for a very different way to think about Albee's plays. Instead of a "linear progression of the realistic play, where the problem is defined, events created to trigger reactions that will lead to a logical or predictable conclusion," Paolucci argues that Albee's work is about the "evolution of spirit" and that the "static action" of his plays is built on the protagonists' attempts to "probe their inner world for 'subjective correlatives' that give certainty and shape to their thoughts and feelings" (163). Looking at Albee's plays from this perspective, Paolucci argues, forces the audience to abandon passivity: "It is an experience aimed at encouraging the discovery of self, at reaching the same freedom that the protagonists of an Absurd play struggle to attain" (164). Whether Paolucci is successful in her argument depends upon the reader, but her goal is lofty, and one is grateful for the coherence and clarity of her vision.

—DAVID A. CRESPY
University of Missouri, Columbia

ॐ

Women Writers of the Provincetown Players. By Judith Barlow. Albany: State University of New York, 2009. 320 pp. $29.95 paper.

Women Writers of the Provincetown Players serves as a welcome addition to the growing body of work on American women dramatists and the Provincetown Players, the influential theatre that began in the summer of 1915 as "an informal group of friends on Cape Cod" (2). While many "little theatres" of this period were producing plays by established European and British playwrights of the era, such as Ibsen, Strindberg, Chekhov, and Shaw, the Provincetown Players were "dedicated to supporting work by American dramatists and involving them in the production" (2). Of their seven-year production period, the majority of works produced were one-act plays by approximately fifty dramatists, sixteen of whom were women. Barlow narrows her focus in this work to twelve women dramatists and thirteen works.

While Barlow acknowledges important earlier works such as Cheryl Black's *The Women of Provincetown, 1915–1922* and Barbara Ozieblo's *The Provincetown Players: A Choice of Shorter Works,* she expands significantly on previous scholarship by providing insightful and engrossing background material of the twelve women in her volume. Not only does she describe these writers individually and the reception of these representative works, she also discusses the degree of each writer's involvement with the Players. Susan Glaspell, a cofounder of the Players and "the most important woman dramatist of the group" (6), saw eleven of her plays produced by the Players. Neith Boyce, Rita Wellman, Djuna Barnes, and Edna St. Vincent Millay each saw three to four of their works produced. The remaining women whose works are represented in Barlow's volume— Louise Bryant, Mary Carolyn Davies, Rita Creighton Smith, Alice L. Rostetter, Bosworth Crocker (Mary Arnold Crocker Childs Lewisohn), Mary Foster Barber, and Edna Ferber—each contributed one work to the Players' repertory.

As Barlow states in her introduction, the plays in this anthology were included for their individual quality and are examples "from each of the women who had a short play presented by the Provincetown Players" (6). Indeed, "they showcase the range and depth of female writers' contribution to the group" (6). Louise Bryant's symbolic morality play, *The Game,* and Davies's parable, *The Slave with Two Faces,* represent thought-provoking abstract pieces, while Boyce's *Winter's Night* serves as a "realistic tragedy about rural marriage" (8). Glaspell's *Woman's Honor* relies heavily on farce and situation yet projects a feminist theme, while Smith's compelling piece, *The Rescue,* addresses issues of independence and family influence. Both Rostetter in *The Widow's Veil* and Crocker in *The Baby Carriage* create urban settings with touching stories of women who are neighbors. Irish characters populate both Barber's *The Squealer,* a play about a husband who has been arrested for involvement with the Molly Maguires, a secret organization of Irish American coal miners, and Barnes's comic work, *Kurzy of the Sea.* Ferber provides a bitter commentary on the relationship between the sexes in *The Eldest,* a tale of Rose, a woman who slaves for selfish family members while still carrying a torch for the man who left her fifteen years earlier; when the suitor returns, wealthy and successful, it is Rose's younger sister he courts.

War provides the theme for three of the plays in this collection. The oft-anthologized *Aria da Capo* by Edna St. Vincent Millay, states Barlow, "is as relevant today as it was when Millay wrote it nearly a century ago; the play shows how the world degenerates while a self-absorbed couple debate clothing, art, and artichokes" (11). Two other plays that occur during wartime are *The Rib-Person* and *The Horrors of War,* previously unpublished plays by Rita Wellman. The *Rib-Person* depicts three distinctly different women, two of whom choose to help in the war effort as correspondent and nurse. Wellman's *The Barbarians* was her first one-act staged by the Players on a "war bill." Although the Players' script of this comedy is apparently lost, Barlow located an earlier version titled *The Horrors of War* and includes it along with a detailed introduction in the appendix. Copyrighted under the name Rita Edgar, this play was likely influenced by Chekhov's *The Three Sisters;* Lisa, Marta, and Sonia, three sisters, whose country has been invaded by enemy soldiers, remain at home in negligees to greet the soldiers because they naively wish for excitement; when the "barbarians" arrive, the men are dashing and handsome, but prove to be well mannered and treat them as sisters, preferring a home-cooked meal to ravishing maidens. Wellman, in satiric fashion, makes fun of those who would romanticize war. The inclusion of these latter two "discovered" works adds greatly to the significance of this volume.

Barlow deftly and interestingly compares these works with those of other dramatists, both men and women, drawing parallels and citing possible influences. In her discussion of *Winter's Night* by Neith Boyce, for example, Barlow suggests a possible influence on the Players' most celebrated playwright, Eugene O'Neill: "Following a paradigm popular in literature throughout the ages, *Winter's Night* is a triangle play about two men in love with the same woman, Rachel Westcott. As in Eugene O'Neill's *Beyond the Horizon,* which may well have been influenced by *Winter's Night,* the men are brothers" (7). Barlow also suggests that Rita Creighton Smith's piece, *The Rescue,* might have influenced O'Neill's

Strange Interlude on the theme of inherited insanity; she also points out striking similarities between Smith's powerful one-act and O'Neill's *Mourning Becomes Electra* (157–58).

Barlow's introductions to both the volume and the individual plays match
the meticulous research and scholarly depth of her previous works, *Plays by
American Women, 1900–1930* (1981) and *Plays by American Women, 1930–1960*
(1994). Her text is pleasurable and interesting reading, as are the plays. And like
those two anthologies, *Women Writers of the Provincetown Players* is sure to become a useful reference and resource for all scholars, teachers, and students interested in American theatre. Assuredly, it is invaluable for anyone interested in
expanding their knowledge of American women dramatists, as well as the Provincetown Players.

—SHERRY ENGLE
Borough of Manhattan Community College (CUNY)

ↄ৯৶

*Women Playing Men: Yue Opera and Social Change in Twentieth-Century Shang-
hai.* By Jin Jiang. Seattle: University of Washington Press, 2009. 352 pp. 26 illus. $30.00 paper.

This well-researched work discusses the rise of Yue opera *(yueju)* as a "minor"
(regional) form of all-male troupes in the Zhejiang countryside around the turn
of the twentieth century, its heyday as an all-female genre in Shanghai from
1930 to 1960, and its decline precipitated by the Cultural Revolution (1966–
76), with emphasis on historical and sociological contexts. Jiang argues that,
compared with male elite genres—Beijing opera *(jingju)* and spoken drama
(huaju)—this product of popular women's culture has been neglected by scholars. Yue opera was molded by the all-female cast and reflected the desires of
its female patrons, providing material to gauge female concerns in twentieth-
century Shanghai. Jiang asserts that the art represents feminine aesthetics and
grew out of the May Fourth New Culture Movement (1915–23), which highlighted women's liberation as an important component of Chinese modernization. As a historian using cultural studies protocols, Jiang draws on newspaper
accounts, fan publications, films, literature, interviews of artists and audiences,
and her own childhood viewings of the form. This clearly written text will be
useful to those interested in Chinese theatre, women and performance, and the
history of modern China.

The introduction outlines basics, arguing that Beijing opera represented a male aesthetic forged in the Qing period to highlight patriarchal values of martial virtue, patriotism, and nationalism; and emergent spoken drama adopted similar themes. While the New Culture Movement took female liberation and love marriage as principles, only popular forms, here Yue opera, document what women experiencing transformations actually wanted. Jiang argues that scripts like *The Butterfly Lovers* (1953) and *Dream of the Red Chamber* (1962) reflect female desire in the new freedom of the urban space. Heroes are "soft" and sympathetic, love is reciprocated, and abused women are ultimately vindicated as their spouses beg forgiveness. Romance *(yanqing)* and melodrama prevail. The genre, perceived as apolitical, developed freely during the Japanese occupation as all-female troupes became the norm. Love, marriage, the family, and modern metropolitan life were themes. The primary audience became women: shopgirls and professional women were fans, while wealthier women served as "adoptive mothers," supporting stars financially. Although males continued as managers and then author-directors, female stars and their audiences molded the form.

Chapter 1 chronicles the art's journey, beginning in 1906 as an all-male form in rural Zhejiang area (Shengxian), arriving in urban Shanghai by 1917, and transforming to an all-female genre by the 1930s: "Broadly viewed, the rise of minor operas in urban centers was a direct response to mass urban migrations, the rhetoric of women's liberation, and women's entrance into the popular market culture" (37). The author notes that the male-to-female transition remains a mystery (51) and was an exception to the twentieth-century movement toward artists playing their biological genders. However, Asian female genres are widespread. Jiang could have usefully compared Yue opera to older genres—household groups of Chinese elite of the Qing period, Indonesia *langendriyan* and Thai *lakhon*—or twentieth-century all-female developments such as Malay *mak yong* or the Japanese Takarazuka Revue. These forms share many of the features of Yue opera ("soft" and sympathetic male impersonator as star, actresses retiring in their twenties to marry, romantic themes, etc.). The author also treads rather lightly in her practical discussion of prostitution, which is historically significant in Chinese theatre for actors and actresses.

In chapter 3, which treats the rise of feminine opera, Jiang does address the public image of the actress and notes that *qingbai* (purity and cleanliness) became "central to the public image of the actress" (61). Paradoxically, the public "demanded chastity from its favorite actresses as it consumed their sexuality" (63). Jiang details the suicide/deaths of Yue actresses Xiao Dangui, Ma Zhanghua, and the film star Ruan Lingyu, who chose death to deflect accusations of sexual laxity. Here Jiang might usefully have explained female suicide as a traditional female strategy rather than waiting four chapters (236); however, using these suicides as a locus, Jiang notes that through the 1940s the actresses struggled for power. The anger of young stars at these deaths inspired them to take greater charge of the content of performances. They banded together to resist demands of male managers and musicians/teachers. Jiang highlights actress Yuan Xuefen, who led peers in purging sex scenes and innuendo from earlier performances in favor of love romances highlighting sexuality in marriage. Jiang argues that this choice reflected desires of female audiences, for whom mutually responsive sexuality in marriage was the ideal. Yuan Xuefen also spurred the use of greater stage spectacle, naturalistic (Stanislavsky-based) acting, the use of directors, and written rather than improvised text. Such innovations were part of actresses' empowerment and modernization.

With the loosening of patriarchy, as Shanghai women entered public spaces, Yue opera became a desirable locale for females to socialize. Given the all-female cast and the largely female audience, women could meet and show their economic or social power without offending propriety. They could enjoy love scenes where, with only women involved, sexual laxity was not an issue. Schoolgirls, college students, and housewives embraced the art. Actresses eventually called the shots and were valued for representing the wishes of the modern female audience. Homoerotic aspects, while touched upon, are not emphasized. Jiang notes lack of evidence for lesbian relationships and sees female sisterly affection as central.

The Communist Party embraced Yuan Xuefen by 1949. Jiang analyzes the 1965 film *Stage Sisters (Wutai jiemei)*, which gives a Marxist Chinese Communist Party take on Yuan's life work of liberating herself and her peers from domination by bosses, in contrast with actresses like Ma and Xiao who were caught under exploitive managers. The film is an interpretation of Yue opera history in which the party's male hero releases the female from bondage, a plot shared with *The White-Haired Girl* and other model opera melodramas. Jiang sees this film as an appropriation of Yue opera history. She finds the 1998 play, a reworking of *Stage Sisters* that focuses on sisterly affection, more accurate to Yue opera history and aesthetics. Modern visual effects and design, emotional acting, beauty, and *yin rou* ("feminine and soft") (218) were central to the genre. *The Butterfly Lovers* (where a couple, when prevented from marrying by parents, dies of love and rises from the tomb as gamboling butterflies), *Dream of the Western Chamber* (where the beauty gets her scholar despite parental resistance), and *Dream of the Red Chamber* (where impoverished Lin Diayu despairs of marrying her beloved and sensitive Jia Baoyu, the scion of the powerful house) are iconic narratives. Yue opera "inscribed its feminine imprint on the culture of love and instilled a feminine sentiment into popular sensibilities regarding the culture of love into . . . gender and sexual relationships in modern China" (250). This book, rich in social and theatre history, puts this understudied genre center stage.

—KATHY FOLEY
University of California, Santa Cruz

❧

Sheldon Cheney's "Theatre Arts Magazine": Promoting a Modern American Theatre, 1916–1921. By DeAnna M. Toten Beard. Lanham, Md.: Scarecrow Press, 2010. ix + 281 pp. $65.00 cloth.

The sea change in the American theatre in the early twentieth century was ushered in by theatre progressives who challenged the day's theatre, which was composed of colonial dramas, minstrel shows, foreign imports, translations, adaptations, small-town comedies, and melodramas of every stripe—with their italicized emotions and exaggerated story lines, peopled with stock characters. It was a theatre best serviced by the star system, directed by businessmen rather than artists. DeAnna M. Toten Beard devotes her volume to those progressives who, before, World War I, were ignored by Broadway—a theatrical system that served the nation easy, digestible, commercial fare, fare made less attractive by the war. The war annihilated the barriers of our cultural isolation and paved the way for an infusion of psychological expressionism and realism more suited to "modernity."

At the same time, theatrical progressives traveled abroad to witness the experiments of Max Reinhardt in Germany, of Jacques Copeau and his Theatre du Vieux Colombier in France, of Stanislavsky and Nemirovich-Danchenko at the Moscow Art Theatre, and the creations of Adolphe Appia and E. Gordon Craig. Thus, a "new" (American) stagecraft was born, embracing the principles of Appia and Craig, marrying theatrical methods to content and accenting the "inner spirit," rather than skimming life's surfaces. The enemy was "Belascoism"— shorthand for David Belasco's flashy productions, thin plotlines, and overwrought naturalistic scenery.

Sheldon Cheney, America's zealous "missionary for modernism," prime mover of the New Stagecraft, led the charge. Author of the 1914 *The New Movement in Theatre,* defining the limits and aims of the new movement, Cheney edited and published the quarterly *Theatre Arts Magazine* from 1916 to 1921.

In the publication, he highlighted the experiments of the nation's Little Theatre groups, published texts of new plays, reviewed books and plays, and invited critical commentary from the day's leading dramatic progressives, upon
which Toten Beard draws for her volume. She provides critical and insightful background to the selected articles in chapters devoted to Sheldon Cheney,
the "Conditions in the American Theatre," "International Influences," the "New
Stagecraft," and "American Plays and Playwrights."

Cheney's editorials occupy a prominent position in the volume. Read here,
they situate Cheney's historic and visionary contribution to American theatre.
In "What We Stand For," Cheney encourages "professionalism": artists working
within the theatre, yet maintaining an "amateur spirit"; he calls for the abol-
ishment of the star system and for drawing clear lines between the commercial and the artistic, or poetic, drama enhanced by simple staging. Elsewhere,
Cheney praises the experiments of the nation's Little Theatres, defines "stylization," argues for a municipal theatre, supports experimental dance, and extols
the Moscow Art Theatre. Cheney ignores actors and the acting profession, real-
izing that they would follow—not lead—the movement.

Cheney's interests gravitated to the visual side of the New Stagecraft, yet
they did not end there—he was aware that the theatre depended not only on
stagecraft but also on strong, modern playwrights and knowledgeable, committed directors to escape being "swallowed by the movies" (21). His mission was
to ignite a theatrical revolution touching all practitioners of drama, his mani-
festo being "to help conserve and develop creative impulse in the American theatre; to provide a permanent record of American dramatic art in its formative
period; to hasten the day when the speculators will step out of the established
playhouse and let the artists in" (2). Cheney's task was Herculean: more needed
to be created than destroyed.

As this volume proves, the path to theatrical reform was uncertain at best.
Kenneth Macgowan questions, were we "to emerge from the war into a new theatre? Will we find ourselves in that theatre of beauty and expressiveness towards
which Russia and Germany and, to a lesser degree, France and England, were
moving in 1914?" (182). (Or would we remain in the clutches of the Schuberts?)
Would we agree with Cheney that following European traditions would be a
mistake, and that we should strike out ahead of Europe—"along parallel but
independent roads" (207)? This volume goes some distance toward answering
what path the theatre took and to closing the gap between today's theatrical
practitioners and our several paterfamilias.

While the volume focuses on Cheney's contribution, it accents the number of other voices shaping our modern theatre. Indeed, besides the author's fine commentary, the strength of this volume is in the assemblage of writers who testify to that breathless moment when the first principles of our modern theatre came into being. These short pieces are refreshing to read, even purifying: the authors frequently convey their idealistic visions in soaring prose. In addition to Macgowan, the author has included articles from Robert Edmond Jones, Walter Prichard Eaton, and Lee Simonson, among others. The volume reads like a family scrapbook of American art proponents and practitioners.

The book's importance to theatre history lies also in the topics discussed. In "Acting and the New Stagecraft," Walter Pritchard Eaton argues that acting "polish" cannot be sacrificed at the altar of artistic expression and imagination. In "The Painter and the Stage," Lee Simonson illustrates how scenic design is integral to illusion. Maxwell Armfield's "Bourgeois Galleries Exhibition of American Stage Design" discusses the use of color (the article should be required reading today). Kenneth Macgowan's "The Centre of the Stage: *Macbeth*" critiques the 1921 Robert E. Jones's production of *Macbeth* and Lionel Barrymore's acting according to New Stagecraft principles. The volume contains fascinating facts—for example, were it not for Macgowan and company financing Robert Edmond Jones's graduation (from Harvard) trip to Europe, Jones would never have been able to study with Max Reinhardt; and the result for theatre?

The final chapter, "American Plays and Playwrights," includes articles on the Drama League, George Pierce Baker, and Eugene O'Neill, whose talents were considered equal to that of Susan Glaspell, Alfred Kreymborg, and Edna St. Vincent Millay. O'Neill's reputation was enhanced when *Theatre Arts Magazine* published *The Emperor Jones* in its entirety in 1921—still, the play was considered "too specific." Only when O'Neill published *The Hairy Ape* was his reputation as an expressionist playwright established.

One understands—thanks to this volume—that were it not for Sheldon Cheney's visionary genius and *Theatre Arts Magazine,* the "modern" American theatre may have taken a different route, or could have been delayed in its birth. The volume is a strong contribution to theatrical history; it challenges one to reflect on the ways in which Cheney's dream has been actualized. Further, it suggests that honoring the aims of our dramatic forebears remains a daunting—yet important—task. Neither they nor the issues that preoccupied them should be forgotten.

—EILEEN HERRMANN-MILLER
Dominican University of California

❧

*The Hanlon Brothers: From Daredevil Acrobatics to Spectacle Pantomime, 1833–
1931.* By Mark Cosdon. Carbondale: Southern Illinois University Press, 2009. xiv + 137 pp.
$28.50 paper.

Researchers of popular theatre performers know well the difficulty of finding
evidence on their subjects, due to the common lack of surviving material and
lack of attention by critics in the performers' own time, and by archivists in
succeeding eras. This makes the extremely detailed research done by Mark Cosdon for his *The Hanlon Brothers: From Daredevil Acrobatics to Spectacle Pantomime, 1833–1931* even more impressive. Cosdon combed playbills and newspapers, mostly the *New York Clipper,* for reviews, advertisements, and relevant
articles, and mined a hundred other sources for minute mentions of the group.
Sources already in existence about the group have proven, according to Cosdon, inaccurate, incomplete, and largely sanitized by family members or fans.

All of this has left a huge chore, and Cosdon largely meets the challenge.
His goal, to "right the historical record" (3), is a hefty one on its own, and he can
perhaps be excused for a paucity of analysis. The recitation of dates and events
is exhaustive, and it appears that no small detail of performance has escaped
notice. The dearth of detailed contemporary information makes it difficult to
draw a personal picture of the Hanlon brothers' characters, but Cosdon is able
to make enough worthy conclusions to paint an intriguing, if spotty, picture of
these performers.

The text is arranged chronologically, a logical choice, but one that at times
leads to a numbing list of dates and occasional confusion when an out-of-
sequence reference results from an emphasis on theme rather than chronology.
Interspersed between chapters are interludes on Jean-Gaspard Deburau, the
Ravels, and George L. Fox. These sections provide some well-structured context for the career of the Hanlons due to their mutual influence. Jean-Gaspard
Deburau revolutionized the character of Pierrot in his pantomimes at the Thé-
âtre des Funambules during the first half of the eighteenth century. His scripts
formed the basis for the highly successful shows that revitalized the career of
the Hanlons after their acrobatics became too imitated and too physically difficult for their aging bodies. The Ravels held the place of the most beloved acro-
bats and pantomimists in the United States in the thirty years prior to the take-
off of the Hanlons. Although he cannot say with certainty, Cosdon makes a
good case for the direct influence of the Ravels on the Hanlons, tracing the
similarities in style and form, and outlining the most popular performances of

the former that could easily have influenced any Hanlon brothers who might have been sitting in the audience. And George L. Fox was the touchstone for American pantomime performance until his death in 1877, with talents for facial transformation and social commentary. Cosdon states that the Hanlons shared those talents and supplemented them with their acrobatics and sizable troupe to make them even more popular than Fox had. Additionally, they occasionally used the Humpty-Dumpty troupes, which sprouted up to take advantage of Fox's pantomime of that name, as training schools, poaching their most talented clowns.

Cosdon spends the majority of his time discussing the Hanlons' most famous pantomime, *Le Voyage en Suisse,* although he makes little of the fact that the play was the only major work in the Hanlons' repertoire not written by them. From Paris to New York and across the United States, Cosdon details the tours, the script changes, and the scenic inventions employed each year to keep the pantomime relevant and appealing to audiences. One of the greatest favors he does the reader is to provide detailed plot synopses and action sequence descriptions for this and other pantomimes, both from the Hanlons' repertoire and others. This offers a glimpse into what the audience would have experienced and is not often available to anyone other than the researchers themselves, poring over old scripts. Cosdon does not attempt to analyze the social relevance or commentary of the plots or technical devices, but he provides enough information on historical context and specific performance conditions to make it possible for readers to do that themselves.

Overall, the book is essentially written as a biographical study and straight history, which allows readers to use the material to draw their own conclusions about historical relevancy. Cosdon might have chosen to theorize on the Hanlons' use of emerging technologies as a source for their popularity (a brief paragraph at the end of the book suggests that the Hanlons' "careers and their lasting influence demonstrate those qualities" [137] of an ambitious American nation) or on how the metamorphosis of their work from simple acrobatics through traditional pantomime to socially relevant, even racy, material paralleled the changes in American popular performance as a whole.

At a brief 137 pages, there would have been room for such conjecture. But Cosdon leaves speculation and close reading to future scholars, providing instead a compendium of fascinating facts about one of the world's most prolific and popular, if under-researched, popular performance troupes.

—SUSAN KATTWINKEL
College of Charleston

⌘

Theatrical Nation: Jews and Other Outlandish Englishmen in Georgian Britain.
By Michael Ragussis. Philadelphia: University of Pennsylvania Press, 2010. vii + 247 pp. $55.00
cloth.

Michael Ragussis's *Theatrical Nation: Jews and Other Outlandish Englishmen in Georgian Britain* offers a fascinating and meticulously researched study of the "ideological work" performed by ethnic types on the eighteenth-century British stage (4). Ragussis questions how the rapid increase in ethnic characters in the English playhouse (Jewish, Irish, Scottish, Yorkshire, Welsh, West Indian, etc.) created an "ethnic spectacle"—one designed to showcase these types as "purely theatrical" by reinforcing the boundaries between the performance of ethnic identity onstage and the performance of "Britishness" outside the playhouse (2). Yet rather than focusing narrowly on how a dominant group used theatre to exert authority over oppressed groups, he also pays careful attention to the "history of resistance" enacted by ethnic minorities who protested their political, social, and cultural marginalization (12). Ragussis incorporates a range of dramatic and popular literature into his study, as well as an impressive array of illustrations, newspaper accounts, and memoirs. He also situates his work firmly in the political history of the period, providing ample background for the reader less familiar with the labyrinthine politics of the Georgian era. The result is an erudite, well-written, and persuasive argument about the changing functions of ethnic types in eighteenth-century British culture.

Theatrical Nation consists of six chapters plus a brief epilogue. Chapter 1, "Family Quarrels," serves as an introduction to the study and explores a nation under siege not from outside forces but from the very groups it had so successfully colonized. Ragussis argues that the battle for control in the Georgian playhouse mirrored a larger struggle to reconceptualize the nation as either "diverse but unified" or "destabilized and internally divided" (14). He suggests that examining "immensely popular but critically neglected plays and performances" and situating those works within larger cultural trends of the period can shed new light on the "consistently comparative nature" of ethnic representation in Georgian England (21). Ragussis is also intrigued by the ways in which the stage helped to promulgate a kind of semiotic shorthand for debates over ethnic identity. These coded signs simultaneously embedded ethnic stereotypes in British culture even while they underscored anxiety that Britons would not be able to spot the markers of difference. This theme leads into chapter 2, which examines the phenomenon of ethnic passing and what Ragussis terms the "multiethnic spectacle" of the Georgian stage (43).

Chapter 2 interrogates both well-known and less familiar play texts, including Macklin's *Love à la Mode*, Sheridan's *Captain O'Blunder*, Mendez's *The Double Disappointment*, Reed's *The Register-Office*, Carey's *The Honest Yorkshireman*, and O'Keeffe's *The Irish Mimic; or, Blunders at Brighton*. While Ragussis notes the importance of outward physical signs (skin tone, ethnic dress, etc.), he argues for dialect as one of the most problematic components of the multiethnic spectacle. The impetus to standardize British speech and the pressure on outside ethnic groups to shed their linguistic markers produced the "ethnic incognito" (58), a dangerously liminal figure hovering at the threshold between "British" and "other." Thus the stage sounded the alarm by exposing characters attempting to pass into a vocal and aural culture to which they did not belong. Ironically, perhaps, the stage also aided in the preservation of various ethnic dialects as the nation succumbed to a kind of dictionary mania, categorizing and archiving regional dialects in danger of disappearing. Critics paid increasing attention to the "authenticity" of a character's dialect. The one notable exception, Ragussis notes, was the stage Jew, whose speech patterns "became an obstacle to the full recuperation of Jewish identity on the stage" (79).

Chapters 3 and 4 focus more specifically on the strange career of the stage Jew. Chapter 3, "Cheeld o' Commerce," links Britain's rapidly transforming capitalist economy to efforts to rehabilitate the stage Jew (which was followed by an equally dramatic backlash against the character in the wake of the "Jew Bill" controversy of 1753–54). By the end of the century it was no longer possible to point to one specific set of stage traits that denoted Jewishness—Jewish characters had emerged as more complicated and fully rounded (if still problematic) figures. Other scholars, such as Richard Braverman, have argued that late-seventeenth-century and even very early eighteenth-century Jewish characters were sometimes used as stand-ins for political dissenters (with the Jewish ethnic identity serving as a kind of catchall for troublemaker and outsider). By the late eighteenth century, Ragussis argues, the stage Jew fulfilled a different role as a figure who had not only mastered the capitalist system but had become a "guardian of tolerance and generosity" (93). Yet, like his African counterpart in America, the kindly stage Jew often appeared less as evidence of racial or ethnic progress and more as an opportunity for Gentile audience members to congratulate themselves on their broad-mindedness in even temporarily accepting the *possibility* that such a character might exist. Ragussis expands on this displaced sentimental identification in chapter 4, describing the peculiar genre of plays featuring Gentile characters disguised as Jews. Describing the Jew as the "signifying body par excellence," Ragussis explores how a range of performers, from rioters to stage actors, co-opted a burlesqued version of the most familiar (stereotyped) associations with Judaism to "re-Judaize" a figure that had come to seem dangerously close to assimilating into British culture (127–28).

Chapters 5 and 6 suggest how authors from different ethnic groups (particularly Scottish and Irish) reconfigured the national dialogue on race, assimilation, and integration from their own points of view. Although chapter 5 focuses largely on the emergence of new ethnic types in the nineteenth-century novel, it still proves valuable to the theatre historian, as Ragussis sees these transformations as "entirely implicated in a theatrical history" that literary scholars have often overlooked (140). He pays particular attention to Maria Edgeworth's *Harrington*, which features a scene in which an anti-Semitic character learns sympathy for British Jews by watching a Jewish woman at a production of *The Merchant of Venice*. As Ragussis notes briefly, Edgeworth's novel was inspired in part by a letter she received from a Jewish reader, protesting her treatment of Jews in previous works. (Given that Edgeworth's irate correspondent was an *American* Jewish woman, it might have been interesting to speculate on the ways in which the circum-Atlantic circulation of stereotypes shifted their meaning—particularly once America moved out of its earlier identity as part of the British empire).

In chapter 6 Ragussis queries not only the ways in which the early-nineteenth-century novel capitalized on and reenvisioned extant stage characters but also how novelists fixated specifically on the ethnic heroine as the character who could overturn destructive stereotypes. Describing these novels as "pedagogic project(s)," Ragussis queries how they simultaneously embraced and deconstructed familiar theatrical devices in order to reposition their audiences' understanding of the function of ethnic types (166). In each case, the beautiful Irish woman, Scottish woman, or Jewish woman becomes the object of adoration (or fixation) by a British man. Ragussis argues that this fascination initially produces a greater sympathy with the traditionally marginalized group but ultimately leads to disturbing questions about assimilation and ethnic identification.

The epilogue examines the afterlife of the Georgian plays and novels discussed throughout the work. Ragussis returns again to his focus on the Jewish character as one who remained consistently problematic (more than his other ethnic counterparts—with the possible exception of the stage African). For Ragussis, the persistence of the "Jewish Question" in British culture and on the British stage underscored the development of British national identity in other arenas. As the Jew remained the perpetual outsider, he or she emphasized the extent to which other, previously marginalized ethnic minorities had achieved some measure of acceptance. Here Ragussis argues that the theatrical repertoire functions as a means of "extending and entering that debate" over ethnic belonging (197). Yet the Victorian era also brought the impulse to historicize some of these ethnic types, so once again they occupied a curiously dual role as living characters in British drama and fiction as well as relics of a bygone era. Ragussis acknowledges several points meriting further study at the end of his work—including the ways in which the figure of the perpetually wandering Jew was recast as a dominant "agent and master . . . of theatrical illusion" by the end of the nineteenth-century (210). Fortunately, his study has laid a strong and imaginative foundation for this continued work.

—HEATHER S. NATHANS
University of Maryland-College Park
Sadly, Dr. Michael Ragussis died of cancer on August 26, 2010. Dr. Ragussis was a professor at Georgetown University for thirty-five years. He was the author of four major books and numerous articles and reviews, as well as the recipient of several significant grants and fellowships, including ones from the National Endowment for the Humanities and the American Council of Learned Societies.

✑

From Winning the Vote to Directing on Broadway: The Emergence of Women on the New York Stage, 1880–1927. By Pamela Cobrin. Newark: University of Delaware Press, 2009. 243 pp. $52.50 hardcover.

In *From Winning the Vote to Directing on Broadway: The Emergence of Women on the New York Stage, 1880–1927,* Pamela Cobrin examines the developing role of women in the theatre of the late nineteenth and early twentieth centuries. By placing the rise of women in theatre within the historical sphere of first-wave feminism, she uses performance as a gauge for the rise, fall, and contradiction of women's fortunes as they broke free of Victorian models of women in society and embraced their evolving role as a political force. Cobrin deftly blends the theatrical with the historical using case studies of five vastly different performance venues to track the development of women in politics and society as they became an increasingly public presence outside the home and outside the prescribed definition of femininity. After introducing the reader to the historical and feminist background of the period, she devotes a chapter to each case study: suffragist parades; Mary Shaw's Gamut Club; the Provincetown

Playhouse; the Neighborhood Playhouse; and the commercial theatre of Lillian Trimble Bradley, Rachel Crothers, Edith Ellis, and Minnie Maddern Fiske.

As a theatre historian, Cobrin hopes to illuminate the "collision of aesthetics, performance practice, and politics" (14) at the turn of the twentieth century. Although she hints at the then-burgeoning theories of gender identity, her discussion is primarily based in performance theory and historical analysis. Nowhere is this more evident than in the first chapter, which examines the inherent theatricality of the suffragist parade. Parades were very popular for celebrating holidays and other events, but they seldom featured women and were rarely planned by women. Perhaps as striking as the suffrage parade itself was the fact that the entire event was planned, choreographed, costumed, and performed by women; and they showed remarkable savvy in knowing what the people wanted to see. The women in the parade were generally attractive, and the costumes and other visuals created an atmosphere of street theatre in which the language of the suffrage movement was displayed as theatrically as possible. The spectacular parades, which occurred between 1910 and 1915, provided entertainment and education for both the women involved and the spectators watching the event.

The second and third chapters focus on theatre organizations that specifically used their resources to promote activism and address political issues facing women. Chapter 2 introduces Mary Shaw's Gamut Club, whose members were encouraged to write and perform plays that were then presented in a home-like community where women could meet and discuss pertinent issues. Chapter 3 presents the Provincetown Playhouse as a "home for wayward radical women" (93). The commune-like atmosphere was appealing to activist theatre women like Susan Glaspell, Neith Boyce, Mary Caroline Davies, and Rita Wellman, who were looking for a place to hone a female-centric voice within the theatre. While other studies have chronicled the lives of Mary Shaw and the women of Provincetown, one of the delights of Cobrin's book is that it places these women side by side within their historical context, allowing the reader a more thorough grasp of the scope of the impact these women had on theatre and society.

Chapters 4 and 5 focus on women who had a profound impact on the theatre world not through their activism but through their mere presence in a world dominated by men. Chapter 4 examines the Neighborhood Playhouse, founded by Alice Lewisohn, Irene Lewisohn, Agnes Morgan, and Helen Arthur. Although it was not created as a feminist project, the fact that it was created out of the settlement house movement added a social and educational component that placed them at the forefront of social change. The feminist activism of the Neighborhood Playhouse arose from the roles its members assumed within the community and the respect their work was given both in the theatre and in New York society in general. Chapter 5 looks at commercial theatre, where the plays themselves were not necessarily feminist or even significantly thought-provoking, but the woman director created a spectacle simply through her presence. This chapter highlights four female directors or "directresses": Lillian Trimble Bradley, Minnie Maddern Fiske, Rachel Crothers, and Edith Ellis. It is in these final chapters that Cobrin's meticulous research truly shines. Each of the women highlighted in chapters 4 and 5 could be the subject of an entire book, but again, Cobrin carefully places them within the historical context, which breathes life into each woman's story.

While there are only a few illustrations scattered throughout the book, the bibliography is a treasure trove of additional research into the historical world of theatre and life. As a whole, this study is an excellent introduction to the emergence of women on the New York stage of the late nineteenth and early twentieth centuries. Moreover, Pamela Cobrin has successfully placed the lives of women in the theatre within the structure of the women's movement, offering valuable insight into the relationship between theatre practice and feminist activism during this era.

—LAURA M. NELSON
University of Missouri

◦◦

The Un-Americans: Jews, the Blacklist, and Stoolpigeon Culture. By Joseph Litvak. Durham, N.C.: Duke University Press, 2009. x + 294 pp. $39.97 cloth, $19.55 paper.

Jews were central figures in the story of the Hollywood blacklist, both as those disproportionately targeted by the House Committee on Un-American Activities (HUAC) and in terms of the predominantly Jewish control of the film studios. It is this aspect of the blacklist era that Joseph Litvak's impressive new book puts center stage for the first time. Beginning in 1947, large numbers of Jews, in the main Communists or ex-Communists, were blacklisted, with many of them avoiding their fate by naming names to HUAC, disavowing, as is argued, a troublesome (for the cold war American state), cosmopolitan tradition of Jewish identity. The book builds on a paradox of the time for radical Jews: that blacklisting and marginalization went hand in hand with the "triumphant entrance of Jews into the American mainstream" (56). Litvak brings an impressive cultural studies armory of theory to bear on the issue, highlighting and embracing what he sees as a lost, stateless tradition of Jewish wit, comedy, and resistance.

The book traces the process of reconstructing American citizenship to key events of the late 1940s, linking the proclamation of the Hollywood blacklist to that of the state of Israel the year after. Exhibiting a mastery of Jewish cultural reference, and drawing particular inspiration from the writings of "culture industry" critics Max Horkheimer and Theodor W. Adorno, Litvak explores the era (in particular from 1947 to 1964) through a close examination of a series of film and Broadway texts dealing with Jewish themes and of the testimonies of key friendly and unfriendly witnesses. The author's background is as a scholar of nineteenth-century literature, and it is the penetrating textual readings that are most striking.

We are shown both Hollywood and the nation dissociating themselves from the radicalism of a particular tradition of Jewish culture, wit, and intellectualism. He calls this tradition *comicosmopolitanism* (3), in a phrase typical of the writer's relentless wordplay, which is often illuminating but occasionally irritating (in the sense that ideas are sometimes suggested rather than fully explained). He links the dangerous "jokers and smart alecks" (155) of the 1950s cultural wars with later minorities, radical academics (like himself), and suspected groups of the post-9/11 era. One is reminded that at the time of the 1951 HUAC appearance of Abraham Polonsky—a key Communist writer-director whose dialectical wit was central to his outlook and writing and who was blacklisted until the mid-1960s—Congressman Harold Velde called him "a very dangerous citizen" (see Paul Buhle and Dave Wagner, *A Very Dangerous Citizen: Abraham Lincoln Polonsky and the Hollywood Left* [Berkeley: University of California Press, 2001]). Yet Litvak goes beyond the blacklist era, linking the sycophancy that he sees as an emblem of the 1950s to the pressure on generations of proudly "irresponsible" feminists, queer activists, and radical academics to cooperate with the state and echo its dominant ideologies.

All this is very valuable, even to those who might question or debate certain aspects of the book. Some readers might prefer more sense of the muddle and chance of historical evolution, in which a series of factors, including the cold war, postwar economic change, disenchantment with the party's ties to the Soviet Union, and a crisis in the studio system all contributed to the dominant (but perhaps less dominant than Litvak suggests) conservativism of American mass culture. There is at times a flattening out of important 1950s differences, so that liberal cultural offerings are rather lumped in with those of the mainstream, while some of the pro-American "sycophancy" of the decade was surely a continuation of the patriotic-sounding rhetoric of the left's earlier Popular Front eras. On the textual front there is much that is illuminating and exciting in the treatment, in particular, of Polonsky and Robert Rossen's *Body and Soul* (1947), the film that drew so many participants to the attention of the FBI, and *Crossfire* (1947), the anti-anti-Semitism film that led non-Jews Adrian Scott and director Edward Dmytryk to their place among the Hollywood Ten. The author mines evidence of his beleaguered tradition, discussing the murder victim Samuels in *Crossfire* (and the "Jew envy" indicated by what is said about him) and the minor character played by Shimen Ruskin in Polonsky's fairy tale of the triumph of old-style Jewish community over ambition and individual American "success."

There is also much else that is interesting, including an extended analysis of *A Face in the Crowd* (1957), the film made by novelist and screenwriter Budd Schulberg and director, "virtual Jew," and notorious cooperative witness Elia Kazan (141). Rather than seeing it as a liberal assault on the way new forces of television and advertising were threatening a kind of American authoritarianism, Litvak sees it as an apologia from two party members turned stoolpigeons, although in my view this reading requires a sometimes strained emphasis on the Walter Matthau character, the Jewish intellectual who stands up to Lonesome Rhodes. Litvak includes other empirical studies, including of the "patriotic show" of the so-called blacklist musicals that appeared on Broadway, climaxing with Zero Mostel's appearance in *Fiddler on the Roof* (1964). There is also material on the "de-Judaizing and de-citifying" (161) of 1950s American television in line with this process, and a good appreciation of the way resistors made *The Front* (1976) in such a way as to rebuild the image of the Jew as both radical and comic.

There is perhaps a nostalgia in Litvak's work for a Jewishness uncoupled from power in both America and Israel, a desire to bring back the Jew of enjoyment (or "en-Jewment") (52), linking them with those women, homosexuals, and "queers" that he sees as standing outside official seriousness and Americanism. Not all his textual disquisitions are equally convincing: the extended discussion on childhood fig throwing, for example (from Schulberg's memoirs), seems rather opaque to this reader. Yet overall this book is an elegant, provocative, and at times brilliant contribution to both Jewish cultural studies and debates about the mix of popular art and politics in the blacklist era.

—**BRIAN NEVE**
University of Bath

∽ঞ

Irish Theatre in America: Essays on Irish Theatrical Diaspora. Edited by John P. Harrington. Syracuse: Syracuse University Press, 2009. xix + 226 pp. $24.95 cloth.

Irish Theatre in America: Essays on Irish Theatrical Diaspora, edited by John P. Harrington, features thirteen essays from the third conference of the Irish Theatrical Diaspora Project, held at New York University's Glucksman Ireland House in April 2006. In his introduction, Harrington asserts that these essays contribute to the "evolving subject area on how Ireland's relationships with the world have been more complex than they are often represented and how the 'wider world' is already developing new relationships with Ireland" (xiv). In addressing such a field, specifically relating to America, the anthology can boast a number of important essays.

Mick Moloney opens the collection with an insightful essay on the late-nineteenth-century Harrigan and Hart phenomena with their comedic and musical *Mulligan Guard* shows. Moloney traces the history of the Ed Harrigan and Tony Hart (Cannon) partnership with the songwriting foundation of Harrigan and David Braham. The essay notes that the Harrigan and Hart depictions of contemporary urban working-class immigrant life "affords us a unique window not just into the evolution of Irish America but into America itself" (18).

Harrigan and Hart are complemented by Maureen Murphy's "From Scapegrace to Grasta: Popular Attitudes and Stereotypes in Irish American Drama," which traces Irish drama in America from 1830 to 1965 as it mirrors immigration and assimilation. Murphy attempts to define the difference between Irish drama in Ireland and Irish drama in America: the former grew from a "legacy of colonialism" or "want of work," while the latter grew from the premise that the Irish in America found work; hence, the appeal of Harrigan and Hart–type entertainments (21–22). Murphy eventually touches on the Abbey Theatre's 1911 U.S. tour, which influenced the American Little Theatre movement, leading her to Eugene O'Neill's *Long Day's Journey into Night* as an example of Irish American drama's "legacy of emigration" (32). Unfortunately, neither Murphy nor any other scholar in the anthology writing on Irish American drama makes mention of O'Neill's *A Touch of the Poet*—that most Irish of Irish American plays.

Two essays that are well coupled are Deirdre McFeely's "Between Two Worlds: Boucicault's *The Shaughraun* and Its New York Audience" and Gwen Orel's "Reporting the Stage Irishman: Dion Boucicault in the Irish Press." McFeely explores the Irish audience that rejected *The Shaughraun*'s imaging, despite the play's New York success, as expressed in a debate of letters in the *Irish World.* The paper's correspondents "wanted an Irish drama to . . . establish the Irish race as culturally different from both the British and Anglo-Americans," with Catholicism, abstinence, and nationalism as ideals (59). Orel provides further context on the overall Boucicault debate in the Irish American press in the 1860s and 1870s by recalling the fact that Boucicault's Irish plays were not admired by Catholic American papers.

One of the highlights of the collection is Lucy McDiarmid's "The Abbey, Its 'Helpers,' and the Field of Cultural Production in 1913." The essay explores the efforts of Lady Gregory and W. B. Yeats to raise funds for the Dublin Municipal Gallery of Modern Art during the Abbey Theatre's early 1913 American tour, using performances of Gregory and Yeats's *The Pot of Broth,* Gregory's *Hyacinth Halvey,* and G. B. Shaw's American work, *The Shewing-up of Blanco Posnet.* McDiarmid relates Gregory's efforts in courting wealthy Americans, the "helpers" who assisted in the fund-raising, and the controversy that resulted when Dublin Corporation voted in September 1913 not to proceed with establishing the gallery to house Hugh Lane's modern paintings (which he was giving to Dublin provided the city build the gallery). Contextualizing her essay through 1913, McDiarmid reveals that the Abbey actors, with the Dublin Lockout as their backdrop, petitioned Gregory and Yeats for the money raised through their performances of the above plays in America. Gregory and Yeats had wanted to retain the money until a later date when the gallery might proceed. Through her revelation of the various machinations of Gregory and Yeats in the crisis, George Moore's *Vale* portrayal of Gregory, and a testimonial dinner for Wilfrid Blunt (all culminating in January 1914), McDiarmid reveals how Gregory and Yeats were "devoted to small easements in the large field of cultural production," which demonstrates "the diasporic spread of the Gregory-Yeats cultural business" (102).

Joan Fitzpatrick Dean's "Mac Liammóir's *The Importance of Being Oscar* in America" and John P. Harrington's "Beckett in America" offer important commentary on the steps Irish drama took in America following World War II. Dean outlines Micheál Mac Liammóir's American tours in *The Importance of Being Oscar* during the early 1960s. Dean suggests, without elaboration, that while the play does not focus on Wilde's Irishness and homosexuality, Mac Liammóir's Wilde "reshaped what American audiences understood as Irish drama" (113). A reshaping of America's sense of Irish drama was also a by-product of Beckett's work. Harrington, while providing American production histories, reveals that Beckett in America has existed through "popular culture in Bert Lahr and Buster Keaton as well as revisionist modernism via Mabou Mines and Morton

Feldman. The relation of none of them to Beckett is characterized by excessive respect of awe, and that is a [*sic*] good for the future of Beckett's work" (123).

Frank McGuinness's *Someone Who'll Watch Over Me* is reconsidered within America during the post-9/11 and Iraq War era by Claire Gleitman in "Another Look at Those 'Three Bollocks in a Cell.'" In the process, she questions recent American productions that have sought a triumphant human spirit amid the play's three Western characters held captive (indefinitely) by Middle Eastern captors. As she concludes, the play reveals that "we are still shackled to a history that we did not start but that we perpetuate" (137).

In "*Faith Healer* in New York and Dublin," Nicholas Grene tackles the "complicated business [of] trying to find out the truth about theatre" (146). Grene astutely endeavors to unravel, amid contradictory perceptions, the reasons why Brian Friel's *Faith Healer* failed in New York in 1979 but triumphed a year later in Dublin.

The anthology does suffer from some copyediting problems, as in the inclusion of "a" in the above Beckett quote from Harrington, and in contradicting statements found on pages 141 and 143. In the former, we are told that Ed Flanders left the 1979 cast of *Faith Healer* before the Baltimore tryout and New York opening, but the latter page includes commentary on the Baltimore and New York reviews of Flanders's acting in the production. The reviews in question actually discussed Donal Donnelly, who had replaced Flanders.

Despite these minor problems, *Irish Theatre in America* contributes favorably to the field of Irish theatrical diaspora. Exploring the role and nature of Irish drama in America—whether imported from Ireland or composed by the Irish American experience—is crucial to the overall understanding of Irish drama. The Irish Diaspora, from colonialism to a world of immediate communication, demands this understanding, and this work is an important step.

—NELSON O'CEALLAIGH RITSCHEL
Massachusetts Maritime Academy

༺༻

Making the Scene: A History of Stage Design and Technology in Europe and the United States. By Oscar Brockett, Margaret Mitchell, and Linda Hardberger. San Antonio, Tex.: Tobin Theatre Arts Fund, 2010. xi + 365 pp. $85.00 cloth.

During a lifetime of collecting theatre art and designs, devoted patron of the arts Robert L. B. Tobin amassed an extensive collection of engravings, illustrated texts, sketches, renderings, and models. Ten years in the making, *Making the Scene: A History of Stage Design and Technology in Europe and the United States* uses his collection as the impetus for a comprehensive overview of scenic design from ancient Greece to the present. It is only part of Tobin's rich legacy and a most welcome addition to the field.

Writing chores are shared by a trio. Oscar Brockett, the venerable author of *History of the Theatre,* takes care of the historical aspects, while Margaret Mitchell, a professor of theatre arts and practicing designer, handles the technical side. Linda Hardberger, the founding curator of the Tobin Collection, acts as editor and writes insightful commentary on the public's relationship to theatre in each period.

As soon as I sat down with the book I was enthralled. It's a class act from the title page. The glossy presentation pulled me in, and I found myself reading familiar information with a renewed sense of wonder. There may not be any theatrical Dead Sea Scrolls here, but the old friends look better. The photography is excellent. Images seem to leap off the page with improved contrast and clarity of color. I have seen countless reproductions of the Giovanni Giorgi etchings of Torelli's designs for *Bellerofonte,* but the hand-colored examples, arranged in chronological order across two pages, are a revelation. The generous size of the book helps. It is especially comforting to those of us who often browse the oversize shelves of bookstores and libraries.

Little is known of scene painting and perspective in Greek and Roman theatre, but the authors offer succinct descriptions of possible precursors to the Renaissance methods. The operative word here is "possible." In this account, and in the work as a whole, the writers have done an admirable job of presenting divergent, conjectural views and planting the seeds for further investigation. When the chronology reaches the late Middle Ages and we start to see images of performance rather than performance space, Brockett really hits his stride. He is particularly adept at describing the flow of the operas and spectacles, placing the engravings in the context of the performance. He may be a historian, but he is able to see the stage with a designer's eye.

The organization of material is almost subliminal. One of the hardest things for any historian to do is to make sense of the myriad intertwining threads of simultaneity, cause and effect. This is a history of design and technology, so the tension between the two continually propels the narrative. What a designer is able to put onstage has always been dependent on available technology, and the artist continually pushes that envelope of technology to discover something new.

As the stage picture evolves we are reminded of connections. Interspersed with the narrative are a chart of developments in ancient scene painting, a description of Renaissance paint formulas, and another chart on the evolution of scenic color. For me, many of the connections were brand new. I was unaware of Daguerre's involvement with translucencies and the development of both the diorama and the panorama. I had not realized that in the 1820s a surge of interest in Shakespeare helped break down the reliance on unity of time, place, and action. I knew of the director Charles Kean but not of the advances in stage machinery necessitated by his vision.

Innovations in lighting theory and technology, from artificial light indoors during the Renaissance to the computer boards of today, are chronicled throughout the text. Of particular interest is a section on how the conversion to gaslight influenced blocking, by opening up hitherto dark recesses of the stage, and scenic design, by exposing the flaws in painted scenery, begging for dimensional ornament.

Until the early years of the twentieth century, lighting was generally the province of the scenic designer, and certainly light was of revolutionary importance to the New Stagecraft designers, but as equipment and ideas became more sophisticated, specialization became the norm. Since 1962, lighting design has been recognized as a separate category by the United Scenic Artists, so it is surprising that no attention is paid to groundbreaking lighting designers. In a book so concerned with the entire stage picture and its attendant technology, I would welcome some mention of Abe Feder, his onetime assistant Jean Rosenthal, her protégé Tharon Musser, and so on. Projection designers are next on the list. As Oscar Hammerstein II said, "Collaboration is the biggest word in the theater."

Making the Scene is refreshingly up-to-date. Current trends such as the use of digital paint elevations, Internet research and sharing, video, and virtual reality are all addressed. I did think it ironic that, after pointing out the problem of archival and authenticity issues when working with computerized drawings, the authors used an AutoCad ground plan for *La Boheme* at San Antonio Opera without designer credit (for the record: David Gano, originally built for New Orleans Opera, 1985).

In all honesty, however, there is little to complain about: a few small typos and oversights that don't diminish the work and, for me, only reveal the human touch, something to be treasured in the art that the book so eloquently describes. It has already been thirty-five years since Donald Oenslager's *Stage Design: 400 Years of Theatrical Invention,* which used material from his personal collection of drawings, and is still one of my favorite books. I'm going to put this one next to it.

Making the Scene is neither a textbook (it's too pretty) nor a coffee-table art book (it's too smart); it is a rare combination of painstaking scholarship and beautiful design that simultaneously informs and delights.

—VAN SANTVOORD
Tisch School of the Arts, New York University

∽⅄

Molière, the French Revolution, and the Theatrical Afterlife. By Mechele Leon. Iowa City: University of Iowa Press, 2009. vi + 184 pp. $39.95 cloth.

In this elegantly written, erudite, lucid, and admirably researched short study of how the French Revolution appropriated Molière to its shifting ideological, political, and cultural purposes, Mechele Leon asks a question that goes beyond the temporal boundaries of her subject and remains of fundamental and universal importance for all Molièristes, be they academics or theatre artists: Who was and is Molière, and where does he and his theatre belong in the history of literature, culture, and theatrical practice? Do we define him as a literary icon, "a coherent and exalted figure suitable for framing and bequeathed to posterity" (11), not to be tampered with, or as a working theatre artist, actor, and producer who is up for grabs? In her richly detailed, fascinating account of how the Revolution redefined, reshaped, refashioned, and reconstructed Molière and his work—how, in her words, "a challenge to the classical order was played out in the revolutionary reconfiguration of Molière's reputation and the performance of his plays" (13)—Leon makes the case for approaching Molière not as an untouchable literary giant but as a living repository of new theatrical possibilities.

The major strength of Leon's study, in my opinion, lies in her choice to see Molière not as a "literary figure" but as a "theatrical figure." That is, she approaches Molière "not as the marker for a stabilized set of printed texts" but as theatre artist, "a shifting protean figure" (10), emerging primarily from theatre production. If, as she says, "Molière functions far more efficiently as a national icon when he is contained as literature" (9), things get interesting when he is freed from the frame of conventional literary definition.

After outlining, with enviable concision and clarity, the theoretical and conceptual framework of her study in her prologue, "The Theatrical Afterlife"— and it is to her credit that she does not shy from citing René Bray (out of fashion) and Michel Foucault (very much in fashion) on the same page—Leon gets to the heart of the matter in six chapters. In the first two ("Repertory" and "Performance"), Leon shows how actors and producers of the Revolution moved the marginal Molière, he of the vulgar farces and potboilers, from the periphery to the center of theatrical production. Doing so, they broke down the established eighteenth-century hierarchy of high versus low by creating a *genre bâtard* that mixed farce with high comedy. In an impressively researched section, Leon rehearses the opposition of established and conventional critics, still under the influence of Voltaire and Rousseau, to these theatrical "monstrosities." In chapter 5, "Life," she traces the continuation of the revolutionary project by showing how the biographical vaudevilles depicting Molière's life "challenged Molière's prestige as literary figure" (115), transforming the iconic figure of the playwright from man of the court to man of the people. To my mind, these chapters contain the essence of her argument and they—indeed the entire book— might be read in tandem with Lawrence W. Levine's *Highbrow, Lowbrow,* which treats the same question of cultural hierarchies with regard to Shakespeare.

If chapters 3 and 4, "History" and "Function," strike me as straying somewhat from the heart of the matter, they are nonetheless well worth the read. "History" deals with how the problematical relationship between Molière and Louis XIV had to be rewritten to remove Molière from the ancien régime. It contains a lively narrative of how producers during the Revolution felt compelled to transform the Exempt's vexing speech at the end of *Tartuffe* from praise of the king to an affirmation of revolutionary values. Chapter 4 offers us an account of how Molièrean comedy was retooled to become a weapon used against the enemies of the Republic. The Jacobins were a grim lot, and their reconstruction of Molièrean comedy took much of the laughter out of his theatre. Of particular interest here is the way the Revolution transformed Molière's Georges Dandin into a version of England's George III.

The final chapter, "Death," involves the various travels of Molière's corpse from place to place during the Revolution (not unlike the fate of Marat's heart), which Leon treats as a kind of eerily comic tale from the crypt. I am not entirely sure what to make of this. Much of the chapter is devoted to an account of Alexandre Lenoir's Musée de Monuments Français during the Revolution. Fascinating stuff to be sure, but not germane to the main question of where Molière belongs within the history and practice of theatre, and thus of more interest to cultural historians than to theatre artists. I suppose one could make a connection between Molière's corpse and the body of his work, which would raise the question of whether conservative academic criticism, by defining Molière as a neoclassical national icon, has embalmed Molière for past and future generations. One goes to see culturally correct productions of his plays much as one would visit Lenin's tomb.

At the end of her book, Leon leaves us with a very fine piece of dissident advice: "Don't touch Molière is a warning that theater directors and historians alike should not heed" (143). This is a book by a theatre historian who clearly has considerable sympathy for theatre practitioners as distinct from those "present-day venerators of Molière" who still govern much of what is written about Molière. The Revolution abolished both the Académie and the Comédie-Française, but they were soon back, functioning at their worst as the crypt within which high culture is entombed. (And that story could be a sequel to this book, which I would like to see Leon write.) Mutable, ever changing, unstable, even incoherent, combining high and low, academic and popular, low and vulgar farce with refined comedy, all of these at once, Molière, as Leon suggests, belongs to all of us, not exclusively to Ces Messieurs de l'Académie. Exhuming Molière, getting him out of the stultifying mausoleum of high culture, remains one of the great joys of working with and playing Molière.

—MICHAEL SPINGLER
Clark University

❧

When Broadway Was the Runway: Theater, Fashion, and American Culture. By Marlis Schweitzer. Philadelphia: University of Pennsylvania Press, 2009. 344 pp. $39.95 cloth.

At the beginning of the twenty-first century, the interrelatedness of fashion and entertainment is ubiquitous. Whether through product placements in movies, performer spokespersons, or the plethora of magazines, television programs, and Web sites dedicated to the close scrutiny of celebrity fashion, we are inundated with examples of how the entertainment industry is intimately connected to and informed by consumer culture. In *When Broadway Was the Runway,* theatre historian Marlis Schweitzer traces the emergence of this phenomenon a century earlier by examining the collaborative, and sometimes competitive, relationship between the theatre and other consumer institutions such as department stores as well as "the more intimate interactions among theatre critics, managers, advertisers, designers, performers, and audiences that influenced the circulation and shaped the meaning of theatrical commodities" (10). Through exhaustive research and engaging prose, Schweitzer exposes the role that commercial Broadway theatre played in modern American consumer culture and addresses the experiences of female performers, designers, and consumers negotiating not only their relationship with fashion but also with modern womanhood.

Schweitzer artfully interweaves the careful analysis of specific examples, such as a vinegar valentine criticizing matinee girls for their love of fashion, with the contextualizations needed to situate the particular in the larger social and cultural landscape. From the "competing discourses on the relationship between art and commerce" to "the standardization and rationalization of labor processes" and from "the effect of foreign commodities on American industry" to "the growing influence of the female consumer," Schweitzer deftly explains changes in professional theatre and gender norms (14). Following in the footsteps of historians such as Dorothy Chansky, Nan Enstad, and Kathy Peiss, Schweitzer shows how concerns over the feminization of cultural institutions fueled the devaluation of female tastes and interests, such as the matinee girl's proclivity toward large hats and frothy romances.

She then turns her attention to the symbiotic relationship between the department store and the theatre. Tracking late-nineteenth-century business partnerships on the Ladies' Mile and the development of separate although still interconnected shopping and entertainment districts (Fifth Avenue and Forty-second Street, respectively), Schweitzer addresses the gendering of consumption in New York City, showing how spectacles of consumer fantasy in both arenas took place against the backdrop of labor unrest. Creative staging and display techniques were used to divert attention away from social strife, offering instead "a new social imaginary that privileged individual choice and expression over collective social advancement" (80). While the department store employed theatrically influenced show windows to dramatize their merchandise, Broadway's commercial theatres relied upon actresses as the primary vehicle for fashion display and as objects of desire. Due to the popularity of theatrical realism, actresses had to sport designer fashions rather than imitations. Actresses such as Ethel Barrymore, Jane Cowl, and Maxine Elliott rose to the occasion, becoming style icons whose opening nights drew society women, dressmakers, and milliners intent on keeping up with the trendsetters. Theatre producers took other cues from department stores, offering free giveaways to entice female consumers or selling production-related goods as a means to advertise their shows. Newspapers and fashion magazines further cemented the relationship between theatre and shopping, thus "training female audiences to read actresses' bodies for design details," "normaliz[ing] the commodification and objectification of female performers," and "obscuring the labor that went into their production as stars" (95).

Like Susan Glenn in her recent analysis of actresses' spectacularization, *Female Spectacle: The Theatrical Roots of Modern Feminism,* Schweitzer considers the consequences, both positive and negative, of women's visibility on the early-twentieth-century stage. She addresses the material costs, such as the financial burden required to appear and continually reappear as fashionable both onstage and offstage, as well as the potential gains in making and remaking oneself as a commodity. Pointing to the emphasis on the artistry of costuming for daily life and the stage, Schweitzer shows how the actress positioned herself as a well-practiced craftsman or artisan (rather than a laborer) with the tools necessary to exhibit her best qualities and remain current while maintaining her individuality. She persuasively argues that, in doing so, actresses were demonstrating their status as modern women and their engagement with changing understandings of personality and the self, particularly in the social sciences, regarding the fluidity rather than stability of human character. "Through their experimentation with the semiotics of fashion," Schweitzer contends, actresses "demonstrated how women of all classes might challenge inscription within consumer society and continue to make meanings for themselves" despite the disciplining aspects of beauty ideals (137). She goes on to suggest that fashion offered women an opportunity for both personal and political expression.

Perhaps one of the most significant contributions Schweitzer makes is her subtle use of performance theory to analyze the complex social and cultural events marking the intersection of theatre and fashion at the beginning of the twentieth century. Treating fashion itself as a performative act, she also points to the performativity of class and race to elucidate the role of fashion in the maintenance or disruption of class and racial distinctions. Similarly, beauty was not something innate or natural but something to be acquired, purchased, and, ideally, democratized. She reads the "copy-acts" of female audience members not merely as imitative but creative in their own right, albeit differently expressed depending on the social status and financial resources available to the women. The presentation of self in everyday life, as well as the constitution of identity categories, underpins her focus on the crafting of public personas via clothing choices, or how "becoming and remaining a fashionable actress necessitated a continual process of reevaluation, reinvestment, and reinvention" (106). *When Broadway Was the Runway* offers a meticulous history of performance and also brings a performance paradigm to the study of theatre history. In her discussion of the "psychology of dress," Schweitzer quotes writer Eleanor Ames saying "it is difficult to say just how great an influence the stage has had in helping the modern woman find herself" (176). Marlis Schweitzer has skillfully surmounted these difficulties, expertly crafting a valuable and enjoyable contribution to the field.

—MONICA STUFFT
University of San Diego

❧

Theatre and Identity in Imperial Russia. By Catherine A. Schuler. Iowa City: University of Iowa Press, 2009. ix + 326 pp. $49.95 cloth.

Identity, in the form of the fundamental national question (Who are we?), emerged as a pressing issue in nineteenth-century Russia as a legacy of the modernization program of Peter the Great, who, through projects great and small, had tried to force Russia's civil and social life to more closely resemble that of its European neighbors. As Catherine A. Schuler notes, the Russian theatre remained inchoate up until the late eighteenth century and even then depended heavily on imported forms. As with other facets of Russian life, however, the theatre began to seek native authenticity, and its representational function implicated the theatre in the larger national search for identity. Schuler shows how modernization and the construction of a distinctive national identity intersected with theatrical representation through three distinct periods: the years leading immediately up to the war of 1812; the interwar period beginning after the Napoleonic Wars and ending with the Crimean War of 1855; and the postwar period immediately following this. Her engaging narrative follows Russian intellectuals and theatre artists as they grappled with evolving notions of national identity and soul. A trend emerges first of Russian theatre's increasing independence from Western traditions followed by the exploration of more complex and contingent negotiations of identity.

Schuler's study covers a lot of ground, and each chapter, after a short preface, begins with a contextualizing account of Russian social history (e.g., the ideals and motivations of the Decembrists circa 1825). While Schuler could likely achieve some of her rhetorical goals with less Russian history at the beginning of each chapter, her prologues do offer the generalist a clear path into the milieu while providing the specialist with a series of connections between political and social classes that often remain stratified in Russian area scholarship. Most notably, Schuler consistently finds and develops meaningful connections between Russian intellectual movements and the theatre. Thus, for example, we come to understand how Vissarion Belinsky's essays on the 1837 production of Nikolai Polevoi's new translation of *Hamlet* served not only to champion the career of actor Pavel Mochalov but also to extol the virtues of a transcendent Russian soul, the *russkaia dusha*. Schuler's extensive discussion of the Russian intellectual tradition attempts to connect the world of elite Russian thinkers with the less exalted social sphere occupied by Russian actors. The breadth of scholarship here should offer several new avenues of investigation for other Russian theatre scholars.

Theatre and Identity in Imperial Russia tracks Russian imperial acting via its actors, coaches, and managers vis-à-vis the evolving sense of nation relative to Western Europe, particularly France. The picture Schuler paints of Russian theatre prior to the prewar tensions with France is not a pretty one. Russian theatre depended, for the most part, on traditions imported from France, Germany, and Italy. Moreover, the country had yet to effectively marshal the talent and bureaucratic organization to allow for the flourishing of a formidable homegrown theatre community; however, the imminence of war with France occasioned reflection about continued reliance on an imported French theatre aesthetic. As the Russian gaze turned inward in response to international tensions, audiences in Moscow and St. Petersburg discovered new and unaccustomed predilections for Russian actors over French ones. Schuler does a fine job identifying actors' techniques onstage as reflective of Russia's evolving relationship with the West. Thus, Aleksei Iakovlev's authentic, masculine, and raw acting style appealed to a nation gearing up for conflict with France. At the same time, audiences increasingly compared an actress like Ekaterina Semenova favorably with the French actress Mlle George in the tense period leading up to Napoleon's invasion of Moscow. Schuler's account of Semenova's victory in this "contest of ideology and aesthetics" between the two actresses highlights the remarkable fact that Russian audiences chose Semenova as their national favorite (53), an emerging emblem of *russkaia dusha,* even as the Russian actress increasingly chose to imitate her rival's French technique.

Meanwhile, the rigid social system separating the majority of serf actors from the westernized elite who ran the imperial theatres remained a major impediment to the advance of Russian theatre. Schuler's account of Aleksandr Shakovskoi delves into the theatre management and acting coaching techniques of the man who sought to bring Russian theatre up to Western European standards. His willingness to work closely with serf actors, crossing an invisible social barrier, Schuler notes, set him apart from prior directors and acting coaches as well as other members of the nobility, who sought to remain aloof from the peasantry. At the same time, Schuler observes that Shakhovskoi retained the social caste system in rehearsal, using the actors' lack of status against them to help manage the rehearsal hall and advance his personal artistic objectives.

Within the realm of acting, Schuler subtly reveals how polarized tensions reminiscent of a nation transfixed both by native talent and foreign sophistication emerge. Actors such as Mochalov and Iakovlev possessed Russian soul, that "elusive quality of authentic Russianness" (61), and a native mentality that helped them occasionally deliver brilliant performances; however, these actors found it difficult to consistently harness their talents and replicate their best moments onstage. Popular and well-regarded actors such as Vasilii Karatygin relied much more on discipline and technique, qualities that, in some detractors' eyes, masked or obscured Russian soul. Actresses such as Polina Strepetova used the mystic qualities of authentic Russian soul to marshal impressive displays of emotion and native talent. At the same time, she immersed herself into her roles so completely that some observers speculated nervously about "possession" (235).

Throughout the book Schuler identifies a series of compelling rivalries among imperial-era actors. In an age of action and reaction, between national and foreign, and between Moscow and St. Petersburg, a good imperial actor usually had an opponent who employed an almost diametrically opposed acting method. In these contests the actor with the greater sense of Russian soul generally prevailed; however, the presence of competing extremes suggests that the theatre continued to grapple with the modernizing legacy put in motion by Peter's reforms. Neither the unvarnished evocation of the Russian soul and its native talents nor the polished and practiced depictions of actors associated with the West would suffice. Nearing the end of the nineteenth century, the answer to the question Who are we?—in the Russian theatre at least—remained a mix of native and foreign influences.

—RYAN TVEDT
University of Wisconsin–Madison

❧

Weyward Macbeth: Intersections of Race and Performance. Edited by Scott L. Newstock and Ayanna Thompson. New York: Palgrave Macmillan, 2010. xvii + 288 pp. $90.00 cloth, $28.95 paper.

The title of Scott L. Newstock and Ayanna Thompson's collection of essays comes from the word used to describe the witches in Shakespeare's play, a word often modernized from "weyward" to "weird." In her introduction to the collection, which developed from a 2008 conference at Rhodes College focusing on racialized productions of *Macbeth,* Thompson sets forth the goal of using the "multiplicity and instability" of the word "weyward" as a way of thinking about "racialized restagings, adaptations, and allusions to" Shakespeare's *Macbeth* (3). Thompson posits that because Shakespeare's play deals with the ontological difference between a king and a usurping other, the play has been, at times, particularly attractive to those who felt marginalized by the otherness of their skin.

The collection of essays is extremely broad, consisting of twenty-five studies—most of which are no longer than ten pages—plus an epilogue and a detailed appendix. The essays are divided into seven sections. The first section, "Beginnings," consists of two essays on race and textuality: Thompson's introduction and Celia R. Daileader's exploration of the texts of *Macbeth* and Middleton's *The Witch,* in which Daileader argues that Middleton's interpolations have created the ambivalent *Macbeth* we know, contributing to racialized readings and stagings specifically through dance and "exoticizing" theatrical additions.

The second section, "Early American Intersections," contains five essays on American productions and allusions to *Macbeth* before 1935. John C. Briggs skillfully charts Frederick Douglass's allusions to and quotations from Shakespeare—especially *Macbeth*—employing Shakespearean language and character to suggest a freedom of spirit. Bernth Lindfors's detailed, engaging essay, "Ira Aldridge as Macbeth," places Aldridge's performance of the role within the larger trajectory of his career and examines his performance style and audience reception. One of the highlights of "Early American Intersections"—and the entire book—is Heather S. Nathans's exploration of the ways *Macbeth* fit the cultural mood in the United States leading up to the Civil War; Nathans shows how the violent imagery from *Macbeth* and Nat Turner, John Brown, and Edwin Forrest (as Macbeth) became conflated in the popular imagination.

Orson Welles's 1935 Federal Theatre Project production, an all-black "Voodoo" *Macbeth* originally staged in Harlem, is the subject of the four essays in the third section. Welles's production, in fact, looms large over the entire collection; as Newstock argues in his essay, Welles's production was transformative, and "it seems that nearly every black *Macbeth* production is expected to situate itself in some relation, however tenuous, to that of Welles" (91). Other essays in this section include Lisa N. Simmons's examination of a 1935 Negro Theatre Troupe production only a half-year before Welles's and Marguerite Rippy's overview of Welles's creation of—and the critical reaction to—this landmark production.

The fourth section examines contemporary racialized productions: Harry J. Lennix's essay is not only an actor's narrative of producing and starring in a

2007 all-black *Macbeth* in Los Angeles but also a theoretical exploration of the challenges black actors must face when approaching "classical" (white) texts. Alexander C. Y. Huang's fascinating essay begins with a theoretical overview of Asian-styled *Macbeths,* which "either map the English imaginary of Scottish incivility onto what is perceived to be equivalent Asian contexts . . . or create a new performance idiom from amalgamated elements from various traditional Asian theatre styles" (121). Huang goes on to examine in detail the 1985 *Shogun Macbeth,* which performs both of the above transformations. Also in this section, Anita Maynard-Losh examines a Tlingit *Macbeth* staged in Alaska, and William C. Carroll discusses, in "Multicultural, Multilingual *Macbeth,*" a production staged by the Kennedy Theatre at University of Hawai'i at Mānoa in 2008.

The fifth and sixth sections of the book examine race in musical and cinematic versions of *Macbeth.* One highlight here is Wallace McClain Cheatham's exploration of why Verdi's *Macbeth* has frequently been staged with performers of color, while many operas never have. Cheatham's essay is a captivating meditation on nontraditional casting in opera. Also notable is Douglas Lanier's "Ellington's Dark Lady," a strong critical rereading of Duke Ellington's often critically maligned late suite *Such Sweet Thunder,* a 1957 work based on Shakespeare. Amy Scott-Douglass, while advocating for color-blind casting in her essay on interracial couples based on the Macbeths in works for film and television, actually shows how race almost always signifies to an audience, despite what producers or performers may intend.

The final sections of the book begin with "Shakespearean (A)Versions": three essays examining responses to *Macbeth* in the works of African American female poets, contemporary African American plays, and black plays about black performers. Philip C. Kolin's essay—on resonances with *Macbeth* in the works of Suzan-Lori Parks, Adrienne Kennedy, Ntozake Shange, and August Wilson—is particularly effective. Following these essays, Richard Burt's epilogue, "ObaMacbeth," examines how all the essays in *Weyward Macbeth* were haunted by the election and inauguration of Obama, just as the 2008 campaign was haunted by the Macbeths, who were used as caricatures for the Obamas, McCains, and Senator Hillary Clinton. The book concludes with an extremely useful appendix, compiled by Newstock and Brent Butgereit, of "Selected Productions of *Macbeth* Featuring Non-Traditional Casting." Over one hundred productions are listed, from 1821 to 2009.

Weyward Macbeth is part of Palgrave Macmillan's "signs of race" series, which "examines the complex relationships between race, ethnicity, and culture in the English-speaking world from the early modern period to the postcolonial present" (xv). Newstock and Thompson's collection accomplishes this goal admirably, both through the quality of most of the essays and the overall breadth of the book. The many essays show that nontraditional casting of *Macbeth* is not just an occasional occurrence or an exception that proves the rule. As with more obviously racialized Shakespearean plays such as *Othello* or *The Tempest, Macbeth* can clearly speak to minority audiences and performers. *Weyward Macbeth* is also a timely book; many essays use the rise of Obama as a parallel, but they remind the reader that the United States is certainly not "post-race." As with the best works of historical scholarship, Newstock and Thompson's collection merges detailed historiography with immediate relevancy, making this a valuable book indeed.

—**DAN VENNING**
CUNY Graduate Center

❧

The Strangeness of Tragedy. By Paul Hammond. New York: Oxford University Press, 2009. xi + 203 pp. $55.00 cloth.

It is refreshing to find a scholar who has a more than passing acquaintance with foreign languages past and present, even more so when these strange tongues are deployed carefully in the service of tragic dramaturgy. Paul Hammond's book-length essay, drawing on modern and postmodern theory alike, reinforces the essential strangeness and elusiveness of tragic language. This is a book that takes us well out of our linguistic comfort zones, but it is one that rewards even as it kicks away at the foundations of our understanding.

With a facility in everything from ancient Greek and Latin to the French of Derrida and Freud's German, Hammond's survey of classic plays explores what he calls "the strangeness that tragedy fashions" (5). As his point of departure, Hammond uses an early essay by Freud, in which the words *heimlich* (familiar, homely) and *unheimlich* (uncanny, strange) are positioned not as opposites but as entwined terms that easily transform into each other. "We ourselves speak a language that is foreign," as Freud once said, to which Hammond adds: "It is pre-eminently the tragic protagonist whose language becomes foreign, who speaks a *parole* which no longer quite meshes with the *langue* of those around him. Tragedy translates the protagonist into his own dimension, separated from the social world around him, and now inaccessible to others" (6). For two thousand years and from one tragic figure to the next, this estrangement is expressed through seemingly normal words that—having multiple or even contradictory meanings—appear reduced to idiolects, sibyl-like rants and ramblings that through their incomprehensibility demonstrate the protagonist's separation from place, time, self, and, in some cases, even his or her own body. The chaos that lies beneath the surface of the original language is often avoided by our translators, whose choices predetermine our somewhat simplistic reactions to the original.

There is also a typographical/cheirographical dimension to Hammond's work, for the tragic figure's strangeness lies not just in the words themselves but in how those words were first expressed on the page. Hammond's discussion of the nuances of the Greek word *daimon* (53–57) reminds us that the first tragic poets reveled in complexity, but the issue of the tragic protagonist's agency becomes more complicated by the fact that (as Hammond points out) until the Middle Ages, literary Greek and Latin were written exclusively in capital letters (uncial), so it is impossible to tell whether the protagonists refer to personified, divine forces beyond their control or to personal emotions (113). The urgent question "Who acts?" becomes impossible to answer even as it is posed, again and again.

Once Hammond establishes his theme, the choices of protagonists—Oedipus, Thyestes, Macbeth, Phedre, and so forth—become self-explanatory in a sense; there's no need for him to argue their estrangement. It's something we instantly recognize. What occurs in each chapter, then, is a detailed exploration of the roots and symptoms of tragic estrangement as evidenced through language, from the basic vocabulary right down to the syntax and grammar. And by demonstrating the awkwardness of contemporary translations (see, e.g., 47–49, on the *Oresteia*), Hammond directs us again and again to the beauty and sphinx-like complexity of the original language. I invite graduate students with anxieties or resentments about having to learn foreign tongues to read *any* chapter in this book, at random, to see what rewards lie in store. Languages are hard work, but they're worth every drop of blood and espresso it takes to learn them.

This being an essay, there is ample room for the reader to disagree with some of the conclusions: much has been made, for example, of the title character's silence at the end of Sophocles' *Electra*, and Hammond (like others) finds her voicelessness to be symbolic of her continued alienation (73). Well, yes and no: tragic form calls for an *exodos*, a final song to accompany the chorus's exit, not a closing monologue. I don't think we even know which cycle *Electra* was part of, or its position within its trilogy. Moreover, pithy three-line odes like the one here would have been sung repeatedly—long enough for the chorus to make their way offstage—and we can only speculate on the effect these lines and any

accompanying tableau may have had on the audience. (Would they have rumi-
nated on the play's meaning, gone out for wine, or simply sung along?) To my
mind it was Euripides more than Sophocles, with his Brechtian habit of repeating the same *exodos* play after play ("The gods take many forms"), who truly
subverted the rhetoric of closure and alienated his audiences from the moraliz-
ing jingles of his predecessors.

Perhaps the most pleasant section for me was Hammond's analysis of Shakespeare's tragedies, in which, among other things, Hammond demonstrates just
how little we know the meanings and structures of the Bard's English. His
chapters on *Macbeth, Othello,* and *King Lear,* in addition to opening these texts
up to new interpretations, argue strongly for the treatment of early modern English as a foreign language in its own right. Positioning Shakespeare immediately after Seneca's *Thyestes,* Hammond also shows how tragic (and linguistic)
alienation was a known quantity in Shakespeare's time, and he handles the issue of Senecan influence deftly indeed, at the levels of language and psychology
alike.

The book has its shortcomings—the lack of a proper bibliography being
one. And it can be intimidating to be confronted with actual Greek lettering in
the early chapters; but a simple online search—two or three clicks will do—will
give the reader a print-ready ancient Greek alphabet, complete with pronuncia-
tion guidelines. And Hammond, aware that many in his audience are Greek-
challenged, transliterates key words and phrases so that you're never in the dark
about what he's discussing.

—ANDREW W. WHITE
American University

◈

Slaves to Fashion: Black Dandyism and the Styling of Black Diasporic Identity.
By Monica L. Miller. Durham, N.C.: Duke University Press, 2009. xiii + 390 pp. $89.95 cloth,
$24.95 paper.

In her introduction to *Slaves to Fashion,* Monica L. Miller points to the significance of "stylin' out" in black culture and the interracial and intraracial importance of dressing to the hilt as a personal and political statement. From the
music industry to sports to churches, images of glittering, impeccably dressed,
and edgily accessorized black men are everywhere in contemporary society. The
epitome of "stylin' out" is the black dandy, whose history Miller traces from the

initial contact between Africans and Europeans that led to the institution of slavery. Dandyism, as explored in Miller's rich and provocative book, becomes a site for examining the ways in which style defines and is defined by black people through shifting political and cultural terrains.

The black dandy is a complex and malleable personage who embodies the performativity of race, class, gender, and sexuality. The power of this figure is his ability to both destabilize and fix normative identity constructs. The dandy, Miller states, "exists in the space between masculine and feminine, homosexual and heterosexual, seeming and being, even when not specifically racialized, [and] an investigation of the black dandy's emergence and perpetuation as a cultural sign of this indeterminacy says much about the politics and aesthetics of racialization and identity formation" (5). Working from this premise, the book's project is to scrutinize numerous literary, artistic, and social instances from eighteenth-century London's Enlightenment to twenty-first-century New York's black cosmopolitanism in which the black dandy is central to the debate around diasporic subject formation.

Slaves to Fashion comprises five chapters and an introduction, and the chapters move fluidly from historical moments, make transatlantic crossings, and draw together popular performances, erudite leaders in arts and letters, and artifacts from visual culture. The first chapter, "Mungo Macaroni: The Slavish Swell," focuses on the emergence of one of the first blackface comic performances in London's patent theatres. Isaac Bickerstaffe and Charles Dibdin's comic opera *The Padlock* (1768) introduced the character Mungo to the stage, and the wildly popular character may be regarded as a prototype for the meticulously festooned, back-talking black dandy who would appear in different guises through theatre history. By the late eighteenth century the Mungo character became closely intertwined in the public imagination through the real-life presentation of Julius Soubise, a freed slave and celebrity London fop who demonstrated the possibility of self-fashioning under oppressive social conditions. Miller explains, "Bringing together the oppositional nature of impertinence with the self-conscious use of style and image, Soubise in Mungo's clothing signals the potential for a black character to constitute identity by actually and figuratively talking back, taking control of his own self-presentation and look" (58).

The following chapter, "Crimes of Fashion: Dressing the Part from Slavery to Freedom," examines the black dandy figure in colonial through nineteenth-century America as he was manifested onstage in Cora Mowatt's *Fashion* (1845), in blackface minstrel theatres, and in the carnivalesque festivals of Negro Election Day and Pinkster. The chapter raises important questions about audience

perceptions and perspectives, showing how the performance of racial stereotypes may at once subvert and liberate them from their cultural and historical
context, while they may also concretize and reproduce "pat definitions of blackness, masculinity, and sexuality" (81).

In chapters 3 and 4, "W. E. B. Du Bois's 'Different' Diasporic Race Man"
and "'Passing Fancies': Dandyism, Harlem Modernism, and the Politics of Vi-
suality," respectively, theatrical performances are placed in the background as
representations of black leadership, modernist subjects, and evolving New York
cosmopolitanism are foregrounded. In one of the most compelling chapters in
the book, Miller offers a close reading of Du Bois's essays and fiction, especially
the novel *Dark Princess* (1928). While engaging Paul Gilroy and Hazel Carby,
Miller makes a strong case for noting the evidence of progressive theories of
the construction of race, sexuality, and gender in Du Bois's work. The analysis
makes the reader reconsider the appellation "Race Man" as it is usually applied
to Du Bois. Additionally, at the height of the Harlem Renaissance many of the
race leaders advocated "authentically" black texts that reflected a definable idea
of blackness and represented by the emergent "New Negro." Miller's reading of
James Weldon Johnson's *Autobiography of an Ex-Colored Man* (1912/1927) shows
that Johnson and other writers were unwittingly pointing to the impossibility
of racial authenticity and the instability of all identity categories, including the
New Negro.

Linking the Harlem Renaissance with the 1990s, the final chapter, "'You
Look Beautiful Like That': Black Dandyism and Visual Histories of Black Cosmopolitanism," begins with a close reading of Isaac Julien's 1989 film *Looking
for Langston*. The chapter then gracefully weaves explorations of contemporary
visual artists—several of whom I had only the barest knowledge of but have
now a desire to learn more about—to weigh the claims introduced in the previous chapters in generally current cultural and social contexts. Miller frames
the chapter with questions about the term "post-black" and provocatively asks,
"Is post-black the new New Negro?" (223). Of course, she does not definitively
answer this question (and I would be disappointed if she tried), but the study
of textiles—often adorning an absent black body—incorporates and recalls the
historicity of the black dandy figure while attempting to forge new expressions
of self-fashioning.

Slaves to Fashion offers an important contribution to cultural, performance, and black studies. There is an epic quality to the book in its scope and
analysis. Miller shows a remarkable ability in gathering rather disparate subjects, such as Julius Soubise, Olaudah Equiano, W. E. B. Du Bois, Iké Udé, Yinka
Shonibare, and Harlem drag ball participants, and making it very clear they be-

long together in the same space. While there may be a few bouts of repetition and occasional reliance on performance studies jargon (e.g., "always already"), the writing is in general lucid and elegant. Copiously illustrated, this book will remain in fashion for quite some time.

—JAMES WILSON
LaGuardia Community College and the Graduate Center—CUNY

৵৶

The Process of Dramaturgy: A Handbook. By Scott R. Irelan, Anne Fletcher, and Julie Felise Dubiner. Newburyport, Mass.: Focus Publishing/R. Pullins Company, 2010. 150 pp. $19.95 paper.

The Process of Dramaturgy: A Handbook, as the authors describe it, is aimed at those who commit "acts of dramaturgy" (ix), as is reinforced throughout. As such, it is a text well suited for classroom use, particularly for students who have minimal exposure to the functions of the dramaturge, whether in a professional or academic theatre setting. This volume is also a welcome prompt for directors, designers, and other theatre artists who might find themselves performing dramaturgical functions in lieu of someone formally designated by that title. While not intended to cover all the possible skills and functions of a dramaturge, it is a well-organized and thoughtfully designed addition to the dramaturgical bookshelf.

This handbook is divided into three parts chronologically, according to the production process, with examples from the authors' own experiences in the field. Part 1, "Pre-Production," devotes chapters to the basics of dramaturgical research, communicating with the director and other collaborators, as well as "Conceptual Frameworks" (mislabeled "Conceptual Sets" in the table of contents), which provides a good introduction to applying critical theory as well as using other approaches to reading a production. Part 2, "Rehearsals," emphasizes the challenges of preparing, culling, and disseminating information to the actors and creative team, as well as assuring continuity in a production. There is also a brief but well-considered guide to working with a playwright on the various stages of a new play. Finally, part 3, "In Production," focuses on outreach efforts, including study guides, program materials, audience talks, and lobby displays. Perhaps most helpful is the case study of work on a university production of *Biloxi Blues;* it demonstrates not only the influence of dramaturgical work throughout the process but also the negotiations between collaborators based on these efforts, as well as their influence on the audience. The final chapter offers advice to the individual seeking to do dramaturgical work, either as a volunteer or a professional.

The appendixes seem geared toward different audiences. Appendix A, "Theatricalisms," identifies characteristics, theorists, and artists connected with early-twentieth-century theatrical movements: naturalism, realism, symbolism, surrealism, and expressionism. It ties in well with the chapter on conceptual frameworks and would aid the undergraduate student as a beginning reference. Appendix B, "Sample Syllabus," is an excellent starting point for the instructor seeking to teach dramaturgy in a methodical manner to undergraduates, including possible projects and activities. Appendix C, "A Resource List," serves as a list of works cited in the text and of other resources to consider; while not exhaustive, it might serve as a good reading list for a graduate student or beginning dramaturge wishing to learn more.

Only a few things distract from this otherwise fine volume (in addition to the occasional typo). The examination of other key dramaturgical texts in the introduction makes no mention of either volume of *The Production Notebooks*, edited by Mark Bly (nor are they referenced in appendix C), a somewhat surprising omission given their detailed, casebook nature, which would be a natural supplement to using this volume in the classroom. Also missing are any publications or Web sites regarding new play development or even the Dramatists Guild.

Despite these quibbles, perhaps the greatest advantage of this volume is the range of experience the authors represent, from academic to freelance to resident dramaturge. All three have generously included examples of their own contributions to a variety of productions, from plays to musicals to new works, and this multiplicity of viewpoints serves their chapters well. They have kept their audience in mind, including a glossary of terms at the end of each chapter and bolding these words in the preceding pages to aid students in learning. Most chapters end with a section titled "So You Want to Be a Production Dramaturg," which summarizes the chapter but also highlights the challenges inherent to the position. They include several built-in exercises well designed for undergraduate learners. The tone throughout is positive without glossing over the difficulties of acts of dramaturgy, making it an excellent resource for the potential instructor and the would-be undergraduate dramaturge-in-training.

—RONALD J. ZANK
Lamar University

BOOKS RECEIVED

Carlson, Marvin. *Theatre Is More Beautiful Than War: German Stage Directing in the Late Twentieth Century.* Iowa City: University of Iowa, 2009.

Cramer, Michael A. *Medieval Fantasy as Performance: The Society for Creative Anachronism and the Current Middle Ages.* Lanham, Md.: Rowman & Littlefield, 2010.

Dash, Irene G. *Shakespeare and the American Musical.* Bloomington: Indiana University Press, 2010.

Leon, Mechele. *Molière, the French Revolution, and the Theatrical Afterlife.* Iowa City: University of Iowa Press, 2009.

Litvak, Joseph. *The Un-Americans: Jews, the Blacklist, and Stoolpigeon Culture.* Durham, N.C.: Duke University Press, 2010.

Powell, Kelly. *Acting Wilde: Victorian Sexuality, Theatre, and Oscar Wilde.* New York: Cambridge University Press, 2010.

Solomon, Rakesh H. *Albee in Performance.* Bloomington: Indiana University Press, 2010.

Toten Beard, DeAnna M. *Sheldon Cheney's "Theatre Arts Magazine": Promoting a Modern American Theatre, 1916–1921.* Baltimore: Rowman & Littlefield, 2010.

CONTRIBUTORS

RICK BOWERS is Professor of English at the University of Alberta, Canada. He has published many articles on Elizabethan literature and culture and is the author of *Radical Comedy in Early Modern England* (2008).

DOROTHY CHANSKY is the author of *Composing Ourselves: The Little Theatre Movement and the American Audience* (2004) and is currently working on a book about domestic labor and food in American theatre. She is Associate Professor in the Department of Theatre and Dance at Texas Tech University.

PATTY S. DERRICK is a Professor of English at the University of Pittsburgh–Johnstown, where she teaches Shakespeare and Renaissance Literature. She is a coeditor of the New Variorum edition of *Two Gentlemen of Verona* and is writing a book on Julia Marlowe's Shakespearean portrayals and interpretations.

KELLY CAROLYN GORDON is the Coordinator of Theatre Studies at Brevard College. She earned a Ph.D. in theatre history, with a certificate in women's studies, from the University of Georgia and a master's degree in directing from Emerson College. She has also studied at Piven Theatre Workshop, La Mama's International Symposium for Directors in Umbria, Italy, and is a trained mediator. Her writing has appeared in *Lighting Dimensions, The Encyclopedia of Modern Drama,* and the *Dallas Morning News*. She is the granddaughter of actor Eddie Bracken.

JENNIFER A. KOKAI is a lecturer at Texas State University. She received her Ph.D. from The University of Texas at Austin in December 2008. She is currently researching Aquarena Springs theme park, the United States' second underwater mermaid show and home of Ralphie the swimming pig.

CONTRIBUTORS

ELIZABETH OSBORNE is an Assistant Professor in Theatre Studies at Florida State University. She has presented her research at IFTR, ASTR, ATHE, ALA, Theatre Symposium, and MATC. Her work appears in *Theatre Symposium, Theatre History Studies,* and the *Journal of American Drama and Theatre.*